Swigatha

A re-read of Agatha Christie

By

Peter Sheeran

Note from the author

Swigatha came about as the result of a re-read by me of all the books by Agatha Christie that I had first encountered as a child. These books were all in paperback editions, published by Fontana and Pan in the UK in the 1960s and 1970s, and most of them were second-hand.

Swigatha contains a review in chronological order of each book, including a brief look at the plot, then the characters and the attitudes of the characters at the time, supported by many quotations from the text. Each one is given a totally subjective *Swigatha* rating, a what-happened-next item and a few notes about some of the on-screen adaptations. It Is designed to be either read In sequence or dipped into, with the result that some background autobiographical details that are relevant to more than one story are repeated.

The review also considers the actual book itself: its front and back covers, its condition and so on. It was a thrill to encounter these books in the versions I had read; some, like the stories within them, have withstood the test of time better than others, but the re-read was for the most part an absolute joy.

Peter Sheeran

CREDITS:

The front cover image is taken from the cover of the 1967 Fontana paperback edition of *The Mirror Crack'd from Side to Side* (artist Tom Adams).

Cover Design: Laura Ingham   *Proof reader*: Anna Haldane   *Photos*: Peter Sheeran

Thanks to Scott Wallace Baker, Tony Medawar and Piers Cardon for their comments.

Inevitably some of the reviews may Indicate quite strongly the Identity of some of the culprits. In such cases a 'spoiler!' warning has been posted.

Contents

Introduction

"You don't read a book, you re-read it."   Vladimir Nabokov

WHY 'SWIGATHA'

Swigatha is short for *Swigatha Whiskey,* a play on the name of Agatha Christie dreamed up by my older brother Bill when he was 13 and I was 11. We were avidly devouring second-hand 1960s paperback detective fiction at the time, and if anyone in the family came across a book by Agatha Christie that we had not seen before they would swoop on it, announcing to the world that they had found 'a new swigatha'. By the time the author died, when I was 20, we had the full set, and had read the lot.

THE BOOKS

It was not just the stories, some of which are magnificent, that attracted us, but also the actual books themselves: the front covers, the blurb on the back, the pages, the print and the *also available* ... pages at the back.

Researching other people's first experiences of Agatha Christie, especially fan pages dedicated to her on Facebook, I have found that 11 is about the median age when people started reading her. It is noticeable the fondness and pride people have for the covers of the books they first read.

RE-READING AGATHA CHRISTIE

I began re-reading Agatha Christie in 2016. It has taken a long time, in part because many of our original copies had disappeared, to track down other copies of the original editions. When I see these editions in a second hand bookshop I feel such a delight of recognition. I do not think I would have reacted to these stories in quite the same way when re-reading them if they had been more modern versions.

I was not surprised to find that some of the books that had thrilled me at the age of 11, such as *The Big Four*, left me cold as an adult; however the reverse also applied: for example, *Five Little Pigs*, which had left little impression on the child, was revealed to be a masterpiece of its ilk to the man.

I re-read the detective fiction in chronological order, and began noting down quotes from the text that seemed, on the surface, to reflect attitudes of the era in which the books were set. Some downright racist comments, as casually expressed in the stories from the period after the end of the First World War, are difficult to read when coming from the pen of a favourite writer, but I jotted them down nevertheless. Although these were increasingly toned down, especially after the end of the Second World War, I maintained my lists of them: one for each decade of her writing career (1916-1973).

Many modern-day readers would defend the author against charges of racism or anti-semitism by stating that the offensive language used was how people spoke at the time. I am not sure this is necessary.

When looking at these quotes in total, one thing leaps to the eye: such comments are never made by any of her narrators or two main characters - Hercule Poirot and Miss Marple. In (almost) every case they are there either to illustrate an aspect of a subsidiary character or mock insular attitudes, rather than being the voice of the author.

The re-read was beginning to become a study.

OF ITS TIME

Most novels, whether intentionally or not, reflect the time and place when they are written. This is certainly true of Agatha Christie's work; the wallpaper of her stories depicts many elements of the ongoing social history of Britain in the middle years of the 20th Century.

So, for the 1920s we have stories featuring an establishment disturbed by the huge levels of social unrest that were a feature of the post WW1 years, with world-domination conspiracy theories rife. We also have what still resemble pre-war country houses, with full complements of servants, their house parties repeatedly mixed up in murder; caught between the two we have a series of plucky young heroines trying to make their way in the world, the first generation of their ilk to have to do so: the Bright Young Things.

By the 1930s the bright lights have begun to dim. The world is in recession, the old families are selling up and the houses are being bought by politicians, actors, soap kings and business magnates; the people of Jarrow are on the march. Miss Marple's home village of St Mary Mead is relatively unchanged, but Poirot spends much of the decade abroad, following his creator on her travels via the Orient Express to North Africa and the Middle East and the various outposts of the British Empire still dotted around them.

The tales from the 1940s are less frivolous than those that came before, unsurprisingly since many were written in London during wartime. Only one is specifically *set* in wartime (*N or M?*), but the theme of totalitarianism is raised in *One Two Buckle My Shoe* and the problem of the returning wartime hero features in *Taken at the Flood* (and is later alluded to in *A Murder is Announced*).

Post-war developments in the UK, such as the decline of the Empire and the colonials' return, the provision of free education for all (and its impact on the 'servant problem'), food rationing, the introduction of the Welfare State and a National Health Service, play a huge background role in the stories set in the 1950s.

Come the 1960s, Miss Marple's previously unchanging village of St Mary Mead has become overlooked by a modern estate known as 'The Development', her neighbour Dolly Bantry's Gossington Hall has been bought by film star Marina Gregg, and The Beatles, Teddy Boys, the Chelsea Arts Set and psychedelic drugs are all being name-checked. One of the stories is even based on the Great Train Robbery of 1963.

Only four stories were written during the 1970s, and two of them (*Postern of Fate* and *Passenger to Frankfurt*) make hardly any sense. The author was, however, by then in her 80s and her finger was maybe not quite so much on the decade's pulse.

DELVING FURTHER

My re-read was supported by a range of background reading, in particular Agatha Christie's *Autobiography* and Middle East memoir *Come Tell Me How You Live*, which helped to highlight some of the recurrent motifs of her detective fiction.

The more I delved into the crossover between her life and her work, the more I came to rely on reference works by the likes of Dr J Curran, Robert Barnard and Mark Aldridge, and the knowledge of the many genuine experts found in some of the excellent social media groups dedicated to her memory.

I knew before I started the re-read that Agatha Christie had long been the most successful author ever in terms of book sales; what I hadn't realised, and what soon became apparent, was quite how enduring a global icon she, and each of her main characters, has remained to this day.

ADAPTATIONS AND TRANSLATIONS

One reason for this is that these stories have inspired an incredible number of adaptations for the cinema, TV and radio, all over the world, for nigh on a century. This shows no sign of letting up. There are even books being written right now, and TV films being made, starring the author *herself* as the sleuth. All this is inspiring ever more 11-year-olds in the 21st Century to pick up, or download, her books. And not just in the anglophone world.

Her works have so far been translated into over 200 languages and dialects. Because of this, and because her style is so easy to understand (and translate), and because the basic stories are so well known, many people use Agatha Christie as an entry point to the study of English as a Foreign Language; similarly, many English people use translations of her books to help them learn European languages, as well as those that use a different alphabet, such as Russian and Hindi.

I began a *swigatha* facebook page at the start of my re-read, and have found that the vast majority of its followers boast English as a secondary or even tertiary language; many of these followers are only just beginning to read the books and are clearly learning English at the same time.

REVIEWS

This book contains a review of each work that constituted the re-read. I should warn that these reviews are *very much* my personal take on them, and not all of the reviews will be glowing. Far from it ...

I should also warn that some will reveal, or make obvious, the identity of the culprit, so don't read the page until you've read the book!

There is quite an emphasis on the attitudes and prejudices demonstrated by the various characters in each title. Authors cannot help but be influenced in some way by the period in which they write; taken as a whole, Agatha Christie's canon is almost a symphonic representation of certain elements of British society, at home and abroad, during the half-century that it spanned.

That is not something that would have occurred to me at the age of 11.

The Mysterious Affair at Styles (1920)

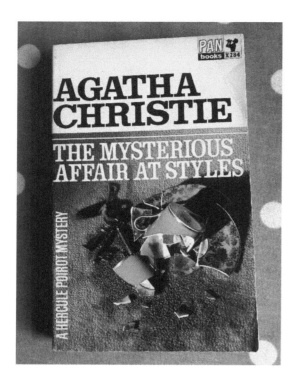 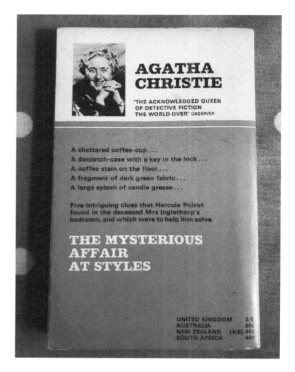

THE BOOK PAN, 1967 pp 190

This is a typical Pan cover from the 1960s. It features a couple of possible clues to the mystery – a crushed mug of coffee and a set of keys. The lead designer for Pan at the time, David Larkin, was responsible for introducing photographic images to replace the somewhat garish artwork from the previous decade.

The lettering is beautiful, and the image of Agatha Christie that he chose is perfect. It used to frighten me: *Oh, Grandma, what big eyes you've got...* she looks like she is watching someone about to drink some tea that had been laced with a noxious substance or two.

THE STORY

The story was written in 1916, at the height of the Great War. Captain Arthur Hastings has been invalided home from the Western Front and invited by his friend John Cavendish to stay at Styles, the Cavendish family home. By chance, Hastings meets an old friend, the retired police detective Hercule Poirot, in the local village. When the owner of the house, the recently re-married Emily Inglethorpe, is poisoned, Hastings persuades Cavendish to call Poirot in to investigate.

This is a classic Christie / "Golden Age" setting: murder in a country house, with plenty of suspects staying in it! Except, of course, that it was the first one she wrote.

As she was often to do, Christie makes full use of what she knows to build her plot: in this case, the attributes of various poisons (she was working in a dispensary at the time she wrote it).

CHARACTERS

In this book we are introduced to Poirot, Hastings and Inspector Japp – Christie's take on Conan Doyle's Holmes, Watson and Lestrade. In time, these characters would become as well-, if not better-known than those that inspired their creation. In comparison, the rest of the cast of characters are somewhat pallid, although Mrs Inglethorpe makes for an unusually sympathetic victim (by Christie standards).

Poirot is a Belgian refugee from the Great War (there were plenty of them around Torquay, where the author lived). Maybe his refugee status made Poirot, unlike just about everyone else with whom he comes into contact during his long career, sympathise with the down-on-their-luck and the dispossessed, and evince absolutely no trace of prejudice or racism.

QUOTES

Agatha Christie is sometimes berated for her racial 'incorrectness'. Certainly, many of her characters carelessly make what we now, 100 years later, would deem to be racist or offensive comments, but never Poirot. Far from it. Here, Poirot discusses Dr Bauerstein (who has just been revealed to be a German spy) with Hastings:

> *"He is, of course, German by birth," said Poirot thoughtfully, "though he has practised so long in this country that nobody thinks of him as anything but an Englishman. He was naturalised about fifteen years ago. A very clever man - a Jew, of course."*
> *"The blackguard!" I cried indignantly.*
> *"Not at all. He is, on the contrary, a patriot. Think what he stands to lose. I admire the man myself."*

Hastings' reaction may be explained by the fact that he had been invalided out of the War; Poirot, who has lost everything as a refugee from the invading German Army, still manages an even-minded assessment of the doctor, whose cleverness is explained by his Jewish origins.

The irony is that the Jews, whether they had fought for their country or not, were blamed by the Nazis after the war for its failure and branded as collaborators with the enemy. Bauerstein had even more to lose than Poirot could have imagined.

SWIGATHA RATING 5/10

It is quite amusing in places, and as ever very easy to read, but Poirot jumps about like a scalded cat, the incriminating evidence plotline is unconvincing, and unless you understand the properties of the various drugs you would struggle to unravel it. 'Styles' was the fore-runner of, and standard-bearer for, the so-called Golden Age of Detective Fiction but, even so, it is not a book that lingers with me.

WHAT HAPPENED NEXT

'Styles' was rejected by some publishers. It first appeared in the UK in serial form in *The Times*, and in book form in the US, in 1920. It was eventually published in the UK in 1921.

Within a couple of years, thanks in part to the income from the book, Agatha and her then husband Archie had bought a house, which they named *Styles*. It was, according to her, 'an unlucky house - everyone who lived there always came to grief in some way...'[1]

She and Archie were to be no exception.

In the meantime, Agatha Christie expanded her repertoire, with adventure mysteries featuring 'bright young things' and short stories featuring Poirot and Hastings. The next novel to feature the pair was *The Murder on the Links*, published in 1923.

ADAPTATIONS

The ITV series *Agatha Christie's Poirot* had for its first two seasons been concentrating almost exclusively on adapting her short stories when in 1990 (in celebration of the 100th anniversary of the author's birth) it produced *Styles*. It was very faithful to the original, apart from the omission of the German-Doctor-Spy Bauerstein.

Poirot, Hastings and Japp (David Suchet, Hugh Fraser and the brilliant Philip Jackson) had already made their mark in the series based on the short stories.

Christopher Gunning's theme for the shorter programmes was a huge popular success. His incidental music for this film adds to its lustre. Much of it was recorded and issued, along with other themes from the early programmes[2].

The only other adaptation I have heard was on BBC Radio, which also featured Philip Jackson in the role of Japp.

NOTES

[1] Agatha Christie, *The Autobiography*

[2] *Agatha Christie's Poirot: Music from the Television Series* (Discovery DMV103)

The Secret Adversary (1922)

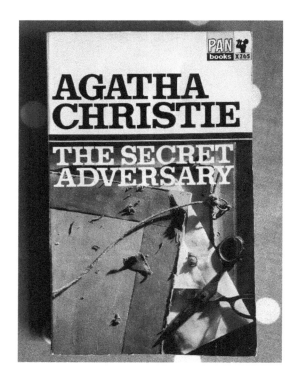 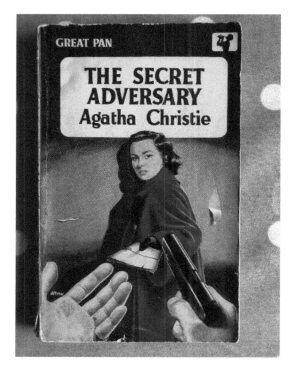

THE BOOK PAN, 1968 pp 221

The photographic cover is a simple depiction of the hiding-place of a "vital secret" document. The book is in great condition for a second-hand 50 year-old paperback.

There is a somewhat patronising dedication: "To all those who lead monotonous lives in the hope that they may experience at second hand the delights and dangers of adventure".

THE STORY

The book opens with the sinking of the Lusitania in 1915. On the basis of "women-and-children-first", a man hands a highly-secret and sensitive document to Jane Finn, a young woman who is more likely than him to survive and deliver it into safe keeping. Years later, WW1 now over, she still has not managed to do that, claiming to have lost her memory.

With widespread unrest and revolution in Europe following the 'end' of hostilities, these papers now present a major threat to the British powers-that-be. Two young people recently demobbed from active and nursing service, Tommy Beresford and Lady Prudence (Tuppence) Cowley, find themselves involved, through a series of coincidences, in the search for Jane Finn.

CHARACTERS AND ATTITUDES - spoiler!

Tommy and Tuppence are not Christie's finest creations, but at least she had the sense to start them young; unlike Poirot and Marple, they are able to age normally, which is just as well because she was still writing about them 50 years later.

Sir James Peel Egerton K.C. was the first of the benign villains from the upper strata of society to feature in her books, soon to be followed by another in *The Man in the Brown Suit* (1924). Albert the page-boy, the mysterious Mr Carter, the multi-millionaire Julius P Hersheimmer (who promises to bankroll a re-creation of the sinking of the Lusitania to jog Jane's memory), the villainous Rita Vandemeyer and her coterie of Borises are all pretty much cardboard cut-out figures.

One oddity: Inspector Japp, doyen of the Poirot stories, is mentioned as wanting to interview Julius, though he does not appear in person.

The Labour Party in the 1920s is represented as a group of dupes, putty in the hands of an unscrupulous villain, and as such a threat to world order. This theme reappears in other stories from this period, and seems almost laughable today, but would not have done so then: after the end of WW1, quite apart from the civil war and consolidation of revolution in Russia, there were left-wing uprisings in Germany, Hungary and Italy. Even so, within two years (in 1924) this same Labour Party formed the British Government.

QUOTES

Agatha Christie's 1920s seeming obsession with national characteristics and life-long interest in genetics are given free rein in this story:

> *He was obviously of the very dregs of society. The low beetling brows, and the criminal jaw, the bestiality of the whole countenance were new to the young man, though he was of a type that Scotland Yard would have recognised at once.*

> *"If that isn't a Hun, I'm a Dutchman!" said Tommy to himself. "And running the show darned systematically, too - as they always do."*

In many of Agatha Christie's stories there is an implied disapproval of the UK justice system. Here is Julius P Hersheimmer's take on the American equivalent:

> *"You will hang if you shoot me," muttered the Russian irresolutely.*
> *"No, stranger, that's where you're wrong. You forget the dollars. A big crowd of solicitors will*

get busy, and they'll get some high-brow doctors on the job, and the end of it all will be that they'll say my brain was unhinged. I shall spend a few months in a quiet sanatorium, my mental health will improve, doctors will declare me sane again, and all will end happily for little Julius."

Christie returned to the subject of justice in the US in *Murder on the Orient Express*, when describing how Cassetti evaded it for the murder of Daisy Armstrong.

SWIGATHA RATING 5/10

The whole book is a bit silly and childish in many ways, and Christie had not certainly established her style by 1922, but I must admit to having quite enjoyed re-reading it. There are enough twists and mis-directions to keep many an 11-year-old today happy.

WHERE IT LED

This book marked the first appearance of Tommy and Tuppence, who later marry and set up their own detective agency with Albert as their receptionist. The Beresfords next appear in 1929 (*Partners in Crime*). It book also set the template for Christie's other 'world-domination' thrillers, which she continued to write until hitting rock-bottom with *Passenger to Frankfurt* nearly fifty years later, in 1970.

As far as the UK Labour Party Is concerned: having swept to power, they managed to keep anarchy at bay.

ADAPTATIONS

The first adaptation was a silent German film from the mid-1920s called *Die Abenteuer GmbH*. This translates as 'Adventurers Ltd' and echoes the 'Young Adventurers' that Tommy and Tuppence style themselves in the book. It is interesting that Agatha Christie's work had spread so quickly into mainland Europe: it makes one wonder how the Weimar Republic readers might have reacted to Tommy's quote about the Hun!

Since then, there have been two British TV adaptations. One, from the 1980s, starred Francesca Annis and James Warwick and was reasonably true to the spirit of the original. The other, from 2014, is pretty dreadful; it appears to have been the brainchild of David Wallians (who played Tommy and was executive producer). It is not always clever to allow the lead actor in a series to have executive producer status (cf. the later episodes of *Agatha Christie's Poirot* and *Endeavour*).

The Murder on the Links (1923)

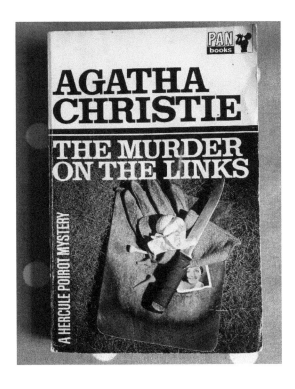 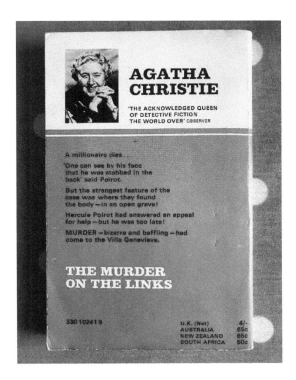

THE BOOK   PAN, 1967 pp 220

It has a fine cover which references some of the story's clues: one of the daggers, Paul Renauld's letter, Bella's photo and the spade to dig the grave. The golf references – glove, tees and ball - are not relevant to the story, but may help to define "links" for those not in the know (or German speakers who think that the murder was committed on the left).

On the back cover: *"One can see by his face that he was stabbed in the back", said Poirot* - who would not want to read on?

THE STORY

Poirot and Hastings are summoned to France by Paul Renauld, who writes that his life is in danger. When they arrive at the Villa Geneviève they find out that he has been murdered. To the consternation of M. Giraud, the detective assigned by the Sûreté to lead the investigation, they decide to conduct one of their own.

A good setting and title – substitute the words 'Golf Course' for 'Links' and marvel at the difference.

CHARACTERS AND ATTITUDES

Poirot battles with Inspector Giraud as much as with the case itself: they even have a bet on the outcome.

The principal characters in this story are Hastings and 'Cinderella', a young girl he meets swearing on a train, and with whom he falls in love. Note that Poirot had foreseen this: in the last line of *The Mysterious Affair at Styles*, he consoles Hastings, who has failed to woo two auburn-haired lovelies, thus:

> *"Never mind. Console yourself my friend. We may hunt together again, who knows? And then -"*

Hastings (who himself must be at least in his 30s) judges that Cinderella is "little more than seventeen". Even so, she surprises some unexpected depths in the good Captain. It reminded me a bit of another Captain: Mainwaring, who is (briefly) transformed when he falls for another woman during the 'Brief Encounter' episode of *Dad's Army*.

Overall, the main characters are incredibly suspicious of each other:

- Hastings is convinced that Cinderella is Bella Duveen and that she killed Paul Renauld
- Cinderella is convinced that her sister killed Paul Renauld
- Bella is convinced that Jack Renauld killed Paul Renauld
- Jack is convinced that Bella killed Paul Renauld

As ever, the *actual* murderer is just about the only character that no-one suspects.

This was the first of Christie's books to be set in France. The local characters here are treated with more respect than she sometimes showed when adding local 'colour' to stories set in England, and this was to continue to be the case. No matter whether the stories were set in the Middle East, South Africa, the Caribbean or the Balkans, you will never find a local character evincing a shred of the fatuity personified by the retired Colonels, politicians, members of the medical profession and seedy gentry during the stories based in England or its shrinking empire.

QUOTES

Poirot's unique (and humorous) English language style develops:

"Some of the greatest criminals I have known had the faces of angels," remarked Poirot cheerfully. "A malformation of the grey cells may coincide quite easily with the face of a Madonna."

"Poirot", I cried, horrified, "you cannot mean that you suspect an innocent child like this!"

"Ta ta ta! Do not excite yourself! ..."

Here he is, admonishing the household of the Villa Geneviève:

"You are an old woman completely imbecile! And Léonie and Denise are no better. All of you are triple idiots!"

SWIGATHA RATING 6/10

In many ways, it is a rattling good yarn, especially for an eleven-year-old to read, but the plot can withstand little scrutiny. Rarely can so many individuals have decided to wander around a golf course at midnight!

WHAT HAPPENED NEXT

Christie packed Hastings off to the Argentine with his wife, possibly to join her sister and Jack Renauld on a ranch. Every few years, Hastings will return to London "for business reasons", then promptly forget them and join Poirot on cases such as *Peril at End House* and *The ABC Murders*.

Christie herself returned to France for *The Kidnapped Prime Minister*, in her first set of short stories, and then again in *The Mystery of the Blue Train* soon afterwards.

ADAPTATIONS

ITV's *Poirot* series adaptation was very close to the original, apart from excluding the future Mrs Hastings' twin sister (much the best thing to do). It is quite amusing, especially in the exchanges between Poirot and Giraud, and Chris Gunning has great fun frenchifying his theme tune.

Poirot Investigates (1924)

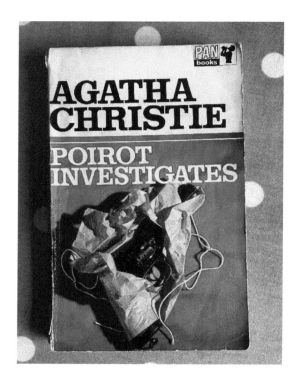 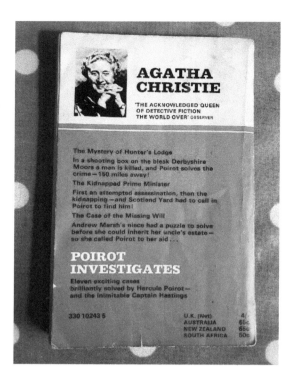

THE BOOK   PAN, 1969 pp 192

The PAN edition which I read has a nice cover but an image that has no relevance to any of the stories in the book. Good condition, though, considering the number of hands through which it has been passed!

THE STORIES

There are eleven stories in this collection. All had been published in *The Sketch* magazine, whose editor, Bruce Ingram, had originally suggested that Agatha Christie have a go at writing short stories featuring Poirot and Hastings.

The Adventure of the Western Star

Poirot investigates the robbery of an exotic jewel, apparently perpetrated by 'a Chink' (the story was written at a time when apparently all Chinamen wore pigtails). PC note: the person who refers to 'the Chink', as is often the case in Agatha Christie's stories when someone disparages people of another race, turns out to be the culprit.

The Tragedy at Marston Manor

Poirot investigates an apparent natural death on behalf of an insurance company. Not up to standard.

The Adventure of the Cheap Flat

Friends of Hastings are offered an in-demand flat for a pittance because of their surname. Very Conan Doyle in concept, and very Holmes and Watson in action.

The Mystery of Hunter's Lodge

Poirot sends Hastings to investigate a murder in the Midlands as he himself is unwell. Hastings reports back his findings and Poirot miraculously solves the case. The murderers get away with it, though.

The Million Dollar Bond Robbery

A million dollars in bearer bonds disappears as it is transported across the Atlantic to New York. For once in this collection, Poirot's deduction is undeniable; all the clues were there.

The Adventure of the Egyptian Tomb

The curse of the mummy's tomb, a story churned out hard on the heels of the 1922 Tutankhamun discoveries. The story has a bit more to it than most in this collection, and also has an early example in Christie of the solution being 'hushed up' afterwards (until, of course, Hastings' narrative is published!).

The Jewel Robbery at the Grand Metropolitan

A simple tale of servants at a Brighton hotel and their activities (or lack of them). A jewel is stolen from under the nose of one of them.

The Kidnapped Prime Minister

Poirot at his best. Set an impossible task - to find a man kidnapped between London and Paris within twenty-four (and a quarter) hours - he abandons the hopeless chase and uses the famed grey cells to work out what had happened.

This is an early example of Agatha Christie directing the readers' attention in a particular direction by playing on her assumptions of their prejudices (with the inclusion as a suspect called O'Murphy from County Clare – this story was written at the time of the Irish battle for independence).

The Disappearance of Mr Davenheim

Another early example of one of Christie's brilliant ideas: in this case, it is the answer to the riddle 'Where is the best place to hide from the police?'

The Adventure of the Italian Nobleman

Unconvincing in the extreme. Poirot solves a case based on the fact that the victim must have drunk some coffee.

The Case of the Missing Will

A slight, but enjoyable tale in which Poirot pits his wits against those of a dead man.

SWIGATHA RATING 4/10

This is a weak collection, which is understandable as these stories are Agatha Christie's first essays in the art. Most of the entertainment is provided by the interaction between Hastings and Poirot, rather than the stories themselves. There are, at least, a couple of ideas that hint at the genius of her plotting that was to come.

Re-reading them today was frankly, boring to me. What irony, then, that these stories, slight though they may be, led indirectly to a huge new global audience for the works of Agatha Christie.

WHAT HAPPENED NEXT

Hastings narrated a further 14 short stories. These were not collected and published for a further 50 years (*Poirot's Early Cases*).

In the meantime, Agatha Christie tried her hand at a variety of short story collections featuring disparate main characters - Tommy and Tuppence, Miss Marple, Mr Quin, Parker Pyne - plus two sets of stories that in the main eschewed the detection element: *The Hound of Death* and *The Listerdale Mystery*. Incredibly, all of these collections were published 1929-34 whilst she was also producing regular (and top-class) full length novels.

ADAPTATIONS

In 1989, ITV in the UK presented the first series of *Agatha Christie's Poirot*. This was a series of one-hour programmes, each based on a short story, featuring David Suchet as Poirot and Hugh Fraser as Captain Hastings. It was a huge success, and encouraged ITV to continue. Further series ensued, until just about every early short story had been covered, and its popularity grew and grew. By 1990, they had started making two-hour films of the novels; within twenty-five years every single Poirot book had been screened. No character in the history of literature has ever been so comprehensively and well-served (for the most part) on TV.

Some of the early stories (such as the ones above) are so slight that the ITV screenplays had to introduce extra elements to fill the hour allocated. The plots would (usually) be fundamentally the same, but with far more background added to the characters of the villain and other suspects. The most significant addition was the inclusion of the characters of Inspector Japp and Poirot's secretary Miss Lemon in almost every one of these episodes.[1]

It proved to be a brilliant move: the characters of Poirot's associates went far beyond what appears on the page and were hugely popular. Because ITV had started with these light short stories, rather than the heavier novels, the actors were given time and space to present their characters to the audience, who in turn took to them immediately.

NOTES

[1] Miss Lemon and Captain Hastings never actually met in any of the original Poirot stories.

The Man in the Brown Suit (1924)

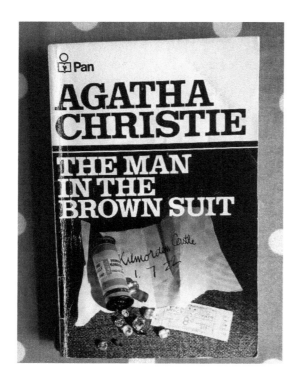 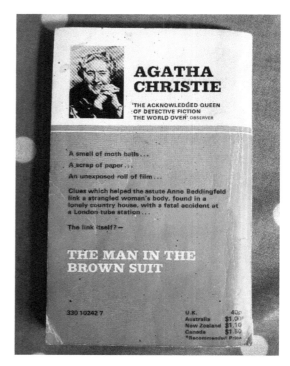

THE BOOK   PAN, 1975 pp 190

The PAN cover depicts the elements that kick the story off - diamonds, a camera film, a London tube ticket - plus, oddly, the misrepresentation of a rendezvous note (it should read 'Kilmorden Castle 1 71 22').

The book is dedicated to "E.A.B." This refers to Major Ernest Belcher, whom the Christies had accompanied on a world tour to promote the British Empire Exhibition of 1923. The tour took in South Africa, during which time Agatha Christie started sketching the notes for this book. Belcher had requested that she include him in it, as the villain, and she obliged.

THE STORY

Anne Beddingfeld finds herself alone in the world after the death of her archaeologist father and sets out to look for adventure. It is not long in coming; she is standing on a platform at Hyde Park Corner underground station when a man, staring fixedly over her shoulder, takes a step back in terror, falls off the platform and is electrocuted. A man in a brown suit, claiming to be a doctor, rifles the dead man's pockets and then rushes off, dropping a piece of paper in the process. Anne picks it up ...

Deeply suspicious of, and intrigued by, what she has seen, Anne plunges her life savings into the hire of a first-class cabin aboard the *Kilmorden Castle* travelling to South Africa, and awaits developments.

CHARACTERS AND ATTITUDES - spoiler!

The heroine Anne is the first of many young-women-on-their-own who get embroiled in outlandish adventures, and the story is one of Christie's earliest who-is-the-hidden-hand-behind-world-political-and-industrial-upheaval plots[1]. Unlike some of the later ones of that ilk, this one is nicely-paced, certainly for the first half of it, and the characters are at least given some time to settle in.

Anne is very-strong-willed and brave, unusually opinionated and, one might think, someone whom Agatha Christie would strongly identify with (or would like to). She is one of the most interesting characters in any swigatha.

The MP-cum-envoy Sir Eustace Pedler is a very amusing character, and particularly reveals this in his diary extracts: Belcher should have been delighted with his portrayal. Suzanne Blair is that rare beast in these books, a society woman with brains; and Colonel Race, unlike in later stories, is allowed emotions and opinions. The caveman figure of Anne's lover 'Harry' seemingly has 'strong silent type' etched on his forehead but his rudeness to Anne when she tends him is beautifully done.

Even so, the discussions of 'what women really want' do go on a bit and a faithful, modern adaptation of this story would attract a great deal of opprobrium nowadays. No reason not to make one - in fact, even more reason to do so.

It must have been quite unusual for a Golden Age crime fiction writer to have two young unmarried people shacked up alone together in the middle of nowhere for a month, and even more unusual for it to have the writer's obvious hearty approval.

QUOTES

Sir Eustace, avoiding deck-quoits and commenting on those who don't:

> *There are many fools in this world. One praises God for their existence and keeps out of their way.*

Anne reacts to Suzanne's suggestion that they take Colonel Race into their confidence:

> *"Do you know Anne, I think the best thing would be to confide in him and tell him the whole story."*
>
> *I objected vigorously to this unsporting proposal. I recognised in it the disastrous effects of matrimony ... Suzanne, by reason of her married state, was yearning to lean upon some man or other.*

Anne explains to Colonel Race why women worship strength:

> *"Papa always said that in the beginning men and women roamed the world together, equal in strength ... They were nomadic, you see. It wasn't till they settled down in communities, and women did one kind of thing and men another, that women got weak. And of course, underneath, one is still the same - one feels the same - and that is why women worship strength in men: it's what they once had, and have lost."*

Here is another interesting take by Anne - she is referring to how relationships develop, but it could equally be seen as an interesting view of human history:

> *"It's the things that are apparently conquered that always do win, isn't it? They win in the only way that counts."*

In the event, the 'apparently-conquered' murderer does in fact win out in the end; Anne is alone in feeling quite pleased about it.

SWIGATHA RATING 7/10

This book starts well but deteriorates into absolute hokum at the end. There is one ludicrous character (whom everyone knows) who manages to variously impersonate a ship's stewardess, the Reverend Chichester, and Pedler's secretary Miss Pettigrew without anyone realising it.

Even so, the book gets a decent overall rating because of the strength of the two main characters, Anne Beddingfeld and Sir Eustace, and because it is a good, and at times interesting, read.

Agatha Christie was always at her best when writing about things she had herself experienced, in this case the southern African continent.

WHERE IT LED

Colonel Race was to re-appear in three future books, alongside Hercule Poirot for *Cards on the Table* and *Death on the Nile*, and then again in *Sparkling Cyanide*. There were also later toned-down versions of the bronzed South African 'Harry' (Stephen Farr, from *Hercule Poirot's Christmas*) and various copies of the young-woman-against-the-world Anne (*The Mystery of the Blue Train*, *Destination Unknown*, *They Came to Baghdad* to name but three).

People staring fixedly over other people's shoulders was also a key element of the plots of *The Mirror Crack'd from Side to Side* and *A Caribbean Mystery*.

ADAPTATIONS

There was a TV production in 1989 which I have yet to see but which was by all accounts dreadful; the Christie family apparently hated it.

NOTES

[1] In the years immediately following the First World War there was a huge level of civil unrest, particularly in Europe in countries such as Italy and Germany; there was civil war in Russia, plus wars of independence in Ireland, Greece, Turkey, across the Middle East and elsewhere.

The Secret of Chimneys (1925)

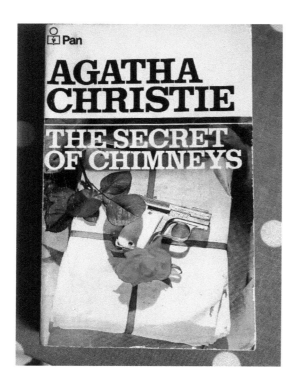
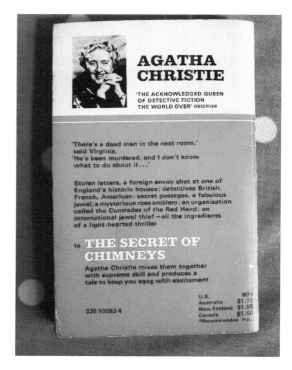

THE BOOK PAN, 1977 pp 220

Another of PAN's rather good photographic covers that were employed for swigathas in the 1960s and 1970s. Beautiful design and lettering, with the cover referring to the memoirs / love letters that open the story, the pistol used in a murder and the rose garden where a missing jewel was buried.

THE STORY

In some ways it is impossible to summarise better than PAN's edition does on the back cover, but I'll take a different tack: Superintendent Battle investigates the murder of a Balkan prince at an English stately home and uncovers a maelstrom of motive, sub-plot and national stereotyping.

CHARACTERS

The characterisation of the house party is Agatha Christie at her best and worst. The nobles portrayed (Lord Caterham, Bundle, Virginia Revel) are very noble, the bourgeoisie (Lomax and Eversleigh) dull and plodding, and the foreigners (Isaacstein, M. Lemoine, Hiram P. Fish and Anthony Cade) all sharp and 'quick on the uptake'; even so, none has a clue what is really going on.

Superintendent Battle, who knows exactly what is going on, watches them all in quiet amusement.

QUOTES

What would today be seen as far worse than casual racism abounds in this book, especially in the descriptions of perceived national characteristics. Jews tended to get the bulk of it in her early books, but the actual Jewish characters themselves are never villains and often the opposite - for example Julius Hersheimmer (*The Secret Adversary*), Jim Lazarus (*Peril at End House*), Oliver Manders (*Three Act Tragedy*), and Isaacstein here.

I think that she sometimes uses the stereotyping as a means of mis-leading her readers, who may well have instinctively shared such notions, which were common-place at the time that the book was published. Here are a few examples from the text:

'Dagoes':

> *"There was a dago whose life I saved ..."*
> *"Just pulled this dago out of the river. Like all dagoes he couldn't swim ..."*
> *"I like to see your righteous heat, James, but let me point out to you dagoes will be dagoes."*

Jews:

> *"Hebraic people. Yellow-faced financiers in City offices ..."*
> *He had a fat yellow face, and black eyes, as impenetrable as those of a cobra. There was a generous curve to the big nose and power in the square lines of the vast jaw ... His voice was deep and rich and had a certain compelling quality about it ...*

Herzoslovakians (see also "Dagoes"):

> *Half a dozen men were sprawling round a table. Four of them were big thick-set men, with high cheekbones, and eyes set in Magyar slanting fashion. The other two were rat-like little men with quick gestures.*

Africans:

> *"Merciful heaven! He has married a black woman in Africa!"*
> *"Come, come, it's not so bad as all that," said Anthony laughing. "She's white enough - white all through, bless her."*

The Rest of the World - the future King of Herzoslovakia explains his planned autocratic style to Battle (who approves):

> "I still believe in democracy. But you've got to force it on people with a strong hand - ram it down their throats. My belief in the brotherhood of man died the day I arrived in London last week, when I observed the people standing in a tube train resolutely refuse to move up and make room for those who entered ... I believe in the brotherhood of man but it's not coming yet awhile ... Evolution is a slow process."

SWIGATHA RATING 8/10

I absolutely adored this book when I first read it as a boy. Twist after twist after twist! I also appreciated the humour. Having re-read it just now, I would still recommend it to children, with maybe a word of caution that attitudes towards people of other nationalities have changed somewhat in the last century.

It is by a mile the best of her 'Gay Young Adventurer' stories, and the final twist is very satisfying, as there are clues a-plenty all the way through that set it up.

WHERE IT LED

Many of the characters - Caterham, Bundle, Lomax, Eversleigh and Battle - re-appear in *The Seven Dials Mystery* (1929). It has none of the wit or charm of *Chimneys*.

ADAPTATIONS

'Chimneys' was the title of Agatha Christie's adaptation for the stage, her first. There have been no screen adaptations yet in which the story is recognisable. Here is a Guardian review of the ITV version, which replaces Battle with Miss Marple and manages to come up with a plot even more ridiculous than the original (at least Christie was playing it for laughs):

> In Julia McKenzie, we have a Marple who gives few signs of consciousness. She sprang to life in the last 10 minutes to deliver the astonishing explanation that the gunshot was not a gunshot but a firework, and that the Marquis of Caterham had both hidden the diamond and accidentally killed the maid 23 years earlier while she was trying to stop him discovering that his wife, who was now dead, had been having an affair with a bloke in an orchestra who now turned out to be the Austrian count who was actually the real father of the marquis's daughter, Virginia[1].

Should anyone ever dare to make a proper version, I hope they keep the racy dialogue of the book and the highly individual characters intact. There is an element of P.G.Wodehouse's Lord Emsworth about Caterham.

NOTES

[1] John Crace, Review in The Guardian, Christmas 2010

The Murder of Roger Ackroyd (1926)

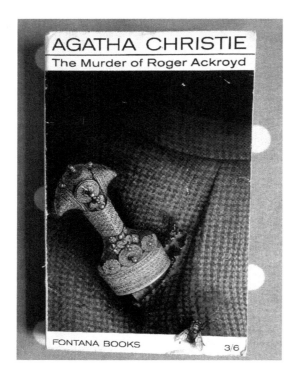
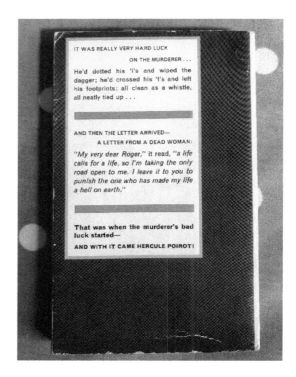

THE BOOK   Fontana, 1963 pp 254 [1]

A great Tom Adams cover, referencing the Tunisian dagger used in the murder and made memorable by the inclusion of the insect crawling up the dead man's back. Insects would feature in many of his later covers. There is a daft and irrelevant spiel on the back cover - for a start, the "letter" precipitated the murder rather than coming afterwards.

THE STORY

Poirot has retired to King's Abbott to grow vegetable marrows. He makes friends with his new neighbours by singular means, and soon becomes involved with them in a murder investigation. The book is narrated by one of the neighbours (Dr Sheppard).

CHARACTERS AND QUOTES - spoiler!

Possibly because this time the narrator is somewhat shrewder than the sometimes vacuous Hastings, the supporting cast is drawn with more care and humour than is often the case.

The different manifestations of the love between Roger Ackroyd and Mrs Ferrars, James and Caroline Sheppard, Miss Russell and Charles Kent, Ralph Paton and Ursula Bourne, Flora Ackroyd and

Hector Blunt keep the plot moving, and enable the reader to overlook some of the absurdities of the *how-dun-it-in-the-time-available*.

The character of the narrator is far more complex and fully-formed than the Hastings that he replaces, and his sister is described with an obvious affection (she became the template for Miss Marple later). Poirot is wonderfully and humorously drawn, starting with his deliberately mangled *franglais* (see below), leading to his increasing use of French expressions (all of which everyone involved is expected to understand), and ending with his anarchic solution: for not the first or the last time, Poirot uncovers the truth and keeps it from the authorities, meting out his own version of justice.

From then on during his career, Poirot's attitude is quite often at odds with the justice system of the time, and not one you would immediately associate with *un bon catholique*.

Here is Poirot introducing himself to his new neighbour (having flung a vegetable marrow over the fence):

> *"I demand of you a thousand pardons, monsieur. I am without defence. For some months now I cultivate the marrows. This morning I suddenly enrage myself with these marrows. I send them to promenade themselves - alas, not only mentally but physically. I seize the biggest. I hurl him over the wall. Monsieur, I am ashamed. I prostrate myself."*

There is a gentle humour underpinning the plot. Here is a typical example:

> *Blunt said nothing for a minute or two. Then he looked away from Flora into the middle distance and observed to an adjacent tree trunk that it was about time he got back to Africa.*

SWIGATHA RATING 9/10

Like many of her novels, this one is perhaps most famous for the ingenuity of its conclusion, but I think it is also among the best-written and funniest of all of them. It is not always appreciated how amusing Agatha Christie's writing can be.

So, the book rates almost - as the Mah Jongg players might say in the Shanghai Club – a "Tin Ho", the Perfect Winning: it nearly got a 10. Unfortunately, however brilliant the idea behind the plot is, I don't think its timing works.

For example, the killer is invited by Roger Ackroyd in the morning to come to supper at 7:30pm. He decides to kill him that evening. His alibi will require him to tamper in his workshop with Ackroyd's dictaphone so that it starts playing at a specific time, and get a stranger he meets in the afternoon to call him at home at another specific time - before he knows what time he will get the chance to be alone with his host.

WHAT HAPPENED NEXT

This is the book with which Agatha Christie came of age as a crime novelist. It was also the one current at the time that she disappeared for 11 days, sparking off a manhunt that, bizarrely, involved Conan Doyle and Dorothy L Sayers (i.e. she was a major celebrity even then). The solution to Ackroyd's murder caused a sensation at the time, and its structure has continued to exercise the minds of academics and critics ever since.

For Agatha Christie, along with the acquisition of global fame came the realisation came that, if she had to stick with Poirot, she could make him a much more rounded figure without Hastings around. The good Captain comes back every few years from the Argentine for the odd "hunt", but some of her finest Poirot stories would have been impossible with him in tow (and narrating). Also, within a couple of years, Caroline Sheppard had been transformed into Miss Marple, with the publication of the first stories that would eventually comprise *The Thirteen Problems*.

WHAT HAPPENED ELSEWHERE

The solution to Ackroyd's murder caused a sensation at the time, and its structure has continued to exercise the minds of academics and critics ever since.

Among those contributing to the debate have been Roland Barthes, Edmund Wilson, Umberto Eco and Raymond Chandler, plus the Sorbonne Professor of Literature, Pierre Bayard.

In 1998, Bayard brought out a book called *Qui a tué Roger Ackroyd?* (which translates as *Who Killed Roger Ackroyd?*). It argued (and argued it almost undeniably well) that Poirot was suffering from delusions, that Sheppard was innocent and that his confession was to protect the real culprit, his beloved sister. It might sound absurd that the minds of the great should be troubled by a whodunit plot twist, but a discussion about what readers can know, and what they have to fill in for themselves, is interesting in the context of any novel, and especially when it is narrated.

ADAPTATIONS

There was an appalling ITV adaptation in 2000 which reflected none of the charm or humour of the book. Worse, it changed possibly the most famous twist and ending of any detective novel, ever, replacing it with a fatuous bang-bang chase sequence. Maybe the screenwriter had been reading Prof. Bayard.

There was a Russian adaptation in 2002 titled *Ne-udatcha Poirot* (which translates as *Poirot's Failure*) that plays it pretty straight. The title comes from Sheppard's *Apologia*:

> *A strange end to my manuscript. I meant it to be published some day as the history of one of Poirot's failures!*

There is also a quite brilliant semi-spoof of *The Murder of Roger Ackroyd* by Gilbert Adair called *The Act of Roger Murgatroyd*. The twist at the end is up there with Agatha Christie's.

NOTES

[1] At the back of Fontana paperbacks of the time there was usually an *Also available from Fontana* section, which listed books of a similar genre with a short, edited extract designed to intrigue the reader. The back pages of this book contained the following, bizarre, blurb:

A QUESTION OF PROOF Nicholas Blake

"Why should anyone? And who? WHO? The Hayfield. A body in it. Ugh! I wonder where? In OUR haycastle? ... Oh, how lovely Hero looked this morning, her body golden in the sunlight ... But not where Hero and I were! ... She may be the headmaster's wife but she's also my own true love ... so don't let them find the body in our haycastle ... PLEASE!"

Incredibly, 'Nicholas Blake' was a pseudonym of Cecil Day Lewis, the UK's poet laureate at the time (and father of actor Daniel).

The Big Four (1927)

THE BOOK PAN, pp 156

Slightly tatty, but it held together - you can tell it's been read by the seaside. It cost me 9d (4p). The cover, alluding to the death of a chess Grandmaster, is better than the contents!

THE STORY

Hastings returns from his ranch in Argentina and drops in on Poirot only to find him packed for a trip to South America ... within minutes someone staggers into Poirot's rooms and dies, but not before revealing the existence of a 'Big Four'[1] conspiracy to provoke world disorder and then take over.

Originally a series of short stories for *The Sketch* magazine, it is another of Christie's "World Domination Conspiracy" plots, but the only one to be foiled by Poirot and Hastings.

The stories were published together in novel form in 1927, but they had clearly been written before *Roger Ackroyd* was published in 1926.

The author herself gives some background into what was clearly a 'rushed job':

Ever since my mother's death (in 1926) I had been unable to write a word. A book was due this year, and having spent so much on Styles I had no money in hand ... It was vital that I should write another book as soon as possible ... My brother-in-law ... suggested that the last twelve stories published in The Sketch should be run together, so that they would have the appearance of a book ... He helped me with the work - I was still unable to tackle anything of the kind. In the end it was published under the title of The Big Four, and turned out to be quite popular[2].

She might also have added that, at the same time, her husband had just walked out on her, leaving her a single parent and thus even more desperate for the money.

CHARACTERS AND ATTITUDES

Countess Vera Rossakoff, who had previously appeared in a couple of short stories on the edge of criminal activity, returns to captivate Poirot further. The individuals comprising The Big Four are mere ciphers; indeed, Li Chang Yen never even appears.

There is also a rare outing for one Achille Poirot, Hercule's 'brother'.

Because of the origins of this 'novel', there is no room for the exposition and development of any of the characters, so there is nothing else to say here.

SWIGATHA RATING 2/10

It doesn't work as a novel, and the ending is just dashed off. The quote from her autobiography above shows how much she thought of it and how little time she spent on it. I "quite enjoyed it" at the age of 12 but it is an embarrassment to read it again as an adult.

WHAT HAPPENED NEXT

Let Poirot tell us:

"Yes, mon ami, together we have faced and routed the Big Four; and now you will return to your charming wife, and I - I shall retire. The great case of my life is over. Anything will seem tame after this. No, I shall retire. Possibly I shall grow vegetable marrows! I might even marry and arrange myself!"

Indeed, Poirot next appears in *The Murder of Roger Ackroyd* as The Man Who Grew Vegetable Marrows and Hastings returns to his ranch in 'the Argentine'. These were the last of the 41

Hastings/Poirot short stories to be written, although some earlier ones were not collected and published in book form until 1974 (*Poirot's Early Cases*).

ADAPTATIONS

ITV produced a version for its final *Poirot* series in 2013. In this adaptation, far from trying to foil a dastardly conspiracy, as in the novel, Poirot sets out to prove that there is *no such thing* as the Big Four. It is a better film than the book deserves (another example!). The Countess and Achille, and various cartoon foreigners, were ditched, mercifully, but Miss Lemon and Inspector Japp were included, thereby allowing a final appearance in these adaptations of the *real* Big Four...

NOTES

[1] In the aftermath of World War 1, there was a huge swathe of civil unrest and civil war around the globe; the expression 'The Big Four', however, was used in reference to the recently victorious Allied Powers (the US, the UK, France and Italy) rather than some background figures apparently orchestrating it all it all. Maybe the author was being mischievous; maybe she was making a subtle point!

[2] Agatha Christie, *An Autobiography*

The Mystery of the Blue Train (1928)

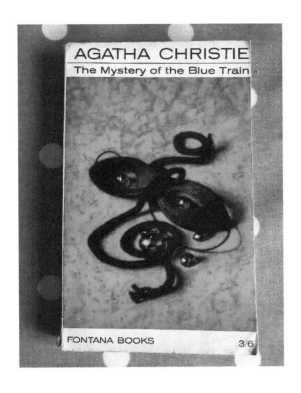
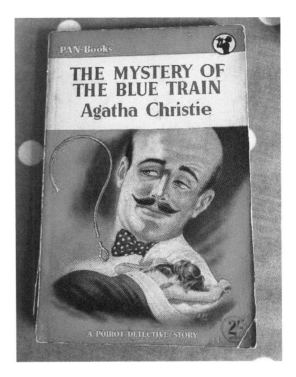

THE BOOK   PAN, 1954 pp 188

The PAN edition is not an attractive one, with a bland and fairly meaningless cover image: the dead woman was completely disfigured by the murderer, Poirot's head is shaped like a pear rather than an egg and the question mark has echoes of both that head and a hangman's rope.

The even blander Fontana cover was painted by Tom Adams, and not one of his favourites. The jewels are the fateful gift from Rufus van Aldin to his daughter, Ruth Kettering.

THE STORY

Katherine Grey comes into a fortune and decides to travel to the South of France on the Blue Train. *En route*, she meets Ruth Kettering, who is later found murdered on the train.

Also on the train is Hercule Poirot, who invites Miss Grey to join his investigation of the crime, Katherine having earlier intimated to him her love of *les romans policiers*.

CHARACTERS

The most sympathetic character is Katherine Grey. Before she came into the money she had spent '*a great deal of her life listening, and those who have listened do not find it easy to talk*'. Katherine is in her 30s, shy and on her own, as was the author at the time - hence the sympathetic treatment.

At least four characters are given forenames or surnames beginning with "K", to facilitate a daft clue about a case with that initial on it.

My favourite character is the "information specialist" Mr Goby, a small, elderly man, shabbily dressed, with eyes that looked carefully all round a room, and never at the person he was addressing:

> *Mr Goby sat down with his hands on his knees, and gazed earnestly at the radiator ...*
> *Mr Goby transferred his gaze from the radiator to the left-hand drawer of the desk ...*
> *Mr Goby smiled understandingly at the fender ...*

ATTITUDES AND QUOTES

Unusually, it is the attitude of the author here that gives one pause. Most of the nationalist or racist comments in her stories are used to delineate the character of the speaker; not here. These quotes are all taken from the *first page* of the book. This is not a first page written by a happy author.

> *A little man with the face of a rat ... In an Empire where rats ruled, he was the king of the rats ...*

> *There was a hint of a curve in the thin nose. His father had been a Polish Jew, a journeyman tailor. It was business such as his father would have loved that took him abroad to-night.*

> *The electric light was shaded with dirty pink festoons, and it softened, but could not disguise, the girl's face with its mask of crude paint. Could not disguise, either, the broad Mongolian cast of her countenance. There was no doubt of Olga Demiroff's profession, nor of her nationality.*

SWIGATHA RATING 4/10

It is readable as usual, but I don't think many would rate it their favourite. Agatha Christie certainly didn't:

> *To begin with, I had no joy in writing, no elan. I had worked out the plot - a conventional plot, partly adapted from one of my other stories... I have always hated the Mystery of the Blue Train ...* [1]

... and it shows; this was the first new novel that she wrote after her mother's death and her husband's abandonment of her.

Even the plot itself isn't original; it is based on that of the short story *The Plymouth Express*, published just four years earlier. The book got the covers it deserved.

WHAT HAPPENED NEXT

Katherine Grey went back to live in the village of St Mary Mead ... there is no record of her ever meeting with a certain Jane Marple, although the Tuesday Night Club stories, set in St Mary Mead and featuring Miss Marple, were being published around the same time.

The 'small elderly man' Mr Goby, as described in this book, evidently shared Poirot's talent for longevity – he is still being employed by him over 40 years later.

The carriage attendant on the Blue Train, Pierre Michel, switched lines: he reappears as carriage attendant on the Orient Express, in time for another murder, six years later.

ADAPTATIONS

An adaptation was made for the ITV *Poirot* series in 2005. It looks good, and is quite amusing, but, understandably because they had already shown *The Plymouth Express*, changes are made to the plot; not all work (the indomitable Miss Grey faces murder attempts by two different people, a group of nuns is added for no obvious reason, and the character of Mr Goby is ditched[2]).

NOTES

[1] Agatha Christie, *An Autobiography*

[2] Although he appeared in five Poirot novels, Mr Goby has never appeared in any of the TV adaptations. Contrast that with Miss Lemon, who appears in only four Poirot novels and two short stories, but features in over 40 *Poirot* adaptations.

The Seven Dials Mystery (1929)

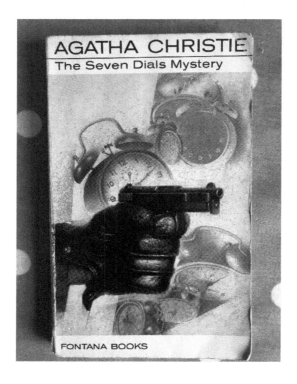 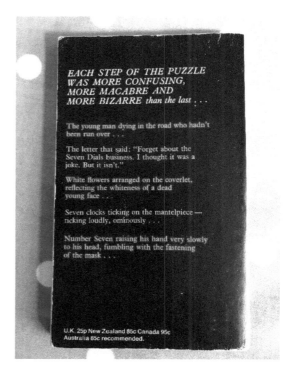

THE BOOK   Fontana, 1967 pp 189

Tom Adams' cover features seven clocks (Seven Dials is a district in the centre of London, but the title refers to a mysterious secret society that meets there). The gloved hand is his own; because he painted right-handed, the gun is held in his left[1].

THE STORY

'Chimneys' is once again the setting for murder when Sir Oswald Coote, who is renting Lord Caterham's ancestral home, hosts a house-party. One of the guests, Gerry Wade, is a notorious over-sleeper, and his friends resolve to give him a shock. They sneak into his room in the middle of the night and leave eight alarm clocks in there.

The following morning, it is they who are given a shock. Gerry Wade is dead in his bed, and one of the eight clocks has been thrown out of his bedroom window.

Lord Caterham's daughter Eileen, known as 'Bundle', decides to investigate further ...

CHARACTERS - spoiler!

One of Agatha Christie's early 'light-hearted' thrillers, *Seven Dials* re-unites several of the characters from *The Secret of Chimneys* with the indomitable, wooden and twinkling Superintendent Battle.

There are the Wodehousean Lord Caterham and his feisty daughter Bundle, their imperious gardener MacDonald, the verbally-diarrhoetic MP George 'Codders' Lomax, the seemingly empty-headed Bill Eversleigh, and the faithful retainer Tredwell.

Added to this mix are that 'amiable youth, Jimmy Thesiger', a Bertie Wooster type with his own Jeeves in his man-servant Stevens, Gerry's sister-who-isn't Lorraine Wade, the industrialist Sir Oswald Coote and his wife (who yearns for the time before he made his fortune) and a few more bright young things with names like Socks and Pongo.

Finally, on the outside of this crowd, there is The Seven Dials, a group of people who sit around a table with bags over their heads that have clockfaces drawn on them.

The dialogue throughout is witty and light-hearted, but somehow the main characters are not as endearing as they had been in *The Secret of Chimneys*.

Christie clearly has a great affection for her 'Chimneys' characters, and cannot conceal her horror at the prospect of the Cootes of this world inheriting their family seats in the decades to come[2].

ATTITUDES AND QUOTES

The opening lines of the book are these:

> *That amiable youth, Jimmy Thesiger, came racing down the big staircase at Chimneys two steps at a time.*

Almost the only thing we discover about Jimmy Thesiger, the main character, at times almost the narrator of the story, is that he is an amiable youth. It is repeated two or three times with exactly the same words. This is typical Agatha Christie, setting up the twist for later.

Lady Coote abhors her new found status, and laments for the times when she and her husband 'knew their place':

> *Lady Coote was a big, handsome woman in a tragic sort of fashion ... She looked as though she had some secret sorrow in her life, and yet if truth be told, Lady Coote had had no trouble*

in her life whatsoever, except the meteoric rise to prosperity of Sir Oswald. As a young girl she had been a jolly flamboyant creature, very much in love with Oswald Coote, the aspiring young man in the bicycle-shop next to her father's hardware store.

Here's a typical piece of advice from Caterham to his daughter:

"You shouldn't shoot people," said Lord Caterham in a tone of mild remonstrance. "You shouldn't, really. I daresay some of them richly deserve it - but all the same it will lead to trouble."

And here, Bundle has just been asked by Coote whether Chimneys might be for sale (her horror at the idea would have been shared by Sir Oswald's wife):

Bundle felt her breath taken away. She had a nightmare vision of England with innumerable Cootes in innumerable counterparts of Chimneys - all, be it understood, with an entirely new system of plumbing installed.

Finally, here is a clairvoyant quote from the amiable youth:

"Oh, I was born to be hanged," said Jimmy.

He said it.

SWIGATHA RATING 5/10

As ever, this is hugely readable and with some amusing moments, but the idea behind the Seven Dials group is ludicrous. Once you have excluded the casts of characters from Chimneys and Seven Dials, there is only really one possible suspect close to home, and the role of his accomplice Lorraine does not ring true at all. Would she really have readily connived in the death of the step-brother she grew up happily with?

WHERE IT LED

That same year, 1929, Agatha Christie published *Partners in Crime*, a book of short stories featuring those other bright young things, Tommy and Tuppence.

After that, she veered away from the 'light-hearted thriller', apart from a last shot with *Why Didn't They Ask Evans?* in 1934. In the interim, she began to emerge as a detective fiction writer on a different level to her contemporaries (and successors).

Agatha Christie's attitude towards the landed gentry became somewhat more equivocal in the 1930s, with characters such as the Lords Edgware, Ferguson (*Death on the Nile*) and Whitfield (*Murder is Easy*) evincing nothing of Caterham's charm.

ADAPTATIONS

There was an ITV adaptation in 1981 with a strong cast, including John Gielgud as Lord Caterham and Cheryl Campbell as Bundle. It more than does the book justice, and is worth watching. The part of Jimmy Thesiger was played by James Warwick, who was to play Tommy Beresford in the same company's adaptation of *Partners in Crime* a few months later.

NOTES

[1] … according to *Tom Adams' Agatha Christie Cover Story*

[2] … what Christie fan Evelyn Waugh would later describe in *Brideshead Revisited* as the 'Age of Hooper'

Partners in Crime (1929)

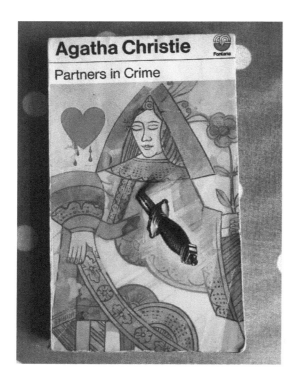 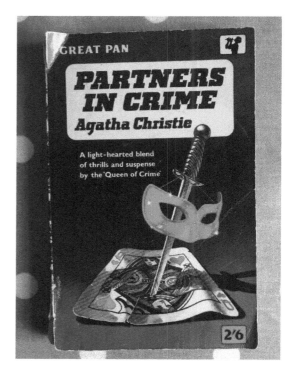

THE BOOK   Fontana, 1971 pp 189

The Fontana book has a remarkably dreary cover that its back proclaims (correctly!) is by Tom Adams. He says that the 'awfully jolly pranks of the amateur sleuths Tommy and Tuppence' are 'lightweight stuff', so he gave it a 'lightweight cover to match'[1].

His cover bears remarkable similarities to an earlier PAN cover. Both focus on the same story ('Finessing the King / The Gentleman Dressed in Newspaper') - unsurprisingly, because it is one of the few that have much of a plot.

THE STORIES

Seven years on from their adventures as recounted in *The Secret Adversary*, Tommy and Tuppence Beresford find themselves bored and desperate for something to happen. Out of the blue, they receive a visit from Mr Carter, a somewhat nebulous character whose outfit has just bought up a detective agency. Mr Carter wonders whether Tommy and Tuppence would like to run it, and at the same time perhaps uncover a secret conspiracy of the kind that infected swigathas in the 1920s.

They agree to do so on condition that they can imitate the antics of other fictional detectives of the time during their investigations.

CHARACTERS

Most of the characters are somewhat stereotypical; perhaps that is not surprising given that some of the stories are very short. Tommy and Tuppence's determination to play each investigation in the manner of different detectives becomes a very tedious element of the book, especially for the 99% of readers who have never heard of most of them.

They run through Thorndyke, Francis and Desmond Okewood, M'Carty, Thornley Colton, Father Brown, The Old Man in the Corner, Hanaud, Roger Sheringham and Dr Fortune before ending up as Poirot and Hastings.

ATTITUDES

Agatha Christie was always interested in genetic engineering:

> *"Tuppence," said Tommy, "you take my breath away. The whole thing is the most immoral business I ever heard of. You aid and abet this young man to marry out of his class – "*
> *"Stuff," said Tuppence. "Janet is a splendid girl - and the queer thing is that she really adores that weak-kneed young man. You can see with half a glance what his family needs. Some good red blood in it ..."*

Agatha Christie rarely had much time for senior officers, retired or not:

> *"Francis Haviland, who always was and always will be one of the most perfect asses God ever made!"*
> *"You forget I used to drive him about during the war, when he was a General. Ah! those were the good old days."*
> *"They were," agreed Tommy.*

It is interesting that both Tommy (who was injured on the Western Front) and Tuppence (who nursed there) find themselves pining for what by all accounts was hell on earth. It was a view shared by many others after they had finally returned to Blighty in 1919-20[2].

Here, Tommy pretends to be able to recognise racial characteristics even when blindfolded. Tuppence confirms it, thereby confirming that she too can discern someone's origins just by looking at them.

43

> *"The man two tables from us is a very wealthy profiteer, I fancy," said Tommy carelessly. "Jew, isn't he?"*
>
> *"Pretty good," said Tuppence appreciatively.*

Finally, Agatha Christie lets slip what she thinks of one of her own creations:

> *"I've a feeling," said Tuppence, "that this particular adventure will be called* The Triumph of Hastings.*"*
>
> *"Never,' said Tommy. "It isn't done. Once the idiot friend, always the idiot friend."*

SWIGATHA RATING 3/10

There are some good ideas and twists in these stories (*The Ambassadors's Boots*, *The Man in the Mist*), but it seems a shame to waste them on such poor material. *The Unbreakable Alibi* features the most obviously breakable alibi one could hope for (very unusual for a Christie).

WHAT HAPPENED NEXT

At the end, Tuppence announces that she is having a baby, due in 1925. When we next encounter the Beresfords, in *N or M* (1941), the baby proves to be a rather remarkable pair of twins: the boy Derek is already an RAF veteran and the girl Deborah is working hush hush.

ADAPTATIONS

The stories were adapted for ITV in the UK, featuring Francesca Annis and James Warwick as the detective duo. It is a slow-paced, light-hearted series that does its best with the light-weight material.

NOTES

[1] *Tom Adams' Agatha Christie Cover Story*

[2] Watch Peter Jackson's documentary WW1 film *They Shall Not Grow Old* for myriad examples of this sentiment.

The Mysterious Mr Quin (1930)

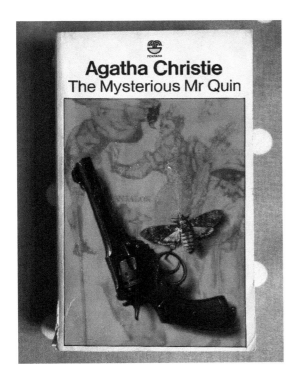
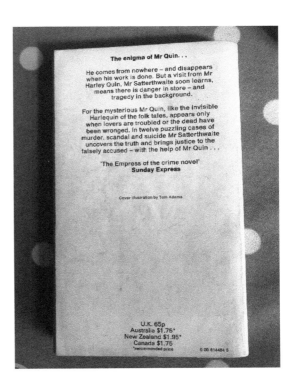

THE BOOK   Fontana, 1977 pp 255

A Tom Adams cover featuring yet another insect (the wonderfully-named Death's Head Hawk Moth) and a revolver pinned to a background drawing of characters from the *commedia dell'arte*, the inspiration for this book's main character, the Harlequin.

THE STORIES

The Mysterious Mr Quin is a collection of 12 short stories, all bar one of which had been published in magazines such as *The Strand* during the 1920s. In terms of the number of pages, it is the longest of any of Agatha Christie's crime fiction books.

There are two characters who appear in each story: Mr Satterthwaite, a dried-up little elf of a man in his 60s, and Harley Quin, a shadowy character who materialises at a crucial moment in each story and disappears just as suddenly after giving those present their cue for action. Mr Satterthwaite had all his life been an on-looker, 'sitting in the stalls', with the world's dramas and tragedies seemingly devised for his own personal entertainment, he himself taking little part in them.

Mr Quin represents the invisible Harlequin of old, one who 'speaks for the dead that cannot speak for themselves' and 'a friend to lovers'. He is also an on-looker, but one unable to intervene in the action. Instead, he plays the silent director who puts Satterthwaite centre-stage, using him as his agent to resolve injustices from the past and prevent those of the future.

Thus Mr Satterthwaite is soon surprised to find himself instrumental in thwarting at least three potential suicides, uncovering a long-lost precious ruby and smoothing the path to happiness of various young lovers.

CHARACTERS AND ATTITUDES

Mr Satterthwaite and Mr Quin were two of Agatha Christie's own personal favourite characters, and they are characterised with more subtlety than many others from the period (the 1920s). But not always... here is Satterthwaite the snob, and apparent anti-semite, anti-foreigner etc (from *The Soul of the Croupier*):

> *Mr Satterthwaite had seen the Countess at Monte Carlo for many seasons now. The first time he had seen her she had been in the Company of a Grand Duke. On the next occasions she was with an Austrian Baron. On successive years her friends had been of Hebraic extraction, sallow men with hooked noses, wearing rather flamboyant jewellery.*

> *"I mean, you know all the Duchesses and Earls and Countesses and things."*
> *"A good many of them," said Mr Satterthwaite. "And also the Jews and the Portuguese and the Greeks and the Argentines."*
> *"Eh?" said Mr Rudge.*
> *"I was just explaining," said Mr Satterthwaite, "that I move in English society."*

Here is Satterthwaite the habitual onlooker - life to him is almost like a soap opera:

> *"In the first place, I doubt if I should have the courage (to commit suicide). It needs courage and I am not at all a brave individual. And in the second place -"*
> *"Well?"*
> *"I always want to know what is going to happen tomorrow."*
> (The Man from the Sea)

And here is Satterthwaite as connoisseur:

> *"Sometimes there are very wonderful things on a rubbish heap," said Mr Quin.*
>
> *"I know, I know," cried Mr Satterthwaite, and quoted with just a trace of self-consciousness:*
>
> *"'Bring me the two most beautiful things in the city, said God'. You know how it goes, eh?"*
>
> *Mr Quin nodded.*   (Harlequin's Lane)

Satterthwaite is proud of his levels of cultural appreciation and here he is quoting from Oscar Wilde's *The Happy Prince* (how many of her readers would now appreciate what he and Quin are getting at?).

But it is a most appropriate comment: in Wilde's story, the 'two most beautiful things' that are brought back to God by his angel are the leaden heart of the prince, and the dead body of his friend the swallow, both found on a rubbish heap, thus presaging the fate of Kharsanova in *Harlequin's Lane*.

AFTERWORD

Mr Satterthwaite's senses are sharpened each time he encounters Mr Quin, and he enjoys his spell in the limelight, but by the end (*Harlequin's Lane*) he realises that he will not allow any of it to have any lasting effect on his own character or way of life:

> *"But I – I have never been down your lane …"*
>
> *"And do you regret?"*
>
> *Mr Satterthwaite quailed. Mr Quin seemed to have loomed to enormous proportions. Mr Satterthwaite had a vista of something at once menacing and terrifying … Joy, Sorrow, Despair. And his comfortable little soul shrank back, appalled.*
>
> *"Do you regret?" Mr Quin repeated his question. There was something terrible about him.*
>
> *"No," Mr Satterthwaite stammered. "N-no."*
>
> *And then suddenly he rallied.*
>
> *"But I see things," he cried. "I may have been only a looker-on at Life – but I see things that other people do not. You said so yourself, Mr Quin …'*
>
> *But Mr Quin had vanished.*

Once each story has finished, as far as the other actors in the drama are concerned, Mr Satterthwaite may as well also have vanished in a puff of smoke along with his friend.

SWIGATHA RATING 7/10

The idea behind this collection - a spirit appearing from nowhere to inspire the righting of an old wrong or the prevention of a new one - is a brilliantly original one. There are no detectives or police in any of the stories.

The quality of some of them is mixed but the good ones - for example, *The Man from the Sea, The Soul of the Croupier* - are among the best she wrote. An overall atmosphere is sustained so that, as a collection, *The Mysterious Mr Quin* hangs together really well. The whole is greater than the sum of the parts.

ORIGINS - THE *COMMEDIA DELL'ARTE*

Agatha Christie's early poetry had included verses inspired by the characters of Harlequin and Columbine; there were a set of *commedia dell'arte* figurines in a cabinet at her home. She returned to these figures a few times in her early writing.

In the original Italian *commedia dell'arte* performances, Harlequin (Arlecchino) was a slapstick servant figure, in love with Columbine, of the kind able to outwit his master each time. The character portrayed by Agatha Christie is more akin to the one that evolved as this piece of street theatre travelled to France and England in the 18th and 19th centuries: from mischievous imp it had developed into something more mercurial and romantic, almost magical.

The Harlequin is not the only member of the troupe to appear in her stories; there are many references to them - for example:

> - the final story in this collection - *Harlequin's Lane* - features a masquerade involving the characters of Columbine, Pierrot and Pierrette
> - In *The Face of Helen*, Satterthwaite is surprised to find Mr Quin attending a performance of *I Pagliacci,* an opera set amongst a *commedia* troupe[1]
> - *The Affair at the Victory Ball*, the first story in the collection *Poirot's Early Cases*, features a fancy dress ball in which all the suspects dress up as characters from the *commedia dell'arte*
> - a Pierrot doll is found in Arlene Marshall's room in *Evil Under the Sun*, and in the Willetts' living-room in *The Sittaford Mystery.*

WHAT HAPPENED NEXT

The mercurial Mr Quin and Mr Satterthwaite appeared once more in the posthumously-published collection *Problem at Pollensa Bay*. Satterthwaite is also to be found in the company of Hercule Poirot in *Three Act Tragedy*.

One of the first *commedia dell'arte* troupes in Italy was founded by Isabella Andreini and her husband, and it may perhaps be not too fanciful to imagine that Agatha Christie used their name for two of the characters in *Murder on the Orient Express*: Count and Countess Andrenyi.

Finally, the germs of two future full-length works are present in some of these stories - *Taken at the Flood* (which uses the main clue from *The Sign in the Sky*) and the beginning of *Towards Zero* (which re-uses Satterthwaite's argument against suicide in *The Man from the Sea*).

ADAPTATIONS

These stories as a group have yet to be adapted for the cinema or TV although the very first silent film of an Agatha Christie story, in 1928, was based loosely on *The Coming of Mr Quinn* (sic).

Many of the stories have been read in abridged form by Martin Jarvis for BBC Radio, and these are repeated on Radio 4 Extra from time to time.

NOTES

[1] The closing line from *i Pagliacci* - '*La commedia é finita*!' - provided Christie with the final line of another opera-based short story - *Swan Song*, from *The Listerdale Mystery* collection.

The Murder at the Vicarage (1930)

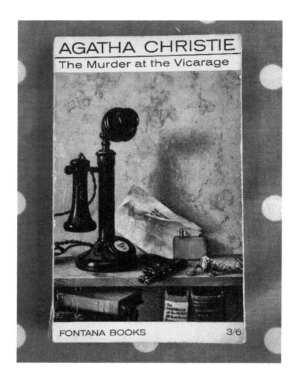

THE BOOK   Fontana, 1964 pp 191

This is an early Tom Adams cover from the 1960s with a somewhat literal take on elements of the story but also book-titles that hint at the involvement of a dig (the Baedeker) an artist (Lawrence Redding) and the Church of England (The Cornhill Magazine - hardly necessary given the title).

THE STORY

This was the first book to feature Miss Marple, although she had appeared in short stories published in magazines during the 1920s.

Colonel Protheroe, the obnoxious churchwarden of the parish of St Mary Mead, is shot dead in the vicarage study. There are a number of local people with different reasons to wish Protheroe harm, a fact acknowledged by the Rev. Clement himself on page one.

Clement is the narrator of the ongoing investigation, during which he comes to appreciate the qualities of his next-door neighbour, whom his wife Griselda had described as 'the worst cat in the village' at the start.

She has changed her mind somewhat by the end ...

CHARACTERS - spoiler!

Apart from Miss Marple herself, the strongest character in the book is the village of St Mary Mead, and there is a map at the front that helps establish it in the reader's imagination.

It is a popular notion that the village of St Mary Mead is awash in murder, but of all the novels featuring Miss Marple over the next 40 years only one other featured a murder that had actually *taken place* in the village (*The Mirror Crack'd from Side to Side*).

St Mary Mead is simply the source of Miss Marple's limitless village parallels and the place where she lives, alongside a wonderful cast of village characters, many of whom re-appear in later stories. Principal among these are Miss Marple's fellow gossip-cum-busybodies - Miss Hartnell, Miss Wetherby and Mrs Price Ridley.

Then there is also the vicarage servant Mary, apparently totally incompetent at every task, and the charming Griselda, who has no idea how to handle Mary but stoutly defends her against any attempts by the vicar to sack her. The vicar himself is a wry and amusing narrator. Here is an example of his ability to bring a character to life in less than a sentence:

> *Miss Wetherby, who is weather-beaten and jolly and much dreaded by the poor ...*

No need to say any more! The author has also managed to conjure up an image of a place that will live long in the imagination in very few words.

There is one interesting comment (for its time) from Dr Haydock, another local who will reappear in later stories:

> *"We think with horror now of the days when we burnt witches. I believe the day will come when we will shudder to think that we ever hanged criminals."*

This comment, from a character much respected by Miss Marple, is particularly interesting because the alternative, locking up convicted criminals for life, is described with similar horror in other Christie novels (*The ABC Murders*, for example).

SWIGATHA RATING 7/10

For the most part this is very much a fun read, but there are a few too many sub-plots, seemingly intended to pad the book out. I think it would read better as a short story, or novella. Anyone who has read swigathas before would guess whodunit like a shot.[1]

WHAT HAPPENED NEXT

There were no more Marple novels for the next dozen years. In 1932, however, she appeared in *The Thirteen Problems*, a brilliant collection of those stories that had been published in magazines in the late 1920s.

ADAPTATIONS

The BBC produced a TV film of the book in 1986, as part of their superb *Miss Marple* series. It sticks closely to the main threads whilst (understandably) ditching one or two of the sub-plots, improving the story thereby.

Robert Lang is superb as the loathsome Protheroe, Paul Eddington makes hay as the troubled vicar, and Cheryl Campbell twinkles as Griselda. Also excellent in a relatively minor role is Rachel Weaver as Mary, the real ruler of the roost at the Vicarage.

NOTES

[1] It is a rule-of-swig that anyone who emerges from a room holding their head in the hands, having just discovered a body, is hugely suspicious

The Sittaford Mystery (1931)

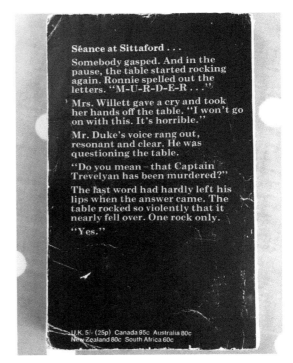

THE BOOK   Fontana, 1971 pp 191

Tom Adams' cover is a bit of a mish-mash. The table that featured in the séance is there, and the worried face of Mrs Willetts, but Captain Wyatt's bull-terrier is for no reason given prominence and it is not obvious who the man grimacing might be. The rest is presumably a depiction of séance emanations.

Nice blurb on the back though ...

THE STORY

Sittaford is a tiny village on the edge of Dartmoor, and as the story begins it is completely snowed in. With nothing else to entertain them, six local people decide to have a table-tapping séance. They are surprised to receive a message that Captain Trevelyan, the actual owner of the house that they are in, has been murdered in a house he was renting in Exhampton, six miles away.

One of the six, Major Burnaby, sets out in the teeth of a blizzard to check that his friend is all right ... he isn't. Trevelyan's somewhat shiftless nephew Jim is arrested for his murder. Emily Trefusis, engaged to Jim, and convinced that he wouldn't have had the guts to do it, travels to Sittaford to find out what really happened.

CHARACTERS AND ATTITUDES - spoiler!

This story has many of the characteristics of a cut-off-remote-village murder mystery (except that the murder takes place six miles away in a town, and one that has not been cut-off). There is a real village atmosphere about Sittaford, with a sprinkling of different characters who are all acquainted with each other without actually knowing each other at all. Sittaford is a village full of people who like to live cut off from everyone else.

Emily Trefusis is by far the most engaging character in the book. Her never-say-die attitude is matched by a gentle ability to manipulate others and re-enforced by a fierce common sense. She has total belief in herself, and, if not contempt, a wry opinion of the character of everyone else (including her fiancé). I think she is one of Agatha Christie's most endearing heroines; if anyone ever gets round to making a decent film of this story, hers would be a plum role.

The other characters in the village are lightly-sketched, almost enigmatic: the misanthropic Captain Wyatt and his servant Abdul; the invalid Miss Percehouse and her shiftless nephew Ronnie; the psychic researcher Rycroft. You get the impression that there is more to come from each of them, but nothing does.

The one other character padded out a bit more is the jealous Major Burnaby. There are quite a few ex-Army officers in the Christie canon; many of them have either gone to seed or are bad hats full stop. One thing Burnaby has going for him is an incredible ability to improvise: within minutes of the decision by the others to indulge in some table-turning, the good major has conjured up a very devious plan, and within half an hour has carried it out.

QUOTES

The early chapters give an interesting insight into some of the attitudes of a well-off village at the end of the 1920s.

> *Major Burnaby was between his hostess and Violet. On the other side of the girl was Ronnie Garfield. A cynical smile creased the major's lips. He thought to himself: "In my young day it was 'Up Jenkins'."*

This seemingly-bizarre thought is actually a reference to an old-drinking game in which members of one team conceal a coin in the palm of one of their hands under a table before slapping them down on the table-top. It is more commonly known these days as *Tippit*. The kind of game that one could only imagine English adults playing, it gave opportunities for coy youngsters to touch hands.

Here, Viola Willett gently joshes Ronnie Garfield, who comes across as a left-over character from *The Seven Dials Mystery*:

> *"Your aunt's very nice, but rather frightening."*
> *"I should think she was frightening. Snaps my head off sometimes. Thinks I've got no brains, you know."*
> *"Not really?"*
> *"Oh! Look here, don't say it like that. Lots of fellows look like fools and are laughing underneath."*

Although they all live close to each other in a remote village, no-one really knows anyone else:

> *Of course, Mr Duke was a very nice man, quite unassuming, but was he, after all, quite - well, quite? Mightn't he, just possibly, be a retired tradesman? But nobody liked to ask him - and indeed it was thought better not to know.*

Mr Duke is revealed at the end to be a retired senior police officer. Whether that would change or re-enforce the locals' attitude toward him is not stated.

Emliy's letter to her fiancé is written in the common parlance of the time:

> *Dearest Jim,*
> *Everything's going to be all right, so cheer up. I am working like the worst kind of n****r to find out the truth. What an idiot you've been, darling.*
> *Love from*
> *Emily*

Women's Lib still had a way to travel in 1931:

> *"Where's that bitch got to? Nice-looking girl." The association of ideas in his mind was quite natural.*

Captain Wyatt is referring to i) his dog and ii) Emily. Or it may be the other way round (naturally enough).

And here Mr Rycroft discusses Mr and Mrs Evans, servants to the dead captain:

> "If you had studied criminology, Miss Trefusis, you would realise the curious effect caused by inbreeding, especially in country districts."

Evans had already been described as having 'very long arms' and 'small, pig-like eyes' (eyes are often a significant character reference in swigathas).

SWIGATHA RATING 7/10

Very entertaining! This is an enjoyable read - a read-in-one-go type of book, in fact. It all seems fairly-clued as long as the readers don't examine the plot too closely as they race through it. If they stop to think, on the other hand, and discard the voices-from-the-other side theory, they might realise that the murderer would have had to be present at the séance - and only one person left it.

It was not obvious to this reader why the murderer should feel the need to shove a pair of the victim's boots up a chimney, and so give Emily the clue to the mystery, but what the heck!

WHAT HAPPENED NEXT

The Sittaford Mystery marked the start of a phenomenal period of output by Agatha Christie. Whether or not this is linked to her marriage to Max Mallowan the previous year is not clear, but she has broken free of the rut she found herself in during 1927-29.

ADAPTATIONS

The only one that I am aware of was a disaster actuated by ITV as part of its *Agatha Christie's Miss Marple* series. This is not Agatha Christie's Miss Marple at all.

This story is crying out for a proper adaptation. It would be a great choice as one of the BBC productions shown in the UK each Christmas.

Peril at End House (1932)

THE BOOK PAN, 1966 pp 191

The book was bought from EGB in Brighton, and so is a surviving "original". Not sure what the picture is supposed to represent; the murder takes place during a firework display in St Loo, but this looks like some kind of Chinese dragon.

THE STORY

Poirot and Hastings take a week's break on the Cornish Riviera and meet a girl who claims to have survived three near-death experiences. By the end you can make that five, with a sixth to come, which it is implied that she would not survive. In between, her namesake cousin is shot.

CHARACTERS

The book features a pretty strong cast, from murderer down to victim, with no ciphers: Fredericka Rice, the enigma, a drug addict treated with compassion; Vyse, the cold lawyer with strong morals; Commander Challenger ("navy man, can't mistake the type", but Hastings of course does); the gentle Maggie Buckley and the shrewd Lazarus. Even the murderer is quite likeable.

Agatha Christie seemingly had little time for doctors and quite often they were disreputable characters in her stories. In this one, the Harley St specialist Dr McAllister is at the centre of a cocaine racket.

Inspector Japp re-appears for the first time in 8 years, the unlikely premise being that he needed to come in person to deliver some information requested by Poirot.

ATTITUDES

Some of Agatha Christie's references to Jewish people in the 1920s books make this reader shudder, so it was with some trepidation that I looked for her characters' descriptions of Jim Lazarus:

> "He's a Jew, of course, but a frightfully decent one."   Nick Buckley

> A tall, fair rather exquisite young man, with a rather fleshy nose and over-emphasised good looks. He had a supercilious manner and a tired drawl. There was a sleekness about him I especially disliked. Hastings

> "He is clever, that one. Note the shape of the head."   Poirot

> "I dismiss the long-nosed M. Lazarus who has offered fifty pounds for a picture that was only worth twenty (it is odd, that, when you come to think of it. Most uncharacteristic of his race)." Poirot

So far, so 1920s. However, this time she has Lazarus emerge as the kindest and shrewdest character in the book, and providing the love interest to boot. At the end, Poirot even asks the clever Lazarus to explain to him something he cannot understand.

SWIGATHA RATING 7/10

Very readable and amusing, as most of the books narrated by Hastings are. It features one of those famous inadvertent comments of his that end up revealing the truth to Poirot, which are always good fun. I loved it as a child.

The identity of the murderer is pretty obvious to an adult, however, and in case anyone fails to spot whodunit, Christie gives it away in the chapter headings, itemising the suspects:

Ch 9.   A to J

Ch 20.   J

Ch 21.   The Person - K.

Unless Poirot, Hastings or Japp is guilty, there is only one person it *could* be, because the suspects listed from A to J had included every other character in the book, even a small 'ghoulish' child.

WHERE IT LED

Peril at End House represents something of a gateway into Agatha Christie's golden-age, especially for those books featuring Poirot. It is on another level from most of the books that she had published in the 1920s. Many elements would recur in her later works, and her seasoned readers would soon realise that, for example:

  - when a letter is shown, scrutinise it very carefully
  - when a character claims someone is trying to kill them, scrutinise them very carefully
  - first names and nicknames can be very misleading

It also led to the toning-down of casual prejudice in future books, and the re-introduction as a regular of Inspector Japp, who would appear in many of the golden-age Poirot stories until his final appearance in 1940 (in *One, Two, Buckle My Shoe*).

ADAPTATIONS

The book was turned into a play by Arnold Ridley in 1940 (a dramatist who later played Pte Godfrey in Dad's Army).

In 1990, *Peril at End House* became the first full-length Christie novel to be adapted by ITV for its *Agatha Christie's Poirot* series (up until then all we had seen were the early short stories). It is one of the very best, paying extremely close attention to the plot (apart from omitting 'J'). All the characters look the part and Polly Walker is terrific as Nick.

The Thirteen Problems (1932)

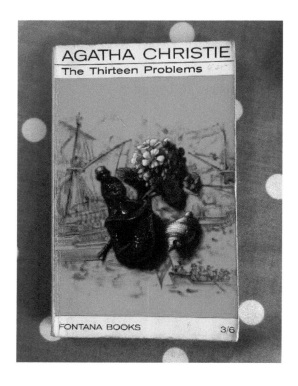 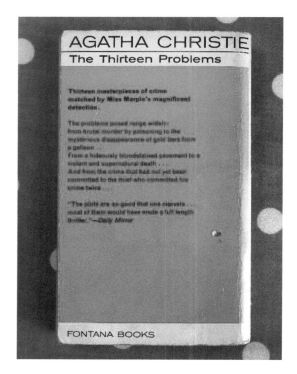

THE BOOK   Fontana, 1965 pp 192

Tom Adams' cover contains images inspired by *Ingots of Gold* and *The Blue Geranium*, two of the stories in the collection. The dedication is to Leonard and Katherine Woolley, whom Agatha Christie had met on her first trip to the Middle East in the 1920s.

THE STORIES

These stories are the first to feature Miss Marple. They were originally published in *Royal* magazine from 1927, the year after the publication of *The Murder of Roger Ackroyd*. The character of Miss Marple was based in part on that of Caroline Sheppard (who had featured in *Ackroyd*), and in part on Agatha Christie's Grannie, who 'always expected the worst of everyone and everything, and was, with almost frightening accuracy, usually proved right'[1].

Six people are spending a cosy Tuesday evening around the fire at Miss Jane Marple's home in St Mary Mead. They form The Tuesday Night Club, and agree that, each week, one of them will relate a mystery, unsolved at the time, and the others will suggest solutions to it.

The party contains Sir Henry Clithering, an ex-Commissioner of Scotland Yard, Raymond West, modernist author and Miss Marple's nephew, his actress girlfriend, a solicitor and a cleric, but it is their seemingly unworldly hostess Miss Marple who homes in on the answer each time. All the characters get so riveted that each of their stories have been told before the first Tuesday night is over.

The following year, Sir Henry is staying with Colonel and Mrs Bantry and persuades them to host a similar evening, insisting (somewhat to Mrs Bantry's dismay) on Miss Marple's attendance. The old lady repeats the trick. Later, again, Sir Henry, who seemingly cannot get enough of St Mary Mead, is staying with the Bantrys when a death occurs in the village ...

CHARACTERS

In a short story format such as this, there is no real opportunity to develop rounded characters, but by the end of these stories Agatha Christie had created in Jane Marple one of the great fictional characters of the 20th century. Apart from her nose for falsehood and her ability to prick the bubble of self-esteem of those who underestimate her, her guiding principle - that human nature is very much the same everywhere - is one of great wisdom. Maybe she has read Alexander Pope:

> *Search thou the ruling passion; there alone,*
> *The wild are constant, and the cunning known;*
> *The fool consistent, and the false sincere;*
> *Priests, princes, women, no dissemblers here.*[2]

The other characters who arouse a smidgeon of interest, only to promptly disappear off the page, are the 'village parallels' that Miss Marple uses to compare the goings-on in these stories. It would have been wonderful to have heard more about them: Mr Badger, the Milkman and Annie, Mr Hargreaves, Tommy Symonds, old Mrs Trout and Mrs Green ...

ATTITUDES AND QUOTES

Although Miss Marple does make reference to 'our own class of life', when it comes down to character and morality she considers everyone equal, to the bemusement of her companions. Here she has guessed that her nephew has just proposed to his artist friend Joyce:

> *"It happened just before dinner, didn't it? When you took Joyce out to admire the sunset. It is a very favourite place, that. There by the jasmine hedge. That is where the milkman asked Annie if he could put up the banns."*

"Dash it all, Aunt Jane," said Raymond, "don't spoil all the romance. Joyce and I aren't like the milkman and Annie."

"That is where you make a mistake, my dear," said Miss Marple. "Everybody is much alike, really. But fortunately, perhaps, they don't realise it."

As is the way with unsolved mysteries, many of these stories refer to characters who still linger under suspicion. The plight of the innocent is a theme of many of Agatha Christie's books, and something she felt strongly about. As Sir Henry says:

"But, you know, it isn't really guilt that is important - it's innocence. That's the thing that nobody will realise."

"I don't understand," said Jane Helier.

"I do," said Miss Marple. "When Mrs Trent found half a crown missing from her bag, the person it affected most was the daily woman, Mrs Arthur. Of course the Trents thought it was her ..."

What started as a parlour-game around a cosy fire becomes something a bit more significant: if the mystery can be solved, then the innocent can be cleared of suspicion.

SWIGATHA RATING 8/10

Although some of the stories stretch a reader's credulity (*A Christmas Tragedy* being a prime example, with dead bodies being swapped around under the disguise of a flimsy hat), this is a significant Christie.

Most of her earlier stories from the 1920s had been set in country houses, London, Deauville, Nice, South Africa and elsewhere; at least two featured plots about world domination. With *The Thirteen Problems*, she created the village setting of St Mary Mead that allowed her to introduce a totally different atmosphere, and it is the one that she is most remembered for today.

Quite apart from the establishment of Miss Marple, these stories contained the germs of plots used in her later works. Here is one example: in the opening story, *The Tuesday Night Club*, a gullible maid is encouraged to tamper with a meal and a death results; a quarter of a century later, in *A Pocketful of Rye*, another gullible maid is encouraged to tamper with a meal, and the same happens. There are more.

The cosiness of the fireside setting in this book works brilliantly - who wouldn't themselves want to curl up in front of an open fire with it? What is particularly impressive is that she repeats the same trick twelve times, but her readers, far from tiring of it, cannot wait to experience the next one.

WHAT HAPPENED NEXT

The next outing for Miss Marple was *The Murder at the Vicarage*, published in 1930 (two years before these stories were collected and published). That story introduced the character of the village itself and its inhabitants. It was the only full-length 'Marple' published during the 1930s, but as the author got older Jane Marple would appear more frequently.

Raymond West was to feature, often in name only, in many future stories ('dear Raymond'). The Bantrys are not seen again until *The Body in the Library* (1942), but they certainly make up for lost time with a spectacular re-entrance. Their friend Sir Henry Clithering also meddles in that case.

The collection was re-issued in 2021 with a change of title – *The Tuesday Night Club*, after the first story in the collection. The change was no doubt occasioned by the huge popularity of Richard Osman's *The Thursday Murder Club*, which had been published the year before. Osman's title is itself a nod to Christie's original.

ADAPTATIONS

Unsurprisingly, because they are far better suited to the radio, only one of these stories has so far been adapted for the screen: *The Blue Geranium* was part of ITV's *Agatha Christie's Miss Marple* series in 2010. Julia McKenzie played Miss Marple as an active participant in the story, rather than an old maid sitting by the fire listening to it. The 'usual strictures' about this series apply.

There is also an audio book that features Joan Hickson reading these stories. It is so refreshing (and unusual) to come across a representation of an Agatha Christie book that changes not one word of the text; every home should have one.

NOTES

[1] Agatha Christie, *An Autobiography*

[2] *The Ruling Passion (Poems of Sentiment)*

The Hound of Death (1933)

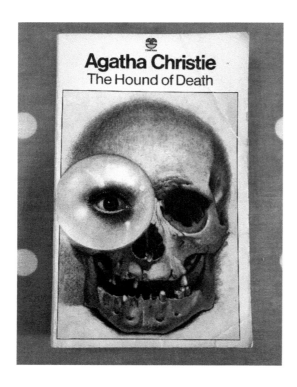
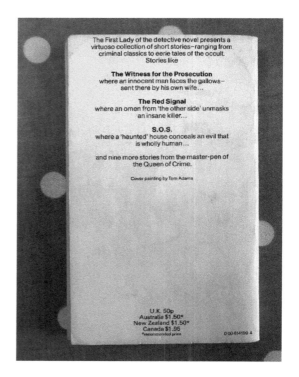

THE BOOK   Fontana, 1976 pp 190

Tom Adams' skull-and-crystal ball cover painting refers (obliquely) to the title story in this collection, in which a nun hallucinates about the 'people of the crystal'. Because of the eye, I had always thought the crystal ball a monocle and the skull that of a Nazi. The book itself came apart on re-reading - so typical of mid-70s copies.

THE STORIES

These stories were mainly written in the 1920s and published in a variety of magazines in the UK. According to Robert Barnard[1], one of them, *The Call of Wings*, was written long before *The Mysterious Affair at Styles*, i.e. before the First World War.

Apart from the central story, *The Witness for the Prosecution*, most of the stories concern the supernatural - there are two seances, four possessions of the soul by an intruder soul, alongside ghostly apparitions and visions of heaven.

There is one story that might have strayed out of *The Listerdale Mystery*: *The Mystery of the Blue Jar*, in which a gormless young halfwit playing golf is deceived into handing over a priceless antique to a pair of crooks, but most are much of a muchness plot-wise.

CHARACTERS

There are plenty of medical men of a charlatanic ilk:

- *Dr Rose*, researching medical disorders (*The Hound of Death*)
- *Sir Alington West*, the 'supreme authority on mental disease' (*The Red Signal*)
- *Dr Campbell Clark*, renowned physician and mental specialist (*The Fourth Man*)
- *Dr Meynell*, who liked attending rich patients (*Wireless*)
- *Ambrose Lavington*, 'Doctor of the Soul' (*The Mystery of the Blue Jar*)
- *Dr Carstairs*, eminent psychologist (*The Strange Case of Sir Arthur Carmichael*)
- *Dr Seldon*, nerve specialist (*The Call of Wings*)
- *Mortimer Cleveland*, expert on the subconscious and member of the Psychical Research Society (*The Call of Wings*)

Agatha Christie never really trusted doctors[2]: 'nuff said!

Among their 'patients' is a nun who is able to coax supernatural powers to destroy a First World War German Army unit that is occupying her convent; a man who is possessed by a cat, is drowned, and then brought back to life, catless; and a man, inspired by the music of a down-and-out, who gives away all his money and sacrifices himself to save a drunken youth who has fallen on to an underground railway track. These stories are, at least, different.

ATTITUDES AND QUOTES

From the title story, a theme returned to often in the other stories:

> *The supernatural is only the natural of which the laws are not understood*

There is one quote that recalls Agatha Christie's recurring childhood nightmare featuring The Gunman, who would turn up during normal family occasions and assume the character of one of her family members:[2]

> *"It all started with a dream I had as a kid. Not a nightmare exactly. She - the gypsy - would just come into any old dream - even a good dream (or a kid's version of what's good - a party*

and crackers and things). I'd be enjoying myself no end, and then I'd feel I'd know that, if I looked up, she'd be there, standing as she always stood, watching me ... " (The Gypsy)

SWIGATHA RATING 5/10

The Hound of Death doesn't work as a collection, unlike, for example, *The Mysterious Mr Quin*, *The Thirteen Problems* or *The Labours of Hercules*, each of which contains one story that establishes the context, with the others following on from it.

In my opinion, one or two of these stories, including the title story, are not worthy of publication. So it came as no surprise to find that the original collection had not been published by Collins, her regular publisher, nor was it available in the shops: to get hold of a copy one had to collect coupons from a magazine.

Most of the individual stories are, however, at least interesting or entertaining and, if one came across one of them in a magazine, one might be delighted.

There is one stand-out story. With *Witness for the Prosecution* Agatha Christie has provided an absolute classic of the genre, and one that would prove to be very lucrative for her.

WHERE IT LED

Nowhere, thankfully, with one blazing exception (see below). Agatha Christie included many of these stories in one of her 'favourites' lists, but not many readers would do likewise.

ADAPTATIONS

Unsurprisingly, given the content, there have not been many, but three of the stories were filmed for *The Agatha Christie Hour - The Red Signal*, *The Fourth Man*, and *The Mystery of the Blue Jar*.

Witness for the Prosecution was adapted into a stage play in the 1950s by the author. It was a huge success and is still performed all over the world. A new production, which invites members of the public to play the jury, opened in London 2017 and has also been a great hit.

The 1957 Billy Wilder film of the play, beautifully filmed in black and white and starring Charles Laughton and Marlene Dietrich, remains one of, if not *the* finest cinematic adaptation of any Agatha Christie work yet.

By contrast, the BBC version from 2016 loses everything in comparison. It adds far too much padding and colour, ripping out the starkness and knife-edge sharpness of the original that Wilder captured so well.

NOTES

[1] Robert Barnard *A Talent to Deceive* (1980): Barnard indicated that in his opinion *The Call of Wings* was 'the best of the rest' (i.e. after *Witness*)

[2] Agatha Christie *An Autobiography* (Part V Chapter One)

Lord Edgware Dies (1933)

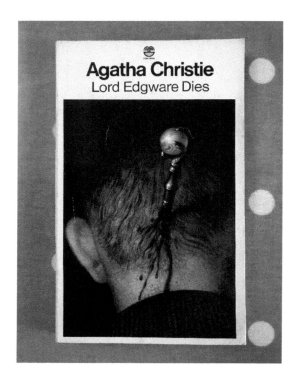

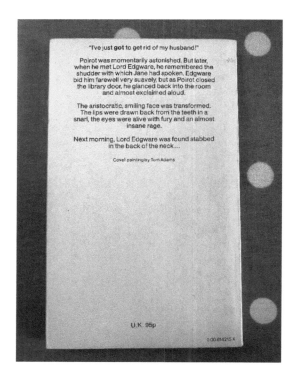

THE BOOK   Fontana, 1980 pp 192

This is a replacement, not the original copy that I read in the 1960s. The cover template is not nearly as appealing a cover as the old "lined" Fontana style from the 1960s, and some of the print is smudged. This is typical of the shoddy 1970s / 80s versions, and that is one of the reasons why I am trying to re-collect the editions that I originally read.

Tom Adams at least gets a credit for the painting on the front, which bears echoes of his cover for *The Murder of Roger Ackroyd*. The head of the victim, however, looks very young for a man with an adult daughter.

THE STORY

Actress Jane Wilkinson asks Poirot to intercede with her husband, who will not accede to her request for a divorce. The husband tells Poirot he is surprised because he *has* agreed to one. He is murdered before it can come about; Poirot and Hastings take it upon themselves to investigate what happened.

The identity of the husband should be guessable from the book's title, a title which is suggested to its narrator, Hastings, by the new Lord.

CHARACTERS

The doomed Lord Edgware's character is possibly the most interesting: apparently honest and believable but with ferocious undercurrents. His bookshelf is filled with the *Memoirs of Casanova*, a volume on the Comte de Sade, another on mediaeval tortures.

His wife is a wonderful study in self-absorption, and Agatha Christie possibly had one of the characters from her imaginary School[1] in mind when she was thinking about her. Edgware's nephew and heir is an impecunious, unthinking racist. His daughter hated and feared her father. What a family!

There are not many instances of the gentry or super-rich appearing in a swigatha, but when they do appear they are often unsympathetically described - as here: Lord Edgware is a sadist, his nephew an idiot, the Duke of Merton weak and ugly, the Dowager Duchess a wilful snob.

The murderer is (again) the most likeable suspect in the book.

The completely different characters of Poirot and Hastings work together beautifully in this book, and some of their interplay is a joy. Inspector Japp plays Inspector Japp.

ATTITUDES - spoiler!

What would be seen today as toe-curling racism is still on show, but at least it is put into the mouth of a drunken buffoon rather than the narrator. Here, the future Lord Edgware introduces himself to Hastings:

> *"What I say is one face is very like another face - that's what I say. If we were a lot of Chinks we wouldn't know each other apart ... Anyway," he said, "I'm not a damned nigger ..."*

He continues with his alibi:

> *"When uncle's lifeblood is flowing, I am whispering cheerful nothings into the diamond encrusted ears of the fair (I beg her pardon, dark) Rachel in a box at Covent Garden. Her long Jewish nose is quivering with emotion."*

Hastings (whose first impressions are usually hopelessly awry) reacts so:

There was something strangely likeable about the young man. (!)

Poirot is well aware of Hastings' capabilities:

> "No human being should learn from another. Each individual should develop his own powers to the uttermost, and not try to imitate those of someone else. I do not wish you to be a second and inferior Poirot. I wish you to be the supreme Hastings. And you are the supreme Hastings."

... and the supreme Hastings once again (inadvertently) provides Poirot with the solution to the riddle.

Jane Wilkinson, the supreme egotist, is allowed the book's final word before she is hanged:

> *P.S. Do you think they will put me in Madame Tussauds?*

SWIGATHA RATING 7/10

The construction of the killer's alibi is Christie at her best, but some of the rest does not bear close scrutiny. For example, the character of Donald Ross, the only person present at both the two crucial dinner parties, introduces himself to Hastings at the second one, under the impression that he had also attended the first, which Hastings had not. The dreaded clue of an initial on a personal effect is used again to no real purpose, and one of the 'Paris' plotlines just fades out.

On the other hand, the main characters in it are terrifically drawn and not many would put the book away before finishing it.

WHAT HAPPENED NEXT

Hastings returned to the Argentine for three years. Poirot makes the first of his trips to the Middle East, from whence he will return via the Orient Express ... This book helped establish Agatha Christie's reputation as the *Queen of Crime*.

ADAPTATIONS

There was a decent version made by ITV for its *Poirot* series, but they obviously decided that there was not enough plot to work with, so they added extra plot lines such as Miss Lemon's filing system and Hastings' bankruptcy (the latter makes a nonsense of the real reason for his eventual return to England).

The two main actresses, when made and dressed up, are extremely convincing in their "roles". Lord Edgware is evilly played by John Castle, better known for his smug portrayal of Miss Marple's godson, Detective Inspector Craddock, in the BBC series.

"Thirteen at Dinner" was the title given to a lamentable outing for Peter Ustinov, aimed at the American market. It portrays Hastings as a complete nincompoop.

NOTES

[1] Agatha Christie, *An Autobiography* (Part II Chapter I).

When she was a child, Agatha Christie populated an imaginary school with children (known simply as *The School*) whose characters she continued to develop in her head well into adulthood. I think that she sometimes used these characters in her books, and you can usually tell because they are the most interesting and well-defined. I think Jane Wilkinson is based on 'Isabel', a *School* character that the young Agatha didn't like, but one who kept coming out on top in spite of her. So, Jane has to be given the final word - and Christie has given her possibly the best last line of any crime fiction book that I have read.

The Listerdale Mystery (1934)

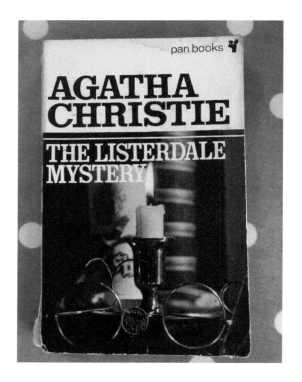
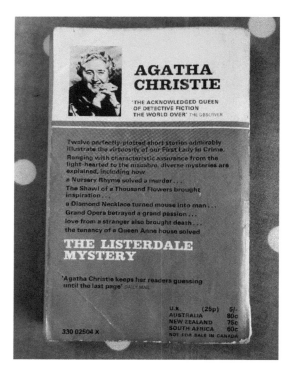

THE BOOK   PAN, 1970 pp 188

The PAN cover design is specifically based on *Sing a Song of Sixpence*, one of twelve stories that make up this collection. The sixpence is surrounded by other trappings of the study of Sir Edward Palliser, QC.

THE STORIES

The stories in this collection were mainly written in the 1920s, in the aftermath of the First World War, a prolific period of short-story writing for the author.

Eight of them involve bright-ish young things desperate for money getting involved in scrapes with a twist, and many of the characters and elements of the plots are interchangeable.

Otherwise there are four tales of death and deception, and two of them have become famous in their own right: *Philomel Cottage* and *Accident*.

CHARACTERS

Here are a few somewhat tongue-in-cheek summaries of the main characters in the non-whodunit stories, but even so it should give some idea of the range (or lack of it) of stories and characters in this collection:

- *Mrs St Vincent* and her (adult) children Barbara and Rupert: genteel, down-at-heel, gentlefolk who are invited to live in a mansion at a peppercorn rent; Mrs St Vincent ends up as Lady Listerdale

- *George Rowland*: a somewhat shiftless well-off young fellow who has hit hard times because his uncle has sacked him; he takes a train and gets involved in a deception involving foreign royalty

- *George Dundas*: a somewhat shiftless young fellow who has hit hard times because his uncle has sacked him, and who finds himself taken in by an heiress and her two chums

- *Edward Robinson*: a mouse of the lower orders who mixes with Lady Noreen and her chums and becomes a lion

- *Edward Palgrave*: a mouse of the lower orders who is persuaded to at least consider criminal activity by his girl-friend when they come across exotic jewellery

- *Jane Cleveland*: a down-on-her-luck young woman who will do anything (including conniving in crime) for money, and is taken in by someone she thinks is a foreign Grand Duchess and her two retainers

- *Anthony Eastwood*: a young fellow with writer's block who is taken in by an exotic foreign woman and her two retainers and has his flat ransacked as a result

- *James Bond*: a young fellow out of his financial depth on holiday who happens by chance to locate a missing jewel and earns the gratitude of Lord Campion.

Take out the nobility and the foreign exotics and there is little left.

ATTITUDES

Here are some quotes from the title story which speak for themselves. They evince a snobbery and disregard for those not of 'our type' which is a characteristic of the whole collection.

73

Here, from the title story, Mrs St Vincent considers the realities of 'genteel poverty':

> *In real life, with a son starting on the bottom rung of the ladder, it means London. Frowsy landladies, dirty children on the stairs, fellow-lodgers who always seem to be half-castes, haddocks for breakfast ...*

Then she considers her daughter Barbara's prospects:

> *"I should like you to marry Jim Masterson," she said. "He is - one of us. He is very well off, also, but I don't mind that so much."*

And then Rupert's:

> *"I should hate it if Rupert got engaged to that dreadful girl in the tobacconist's. I daresay she may be a very nice girl, really. But she's not our kind."*

Now a quote from *The Girl on the Train*: a railway guard's training in the 1920s must surely have been different from today!

> *The guard looked from one to the other. His mind was made up. His training led him to despise foreigners, and to respect and admire well-dressed gentlemen who travelled first-class.*

And finally, a description of Mr Cowan, the main observer of *Swan Song* (and possibly the nicest character in it):

> *He was a tall man, clean-shaven, with a frame rather too well covered, and clothes that were rather too faultless. His hair was very black and shining, and his teeth were aggressively white. When he spoke, he had a way of slurring his 's's which was not quite a lisp, but came perilously near to it. It required no stretch of imagination to realise that his father's name had probably been Cohen.*

SWIGATHA RATING 4/10

Many people will really like this collection but most of it feels very churned out to me. The snobbery throughout the whole of the title story made me shudder. Having said that, there are one or two top-notch tales that make it worth reading; I particularly enjoyed *Swan Song*.

There was to be a sea-change in the representation of social attitudes in her books once she started spending more time in the Middle East, and especially after the outbreak of World War 2 in 1939.

WHERE IT LED

The bottom of the barrel of old short stories was being scraped. After the uninspiring collection *The Hound of Death* (1933), then this set and *Parker Pyne Investigates*, both published in 1934, Agatha Christie's publishers concentrated on the full- length novels that were to consolidate her status as the most popular crime fiction writer of that time (and this!).

She produced a dozen of them in the next five years, all of them of good quality and some of them the most famous of their ilk ever-written.

ADAPTATIONS

Three of the stories in the collection, *The Girl in the Train*, *Jane in Search of a Job* and *The Manhood of Edward Robinson*, were adapted for by ITV's Thames Television in 1982 as part of their ten-part programme *The Agatha Christie Hour*.

The story of *Philomel Cottage* was hugely successful. In the US and UK alone it was twice adapted for each of radio and TV, once for the stage and twice for the cinema. It usually went by the name given to the stage adaptation: *Love from a Stranger*.

Parker Pyne Investigates (1934)

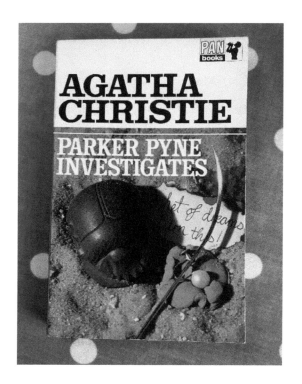

THE BOOK   PAN, 1968 pp 186

This book is a bit of a mish-mash of short stories: some tragic, some very light-hearted. PAN's photographic cover includes the eponymous *Pearl of Great Price*, a sock used to bludgeon a man to death (once filled with sand!) and a note from a murderer. I am not sure what the rest refers to - not a particularly successful cover.

THE STORIES

J. Parker Pyne advertises his services in The Times: 'Are you happy? If not, consult Mr Parker Pyne'. This collection features eleven cases in which he is consulted, and one, the final one, where he is not (but for good reasons decides to get involved).

Parker Pyne has an office in London and staff who have been trained in the art of spicing up the lives of others. They are employed to do so in the first six cases.

Those stories were published in various magazines from 1932. They are reminiscent of some in *The Listerdale Mystery*, which was published the same year: light-hearted and romantic, with just a touch of humour.

The remaining six stories find Parker Pyne on the Mallowan trail: firstly on the Orient Express, and then to Syria, Egypt and Greece. Each time he finds himself interrupting his tour to investigate local crimes. This change of tack was presumably occasioned by Agatha Christie's increasing fascination with the Middle East following her marriage to the archaeologist Max Mallowan in 1930.

CHARACTERS

It is in the nature of these types of stories that, short though they are, they each need a cast of characters, and there is not much room to describe all of them. Agatha Christie is brilliant at evoking in one sentence a character that the reader can easily visualise. To do so, she plays to her readers' imagined prejudices.

For example, in one story (*The Pearl of Price*), we are introduced to the following seven people in the space of eleven lines: a stout and prosperous American magnate; his dark and good-looking, if somewhat taciturn secretary; a tired-looking English politician; a world-renowned elderly archaeologist; a gallant Frenchman on leave; Parker Pyne, 'not perhaps so plainly labelled with his profession', and a pretty, spoiled young woman who is extremely sure of herself.

The twist, of course, will come when one of them belies their description.

Parker Pyne, however, appears in every story, so there is space to portray him in more depth. Unfortunately, we know no more about him by the end than we did at the beginning. The same could be said for his go-to team - the vamp Miss de Sara and the gigolo Claude Luttrell.

ATTITUDES AND QUOTES

The world is introduced to Miss Lemon (*The Case of the Middle-Aged Wife*):

> *When she had gone he pressed a buzzer on his desk. A forbidding-looking young woman with spectacles answered it. "A file, please, Miss Lemon ..."*

... and the world is introduced to Mrs Oliver (*The Case of the Discontented Soldier*):

> *Mr Parker Pyne tapped on the door and entered. Miss Oliver sat at a table on which were a typewriter, several notebooks, a general confusion of loose manuscripts and a large bag of apples.*

Here, Parker Pyne ladles out advice on a matrimonial washout (*The Case of the Discontented Husband*):

> *"Never adopt an apologetic attitude with a woman. She will take you at your own valuation - and you deserve it."*

Parker Pyne doles out some more advice about what constitutes a happy marriage (*Have You Got Everything You Want?*). Was he himself married? We are not told.

> *"It is a fundamental axiom of married life that you must lie to a woman. She likes it! Go and be forgiven, my boy. And live happily ever afterwards."*

Now for some genuine insight (from *The Case of the City Clerk*):

> *"I've a great deal to be thankful for."*
> *"We all have," said Mr Parker Pyne. "But when we have to remind ourselves of the fact it is a bad sign."*

An unusually long introduction to this character sets up the twist at the end of *The Case of the Rich Woman*:

> *Mrs Rymer was a tall woman, big-boned. Her figure was ungainly and the velvet dress and the heavy fur coat she wore did not disguise the fact. The knuckles of her large hands were pronounced. Her face was big and broad and highly coloured. Her black hair was fashionably dressed, and there were many tips of curled ostrich in her hat.*

Parker Pyne / Agatha Christie seems to foresee the crisis of capitalism during the 21st Century in *The Pearl of Price*:

> *"A man who makes money benefits mankind," said Mr Blundell sententiously.*
> *"Mankind," murmured Mr Parker Pyne, 'is so ungrateful."*

SWIGATHA RATING 3/10

Having re-read the book on a Saturday, I struggled to remember much of it on the Sunday. Only two stories stuck in my mind: *The Case of the Rich Woman*, and *The Oracle at Delphos*. Unusually for Agatha Christie, the main protagonist has no character at all.

My feeling is that Parker Pyne was a try-out for a new character to replace Hercule Poirot, of whom Agatha Christie was getting heartily sick. She then realised that the character didn't work, or was dissuaded from continuing with him. The characters of Miss Lemon and Mrs Oliver, introduced in these stories, did work, and so they were swiftly transferred into Poirot's world.

WHAT HAPPENED NEXT

J. Parker Pyne re-appeared in two posthumously-published stories in the collection *Problem at Pollensa Bay* (*The Regatta Mystery* and the title story). He had by then changed the initial of his first name to 'C'. Both of those stories had originally been published in the UK with Poirot as the protagonist.

Miss Lemon made her debut alongside Poirot in the short story *How Does Your Garden Grow*?. This was written in 1932, the same year that the Parker Pyne stories were first published in magazines in the US and UK. It was included in the 1974 collection *Poirot's Early Cases*.

Mrs Oliver next appeared, alongside Poirot, in *Cards on the Table* (1936).

As far as Agatha Christie is concerned, she abandoned the romantic short story style prevalent in *Parker Pyne Investigates* and *The Listerdale Mystery* at the start of the 1930s, instead devoting her talents to producing full-length romantic novels under the name of Mary Westmacott. The first of these had appeared in 1930.

ADAPTATIONS

The first two stories in the Parker Pyne collection appeared as episodes in the series *The Agatha Christie Hour* on ITV in 1982, with Maurice Denham in the title role. The rest of that series was made up of stories from *The Listerdale Mystery*; Parker Pyne was abandoned. Maurice Denham, however, returned to wonderful effect as Luther Crackenthorpe in the BBC's production of *4.50 from Paddington*.

Murder on the Orient Express (1934)

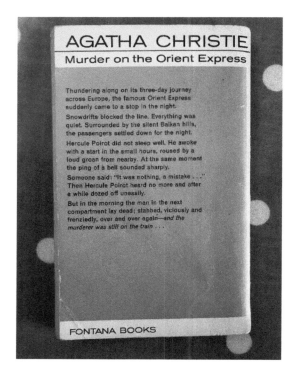

THE BOOK Fontana, 1966 pp 191

A typical Tom Adams cover featuring items found in the murdered man's carriage, with a map of Macedonia in the background. The orange line shows the Orient Express's route through the towns of Vinkovci and Brod.

It is dedicated to "M.E.L.M, Arpachiyah 1953" - the year is a misprint. The initials are those of Max Edgar Lucien Mallowan, Agatha Christie's second husband, who had organised a dig at Tell Arpachiyah (Nineveh) the year before the book was written (i.e. in 1933). They would have travelled out and back by the Orient Express.

THE STORY

Travelling back from Istanbul, Hercule Poirot manages to secure the last first-class berth on the Calais coach of the Orient Express, much to the consternation of some of his fellow-passengers, who had booked the carriage in the name of 'Mr Harris'[1].

One of the passengers, named Ratchett, tries to secure Poirot's services to protect him while on board, but Poirot refuses. During the night, Ratchett is stabbed to death.

80

The train had come to a standstill, caught in a snow-drift somewhere between Vinkovci and Brod. It becomes apparent that the murderer must still be on the train, and M Bouc, director of the line, implores Poirot to investigate.

THE TITLE

It is a pretty obvious title but still a good one, one that entices a reader to find out more. Murder on a train or a plane, when there is not obvious means of immediate escape for either the murderer or potential victim, is always a good plot device, but also The Orient Express was the glamour means of travel in the early 20th century and had an amazing history[2].

Also, the title scans: just add the word 'The' to the beginning and see what a difference it makes.

CHARACTERS

The nature of the story is such that its range of characters covers a wide variety of nationalities and social positions, from Russian Princess Dragmiroff to Italian chauffeur Foscarelli via the Hungarian diplomat Andrenyi. The victim is possibly the nastiest person to appear anywhere in the Christie canon: the kidnapper and murderer of Daisy Armstrong, a two-year old girl. He displays no hint of humanity or remorse in his brief appearance in the book.

There are twelve suspects to investigate, and each is given a chapter to themselves as they are interviewed. They are somewhat stereotypical, but then each is playing a part. The star part is taken by the American matron Mrs Hubbard, who is given the opportunity to decry everything and comes to dominate the story.

Everything described in the book is as observed by Poirot. There are no scenes in which the other characters talk to each other, apart from one exchange between Colonel Arbuthnot and Mary Debenham, and even that is overheard by Poirot.

ATTITUDES

There is not a single person on the train (including Poirot and the director of the Orient Express line) that believes in the sanctity of the legal justice system, whether in the US or Europe; Ratchett had previously been arrested for Daisy's murder, but managed to use his wealth and underworld contacts to bribe his way out, and everyone knew it.

The Yugoslavian police are not to be trusted either, apparently, so Poirot is urged to come up with a(ny) solution before the snow clears and they arrive at Brod.

QUOTES

Here, Poirot and M Bouc discuss Mr Ratchett, presumably talking in French, translated for us by the author. People on the train (apart from the victim) seem to have a wonderful command of languages, especially Poirot, who conducts interviews in English, French and German.

> *"And yet he looked altogether of the most respectable."*
> *"Précisément! The body - the cage - is everything of the most respectable - but through the bars, the wild animal looks out."*

Poirot turns down a client:

> *"What's wrong with my proposition?"*
> *Poirot rose. "If you will forgive me for being personal - I do not like your face, Mr Ratchett."*
> *And with that he left the restaurant car.*

It is extremely rare for Poirot to be directly rude to another character in any of his stories – in fact, I cannot think of another example.

Mrs Hubbard vents her opinion on everything un-American, from dinars to Turkish cuisine. Here, she is upset at the train becoming stuck in a snow-drift:

> *"What country is this anyway?" demanded Mrs Hubbard tearfully.*
> *On being told it was Yugoslavia, she said: "Oh! One of those Balkan things. What can you expect?"*

Here she explains Greta Ohlsson to Poirot:

> *"Poor creature, she's a Swede."*

Miss Ohlsson takes a bit of stick in the dialogue (she is later referred to as 'that Swedish creature', and twice described as a sheep, one who 'gets anxious and bleats'), but actually the others are being protective of her.

There is much discussion about which nationalities have a predilection for stabbing and which ones do not ("The English – they do not stab"). One of the main clues is sneaked in beautifully around a dismissive remark about the knife-happy natives of Corsica and Sicily:

"In fact, Colonel Arbuthnot, you prefer law and order to private vengeance?"

"Well, you can't go about having blood feuds and stabbing each other like the Corsicans and the Mafia," said the Colonel. "Say what you like, trial by a jury is a sound system."

He has a funny way of showing it.

SWIGATHA RATING 9/10

This is one of the very best swigathas, if not quite top-drawer. It has a brilliant setting (Agatha Christie was always at her best when writing about what she knew, and she knew the Orient Express) and a series of colourful characters, each playing their part with gusto.

The unity-of-time-and-place element, however, means that there can be no plot or character development; the bulk of Part 2 consists of twelve consecutive chapters of interviews, followed by a (necessary) chapter summarising them.

These chapters never drag, though, and the solution is another of her stone-cold classics, and totally original. On re-reading it I felt that it should be obvious to any first-time reader whodunit by half-way through, but the vast majority will not get it when they first come to it.

This is one to curl up with in front of a blazing fire in winter.

WHERE IT LED

Poirot was by now huge business. In the following four years, no fewer than nine full-length Poirot novels and a collection of medium-sized stories (*Murder in the Mews*) were written and published.

Many of these are absolute classics of the genre.

ADAPTATIONS

There have been six cinema adaptations so far (in English, German and Japanese)[3] with the most recent being the Kenneth Branagh film released in November 2017; that was the one with the ballet-dancing, kick-boxing Count Andrenyi.

The British film released in 1974, directed by Sidney Lumet, was very much more respectful of the plot and atmosphere of the book. It is an enjoyably cosy all-star romp that featured a stunning performance by the 38-year-old Albert Finney as Poirot. It has a great theme tune by Richard Rodney Bennett, luxurious sets and a cast who seemed to be enjoying their (minor) roles enormously: they add a lot to their characters, so much so that Ingrid Bergman won the Best Actress Oscar for her portrayal of the 'Swedish creature'.

For a while, it was the top-grossing British film of all time.

The 2010 film for ITV's *Poirot* series was careful to distinguish itself from the film. It thus turned Ratchett into a man feeling scared and remorseful, and emphasised Poirot's struggle with his Catholic conscience as he considers the right solution.

This programme is much darker in all senses than the 1974 film. The killing of Ratchett is sadistically carried out: he is deliberately kept semi-doped and powerless so that he can witness his own murder.

Poirot is threatened by the passengers; this is no cosy carriage. The train's services deteriorate, the water freezes in the pipes and the passengers sit around in a half-light wondering what will happen to them.

The Branagh film follows the tone of the TV version. Even so, I prefer the Finney to either of them, by a mile.

NOTES

[1] When he hears this, Poirot says: *A name of good omen, Harris. I read my Dickens. He will not arrive.* Poirot is referring to Mrs Gamp's imaginary friend Harris, from Dickens' *Martin Chuzzlewit*.

[2] One of its first-class carriages was de-trained and used for the German surrender at Versailles at the end of WW1. Thus, when France surrendered to Hitler in 1940, the latter insisted on the ceremony being conducted in the same carriage. When it became apparent Germany was going to be defeated, Hitler ordered the carriage to be destroyed (it wasn't).

[3] Mark Aldridge, *Agatha Christie on Screen*

Why Didn't They Ask Evans? (1934)

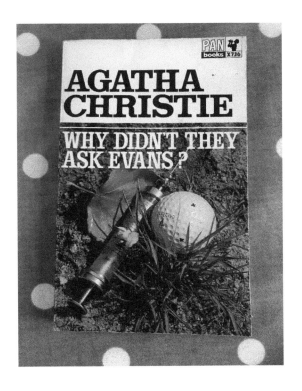 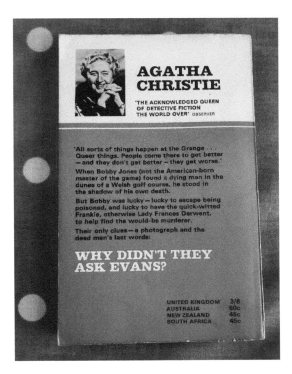

THE BOOK PAN 1968 pp 188

The very recognisable PAN photographic covers were introduced in the 1960s by David Larkin, possibly to distinguish them from the hugely popular Tom Adams covers of books by the same author for Fontana.

This particular one is a beautiful book and, fifty or more years later, still in great condition.

THE STORY

Vicar's son Bobby Jones is playing golf with his friend Dr Thomas when they discover an unconscious, dying man at the bottom of a cliff. Bobby is left at the scene while the doctor goes to summon help. The man wakes, declaims "Why didn't they ask Evans?", and dies.

Bobby's suspicions are aroused when the Caymans, a couple purporting to be the dead man's relatives, visit the vicarage to ask whether he had left any final messages before he died. He shares his doubts with Lady Frances Derwent ("Frankie"), an old childhood friend, and they determine to investigate further, if only to find out who Evans was.

CHARACTERS

Bobby and Frankie form a familiar partnership. Familiar, that is, to those of Agatha Christie's readers who had come across Tommy and Tuppence in their 1920s incarnation. This time it is the boy, not the girl, who is the child of a vicar, but otherwise the two pairs of characters could almost be interchangeable (ITV obviously agreed because they used the same two actors for each pair of characters in their 1980s adaptations).

There are other characters who seem recognisable from the earlier 'light-hearted' thrillers: the sinister doctor Nicholson, the terrified damsel in distress, the witless Wodehousean Badger, the affectionately-portrayed old buffer of a father … not to mention a villain who escapes justice, and at the end writes to the lead girl explaining all (as had also happened in *The Man in the Brown Suit*).

QUOTES AND ATTITUDES

The issue of class permeates the book, in part because of the long-standing, awkward friendship between a vicar's son and the daughter of a Lord:

> *The Derwents were, perhaps, a shade more friendly than they need have been as though to show that "there was no difference". The Jones, on their side, were a shade formal, as though determined not to claim more friendship than was offered them.*

People in those days, seemingly, knew their place (until the final page!). When a couple claiming to be the dead man's relatives do not conform to the class stereotypes, Bobby's suspicions are aroused:

> *"The Caymans were a different class altogether. The dead man was … a pukka sahib."*
> *"And the Caymans most emphatically weren't?"*
> *"Most emphatically."*

Here is Frankie reasoning, with undeniable if unfeeling logic, that Bobby will get away with his chauffeur's disguise:

> *"Nobody looks at a chauffeur the way that they look at a person."*[1]

Bobby makes an interesting observation, one that could apply to all amateur detectives:

> *"It's as though we'd walked on to the stage in the middle of the second act and we haven't really got parts in the play at all, but we have to pretend, and what makes it so frightfully hard is that we haven't the faintest idea what the first act was about."*

With this observation, Agatha Christie is anticipating Tom Stoppard's play "Rosencrantz and Guildenstern are Dead" by about thirty years.

SWIGATHA RATING 6/10

It is all a jolly enough story, and (as is often the case with Agatha Christie novels) the beginning is inspired, as is the book's title, but the extremely convoluted plot takes some swallowing. There is a bit too much padding (pages and pages of Bobby and Frankie speculating about Dr Nicholson and various Bassington-ffrenches), but I guess that is understandable: this was to be the third book out of four to be published under her name in the same year (1934).

On the plus side, some of the observations in the book are very sharp and in a different league to the-bright-young-thing works of the previous decade, and the final twist at the end is very clever (and funny).

WHERE IT LED

This was the end of the line for Christie's light-hearted thrillers. Things were to get much darker from then on.

ADAPTATIONS

There was a three-hour ITV adaptation in 1980 with a phenomenal cast, including John Gielgud, Eric Porter, Joan Hickson, Connie Booth, Leigh Lawson and Lynda la Plante (who later became one of the UK's most successful crime-thriller writers). The parts of Bobby Jones and Lady Frances Derwent were played by James Warwick and Francesca Annis, who graduated from this to play another pair of bright young things in the Tommy and Tuppence series *Partners in Crime*.

NOTES

[1] Having served at table for a charity at a high-class feast at Madresfield Court recently, I can confirm that this observation still has the ring of truth to it. I knew many of the people there well but I don't think many, if any of them saw me as I served them drinks.

Three Act Tragedy (1935)

THE BOOK Fontana 1970 pp 192

This is the original 1970 Fontana edition I got from the Bromley South Station bookstall. It really is evocative; I can still remember being on Brighton beach and reading the bit where Poirot hears of Bartholomew Strange's death. Poirot himself was on a beach in France at the time, bored …

THE STORY

Poirot is invited to a drinks party by retired actor Sir Charles Cartwright, at which the gentle, likeable cleric Stephen Babbington dies after drinking a cocktail. Sir Charles is alone in suggesting foul play, and seems to be justified when, weeks later, another of his other guests dies elsewhere in similar circumstances. From then on, Sir Charles directs and stars in the investigation.

CHARACTERS - spoiler!

The character of Sir Charles Cartwright dominates the story. Throughout it, he is playing different parts, from "Retired Naval Man, can't mistake the type", to thwarted lover, to amateur sleuth, and directing the attentions of his companions to what he wants them to see and think. When I first read this, I kept seeing Charles Laughton as Cartwright.

Mr Satterthwaite, who had appeared as amanuensis in the *Harley Quin* stories, re-appears here in his usual role as onlooker. He watches his friend's play-acting with amusement, but is nevertheless taken in.

Cartwright has a love-interest, known to all as Egg. She discovers that Cartwright is his stage name, and that he was born Mugg. She would have welcomed a marriage proposal from Sir Charles; it would not have occurred to her that, should that have transpired, her name would be Egg Mugg.

Most of the other characters are bit-parts there to fill the pages, apart from the playwright Muriel Wills ("the chiel' among ye taking notes") and the unfortunate Mrs de Rushbridger, who doesn't appear in person in the book and is murdered because she doesn't know anything.

ATTITUDES AND QUOTES

Agatha Christie's seemingly equivocal toned-down-from-the-1920s attitude towards Jewish people re-appears in this story:

> *Egg Lytton-Gore's voice rang out: "Oliver - you slippery Shylock!"*
> *"Of course," thought Mr Satterthwaite. "That's it - not foreign - Jew!"*

This exchange would sound excruciating to us today, but Egg is being affectionate, and at the end she and Oliver depart the story arm-in-arm: Oliver had poached Egg ...

There's an amusing interchange as Poirot mocks the awkwardness of the correct use of English personal pronouns and retreats into French.

> *Miss Milray came out. She started when she saw Poirot.*
> *"You!"*
> *Poirot smiled. "Me! Or is it I? Enfin, moi!"*

SWIGATHA RATING 7/10

A rattling good yarn that drags a bit in the middle. The motives for the murders are superbly original. None of the three murdered people had ever knowingly done anyone any harm, or threatened to, which adds a darker side to the book: their deaths *are* a tragedy.

Once again we have a swigatha in which, logically, the only person who could possibly have done it is right at the centre of events throughout, but there will not be many readers who are not taken in. Fantastic mis-direction, in this case effected by having the actual killer direct the show.

WHERE IT LED

Mr Satterthwaite and Poirot teamed up again for one of the stories in *Murder in the Mews*.

In the summer of 1970, my boyhood friend David Hatton and I conspired to write a swigatha of our own: *The Little Dog Laughed*. We got the title from the name of the Muriel Wills play that is being rehearsed in the third act of this tragedy. It is the mention of the dress rehearsal for *Little Dog Laughed* that inspires Poirot to work out what must have happened.

Also, and somewhat incredibly, the crossword in the July 1, 2016 issue of the Times Literary Supplement had the following clue:

> *Dress circle to see Babbington in three act tragedy? (6).*

God knows what the American academics that make up much of the TLS readership made of that! No doubt some came up with the answer, '*cleric*', an anagram of 'circle'; the reference is to the first murder victim, Rev Stephen Babbington.

ADAPTATIONS

The 2010 UK ITV adaptation was pretty close to the original, but dispensed with a couple of characters (including 'and' Mr Satterthwaite, presumably to give Poirot a larger role). It is such a pity that some of Agatha Christie's favourite repeat characters, such as Mr Satterthwaite and Mr Goby, are never included when adaptations of the books in which they appear are made.

A US production was made using the US title: *Murder in Three Acts*, starring Ustinov's Poirot and Tony Curtis as Cartwright: the casting alone gives the game away ...

Death in the Clouds (1935)

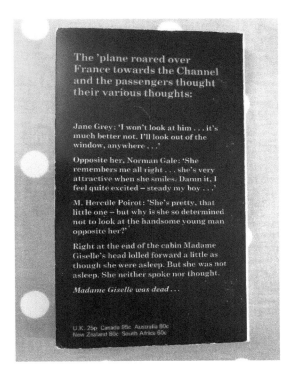

THE BOOK Fontana 1971 pp 190

This book is in beautiful condition for a half-century-old paperback and it was a pleasure to re-read it. The cover is another of the Tom Adams "insect" covers, this time one that is particularly relevant to the story inside.

The scene-setter on the back is a classic of its time.

THE STORY

Mme Giselle, a notorious moneylender, is found dead on an aeroplane travelling to Croydon. It soon emerges that she was poisoned by a dart during the journey; three of the passengers on board - Hercule Poirot, Jane Grey and Norman Gale - join forces to investigate how that could happen, in a crowded cabin, without anybody noticing it.

CHARACTERS

The most interesting character for a Christie student is that of Jane Grey. She appears to be something of a reprise of Katherine Grey, who appeared in the *Mystery of the Blue Train* seven years earlier. Both are single women working to support themselves in menial jobs, both come into a windfall that enables them to travel, both are viewed by Poirot as *sympathique*, both fall for the killer and both escape to the promise of a happier life.

I think that Agatha Christie wrote something of her post-Archie-Christie self into each of them; Jane Grey even ends up travelling to the Middle East with an archaeologist ...

The French police (in the character of Fournier) are portrayed as somewhat more intelligent than Inspector Japp: they actually reason Poirot's hints for themselves and come out with the right answers. Otherwise the characters are straight from central casting. The villain even 'throws back his head and laughs' - a sure giveaway in a swigatha.

ATTITUDES

Although half of the story takes place in France, there is little of the national stereotyping that one can find elsewhere. Agatha Christie obviously had a healthy respect for that country. There is a mention of "Ikey Andrew" at the hairdressers where Jane worked, and then there is the quote below... analyse that!

QUOTES

Two young people on a first date. How sweet ...

> *They liked dogs and disliked cats. They both hated oysters and loved smoked salmon. They liked Greta Garbo and disliked Katherine Hepburn. They didn't like fat women and admired really jet-black hair. They disliked very red nails. They disliked loud voices, noisy restaurants and Negroes. They preferred buses to tubes. It seemed almost miraculous that two people should have so many points of agreement.*

Japp's French is coming along nicely:

> *"You mean?"*
> *"Chantage."*
> *"Blackmail?" echoed Japp.*

Here is a great couple of lines featuring Poirot and the original instance of entrapment (this would not be admissible evidence in court today):

"You even left your fingerprints on the bottle."

"You lie. I wore -"

"Ah, you wore gloves...? I think, Monsieur, that little admission cooks your gander."

SWIGATHA RATING 6/10

A very distinctive setting, and an unusually fair set of clues, but somehow the story never takes off (ironically!). It seems cobbled together with bits and pieces from elsewhere, so it gets an average mark. In the period from 1934-38 Agatha Christie published 11 full-length novels (9 featuring Poirot) and 3 books of short stories, as well as writing two plays for TV and radio. Many of these works are masterpieces of their kind, but this is not one of them.

WHAT HAPPENED NEXT

The aircraft Prometheus is the second of the three "International Transport" Poirot murder scenes from the mid-1930s, following the *Orient Express*, which Poirot had boarded the previous year, and preceding the steamer SS Karnak in *Death on the Nile* two years later: murder In the air, on water and on land.

It is also the second of three in which he teams up with the potential suspects to investigate, following *Three Act Tragedy*, published in the same year, and with *The ABC Murders* to be published a year later.

ADAPTATIONS

ITV provided a reasonably faithful adaptation, but added Captain Hastings, huge extra lashings of Parisian local colour and the French Open Tennis to fill in for those parts where the plot sags. At one point, while in Montmartre, Poirot even takes time out to explain the Surrealists to Jane Grey ...

The ABC Murders (1936)

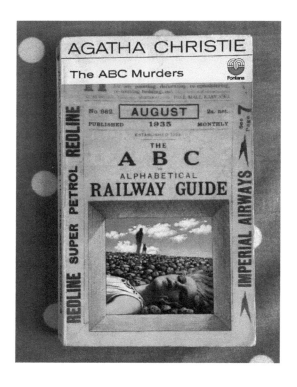
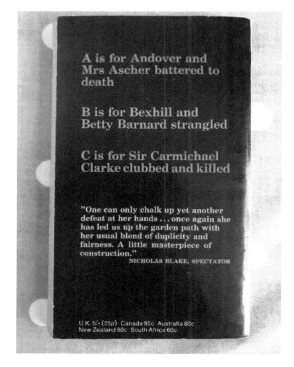

THE BOOK   Fontana, 1972 pp 192

The Tom Adams cover shows the body of victim B, Betty Barnard, on the beach at Bexhill framed on a 1935 Railway Guide. The blurb on the back is perfect (what great alliteration!).

THE STORY

Captain Hastings returns from the Argentine on urgent business to do with his ranch there, which he promptly forgets when he meets up with Poirot again. Poirot receives a letter from "ABC", taunting him with a hint of a crime to take place in Andover, which turns out to be the senseless murder of Alice Ascher.

It becomes clear that ABC has in mind a series of similarly random murders, with the location and victim chosen by dint of their initials. Before each murder takes place, ABC writes to tell Poirot where and when it will happen. By the time we get to the letter D, Poirot has formed an investigative band, his Special Legion, made up of the people primarily affected by the murders A, B and C. They go to Doncaster to join the hunt ...

CHARACTERS

The characters in this book are among the more interesting created by Agatha Christie - few cardboard cut-outs here. Alexander Bonaparte Cust is a brilliant study of the quintessential societal victim; Lily Marbury, with whom he lodges, unexpectedly takes pity on him and warns him that an Inspector will be calling to see him, even though it must be apparent to her that he is possibly a serial killer; Megan Barnard is a hugely strong-minded woman who has no qualms about (successfully) pricking Poirot's self-important waffle, and announces that she hopes the killer will not be found ... and so on.

To make the characters so distinctive is quite an achievement because the cast-list in this 192-page book is a huge one. There is yet another single young woman joining forces with Poirot named Grey (Thora), following on from Jane (*Death in the Clouds*) and Katherine (*Mystery of the Blue Train*). She is, however, less sympathetically treated.

ATTITUDES AND QUOTES

My selection of quotes for this book is very different to those for all the other swigathas because it is the attitudes of Poirot, Hastings and the author that come through most clearly in it, rather than those of the other characters, and they are not by any means a reflection of attitudes prevalent at the time the story was written.

For example, here are Poirot and Hastings discussing the character of the serial killer ABC:

> *"No, the poisoning of life for the innocent, that, at least, we cannot lay at ABC's door."*
> *"You'll soon be making excuses for the man!" I said bitterly.*
> *"Why not? He may believe himself fully justified. We may, perhaps, end by having sympathy for his point of view."*

This is a somewhat unexpected statement for Poirot to make about a serial-killer, but Agatha Christie often seemed more concerned for the innocent survivors than the victims of crime.

Here is another exchange from the same scene, when Hastings berates him for his lack of action:

> *"In the meantime people are dying right and left."*
> *"Three people. And there are, what is it - about 120 - road deaths every week?"*
> *"That is entirely different."*
> *"It is probably exactly the same to those who die ..."*

Having forgotten his urgent business concerning his Argentine ranch, Hastings also seems to have forgotten his wife Bella - here Poirot mocks his eye for a pretty girl (in this case the Nordic-looking Thora Grey):

> *Some of the time I love a brunette*
> *Some of the time I love a blonde*
> *(Who comes from Eden by way of Sweden).*[1]

Poirot overhears children singing 'And catch a fox and put him in a box and never let him go'.[2] He asks Hastings what he thinks of fox-hunting:

> *"I suppose it does sound cruel, but really -"*
> *"The fox enjoys it? Do not say* les bêtises, *my friend.* Tout de même - *it is better that - the quick, cruel death - than what those children were singing... To be shut away - in a box - for ever ... No, it is not good that."*

Poirot is considering the likelihood that ABC, when caught, will be judged insane and spared the hangman's rope. He returns to this theme just before Cust's trial:

> *"With insanity there can be no acquittal. Imprisonment during His Majesty's pleasure is hardly preferable to death."*

Agatha Christie shared Poirot's horror at the concept of life imprisonment, as well as doubts as to the merits of a drawn-out legal process that would end in a capital sentence, which is why she/he often allows the guilty party to take their own way out.

SWIGATHA RATING 10/10

Not only is this a brilliantly constructed story, with a unique idea at the heart of it, but it is one of the best-written, and, yes, most exciting books that she ever wrote. There is no padding whatsoever. Simply first-rate, and the best of the Poirot-Hastings tales by a mile, which is a bit surprising as she had long tired of the pairing.

WHERE IT LED

These days, just about every crime thriller that is published anywhere or televised seems to be based around the character of a serial killing mastermind taunting the police with their brilliance.

That was not the case in the 1930s: Agatha Christie's plot was hugely original, and was unique for the genre because it is about a serial-killer-that-wasn't. She brought the world a real serial killer three years later, in the book now known as *And Then There Were None*.

There is some confusion as to when, and in what order, this story and *Cards on the Table* were written, because characters in each refer to events in the other; both were first published in the UK in 1936. Whichever the way round it was, this book came out in the middle of a run of Poirot classics from the pen of Agatha Christie.

ADAPTATIONS

ITV *Poirot* series, 1992 : the story works well on television, and this is one of the best, if not the best, of the 'Suchet Poirots'. The portrayal of Cust, by David Sumpter, is really impressive.

Then there was one of those dreadful 1960s adaptations - *The Alphabet Murders* - which has Poirot meeting up with Margaret Rutherford hamming it up as Miss Marple. More recently, the BBC made a TV film with John Malkovich playing Poirot as a tortured ex-priest trying to prove himself.

I have no problem with adaptations trying to leave their own mark on a work, but, really ...

NOTES

[1] Poirot is quoting (not totally accurately) from "*Some Sort of Somebody*", a song by Jerome Kern and Elsie Janis written in 1915.

[2] From the Children's nursery rhyme "A-Hunting we will go". Note that the version used in schools today reads:

> *And catch a fox*
> *And put him in a box*
> And then we'll let him go

Cards on the Table (1936)

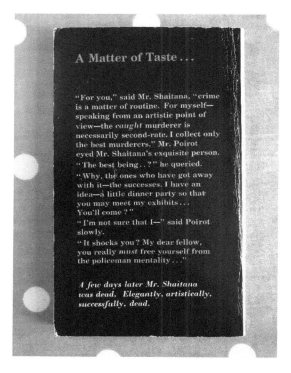

THE BOOK Fontana, 1969 pp 192

A cover by Ian Robinson rather unexpectedly showing a weasel, presumably a reference to the character of the murder victim? The court cards refer to the four card-playing suspects, two women and two men. Ian Robinson was asked by Fontana to imitate Tom Adams' style when the latter was unavailable.

THE STORY

Mr Shaitana, collector and connoisseur, invites four criminal experts and four successful murderers to dinner, and announces that at the end of the evening he will have a surprise announcement to make. After dinner, he leads the two groups into two card rooms to play bridge. Shaitana sits by the fire in the murderers' room. He never gets to reveal his surprise ...

CHARACTERS

The four 'sleuths' are a detective super-group: Poirot himself, Colonel Race, last seen in *The Man in the Brown Suit*, Superintendent Battle, of *Secret of Chimneys* fame, and the crime-writer Ariadne Oliver, who in later years becomes a replacement Hastings for Poirot.

The four apparently-successful killers - Dr Roberts, Mrs Lorrimer, Major Despard and Anne Meredith - are surprisingly un-bloody in character, but, for once in a swigatha, each has a believable motive and opportunity to commit the crime, and all Poirot has to go on are the bridge score-sheets. Time for him to use his fabled 'psychology'.

ATTITUDES AND QUOTES

Agatha Christie clearly enjoyed herself writing this book. First, she delights in her ridicule of the Anglo-Saxon attitude toward 'that damned Dago, Shaitana'. His appearance and attire are mannered, almost Dali-esque:

> He deliberately attempted a Mephistophelean effect. He was tall and thin, his face was long and melancholy, his eyebrows were heavily accented and jet-black, he wore a moustache with stiff waxed ends and a tiny black imperial...

> Every Englishman who saw him longed earnestly and fervently to kick him ... Whether Mr Shaitana was an Argentine, or a Portuguese, or a Greek, or some other nationality rightly despised by the insular Briton, nobody knew.[1]

She introduces Ariadne Oliver, a mocking self-portrait of herself who had briefly appeared in a Parker Pyne story, into the world of Poirot:

> "I've written 32 books by now - and of course they're all exactly the same really, as Mr Poirot seems to have noticed - but no-one else has."

Agatha Christie is being unduly modest here, having written 30 or so herself by then. Certainly, some elements in her plots are re-used once or twice, but it is incredible how distinct the books written in her prime are from each other.

Her schoolgirl French has come flooding back - in this example, Poirot has just survived a visit to Mrs Luxmore:

> "Quelle femme!" murmured Hercule Poirot. "Ce pauvre Despard! Ce qu'il a dû souffrir! Quel voyage épouvantable!"

The most amusing, and gripping, chapters deal with Poirot's encounter with Mrs Lorrimer: she confesses to the murder and he refuses to believe her. There is a fantastic flow to her writing here:

"The question is", he said, "can Hercule Poirot possibly be wrong?"

"No-one can always be right," said Mrs Lorrimer coldly.

"I am," said Poirot. "Always I am right. It is so invariable that it startles me. But now it looks, it very much looks, as though I am wrong. And that upsets me. Presumably, you know what you are saying. It is your murder! Fantastic, then, that Hercule Poirot should know better than you how you committed it."

"Fantastic and very absurd," said Mrs Lorrimer still more coldly.

"I am, then, mad. Decidedly I am mad. No - sacré nom d'un petit bonnehomme - I am not mad! I am right. I must be right ..."

Mrs Lorrimer said sharply: "I really believe you are mad, M Poirot..."

Chapter 26 ends with Poirot wringing some truth out of her:

"How can you be so sure? How do you know that it was Anne Meredith who killed Mr Shaitana?"

A deep sigh broke from Mrs Lorrimer. Her last resistance had gone down before Poirot's insistence. "Because," she said, "I saw her."

Suddenly Poirot laughed. He could not help it. His head went back, and his high Gallic laugh filled the room.

In a 50-year career, Poirot is rarely to be seen laughing, and so to find him almost crying with laughter, as here, is unique. What is so funny?

It had been a challenging case. There were no incriminating clues: any of the suspects might have done it. Poirot had thought that the only way to identify Shaitana's murder would be via a thorough understanding of each suspect's psychology, of how they would be most likely to behave in the peculiar circumstances of that evening. So he, somewhat laboriously, had used the bridge scores and questions about their powers of observation to build up a profile for each of the suspects ... only to discover that someone had (apparently) witnessed the killing.

I think Poirot's laughter here is an indication of how much the author enjoyed writing this book.

SWIGATHA RATING 7/10

Agatha Christie writes in her Foreword to *Cards on the Table* that it was 'one of Hercule Poirot's favourite cases. His friend, Captain Hastings, however, when Poirot describes it to him, considered it very dull. I wonder with which of them my readers will agree'.

The crime fiction writer Robert Barnard, in his *Agatha Christie: A Talent to Deceive*, describes it as 'on the very top rung'.

I incline more to Hastings' opinion than Poirot or Barnard's. The idea for the setting is, yet again, brilliant: four sleuths and four murderers invited to form bridge fours by a devil-like character, who promises to reveal some secrets when they finish playing ... take it away!

But it drags somewhat after that. There is too much padding - the ridiculous circumstance of the murder of Mrs Lorrimer has no place in this story and looks designed to drag Agatha Christie over the line to 'page 192'.

The sleuth super-group is unconvincing, and it seems that Race realises it, because he has disappeared to some 'remote part of Empire where there's trouble brewing' well before the end. I would have gone for 6/10 were it not for Chapter 26.

WHAT HAPPENED NEXT

The supergroup disbanded. Race met up with Poirot again the following year on the Nile; Battle returned for *Towards Zero* wondering what 'keeps putting Hercule Poirot into my head', and Mrs Oliver re-emerges 16 years later when Poirot investigates the death of Mrs McGinty. Two of the characters, Major Despard and Rhoda Dawes, marry and turn up again with Mrs Oliver in *The Pale Horse*.

ADAPTATIONS

ITV, 2005. Some of the ITV adaptations seem not to trust the original story too much. This one is a classic example; here are some of the 'improvements' in the screenplay:

- Colonel Race and Superintendent Battle are replaced by Colonel Hughes and Supt Wheeler (why?!)
- Dr Roberts apparently killed to prevent the fact of his homosexuality being made public
- One of Shaitana's four murderers, Anne Meredith, hadn't done anything
- Her friend Rhoda Dawes proves to be a homicidal nutcase and drowns (which explains why she doesn't appear in any of the TV productions of *The Pale Horse*)
- Mrs Lorrimer survives and turns out to be Anne Meredith's mother.

It is a difficult story to stretch over two hours, admittedly, but these changes are witless. The character of Shaitana, however, is beautifully captured by Alexander Siddig.

NOTES

[1] The apparent English urge to kick Argentinian, Portuguese and Greek people Is also on display elsewhere In Agatha Christie's work, notably in *Dumb Witness*, published the following year.

Murder in Mesopotamia (1936)

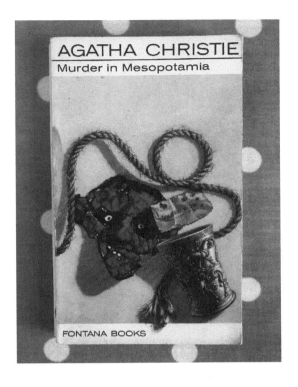
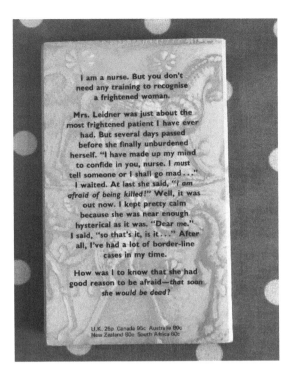

THE BOOK   Fontana, 1971 pp 190

Another cover by Tom Adams, featuring elements from the plot: death mask, threatening letter, fake goblet and the first of his 'ropes' (see also his painting for *Towards Zero*).

This was the first of Agatha Christie's novels to be set in the Middle East. She had married archaeologist Max Mallowan six years previously and hugely enjoyed accompanying him on his expeditions. The book is dedicated to "my many archaeological friends in Iraq and Syria". The original cover for the first UK edition was designed by Robin Macartney, who was often the expeditions' architect.

THE STORY

Dr Leidner is accompanied by his wife on an archaeological expedition to Iraq. Her behaviour becomes increasingly erratic, and he hires Nurse Amy Leatheran to help care for her. Mrs Leidner confides to the nurse that she is in fear for her life, and indeed that fear proves to be justified. The local (British) authorities ask Hercule Poirot, who happened to be visiting Baghdad, to investigate her murder.

A couple of years later, Nurse Leatheran is persuaded to write her account of the affair.

CHARACTERS spoiler!

Agatha Christie usually claimed that she was unable to base fictional characters on people from her own personal circle, but one or two in this book reflect, at least in part, people that she came across on expedition. She had come to know her subject and was thus able to describe with accuracy the roles and responsibilities of the people involved at the dig.

Thus, Mrs Leidner is based upon the character of Katherine Woolley, whom the author met on her trips to Baghdad and Ur and who became a firm friend. Other characters from those trips re-appear in this book - the character of Carl Reiter seems to be based on that of the architect Whitburn, and the calm David Emmott could be Max Mallowan himself[1].

Mrs Leidner is portrayed as a fascinating woman, a prima donna type whom you could be repulsed by and yet devoted to simultaneously. The fact that she does not recognise that her second husband is the same person as her first can only be explained by her total self-absorption ...

ATTITUDES AND QUOTES

The most interesting character is Nurse Leatheran, the narrator, who tells everything as she saw it at the time, rather than with the benefit of hindsight. This gives a very refreshing feel to her narrative style, and allows her to make some very amusing asides. She is yet another single, thirty-something young woman teaming up with Poirot on a murder enquiry, but the first to let us know what she thought of him.

Here she explains her diary-like approach to narration.

> *Looking back as I do from my present standpoint of knowledge I can see a good many little signs and indications that I was quite blind to at the time. To tell the story properly, however, I think I ought to try to capture the point of view that I actually held - puzzled, uneasy and increasingly conscious of something wrong.*

And here she describes working with Poirot:

> *I'd got the feeling, you see, by this time, that M. Poirot and I were the doctor and nurse in charge of a case. At least, it was more like an operation and he was the surgeon. Perhaps I oughtn't to say so, but in a queer way I was beginning to enjoy myself.*

And here Sheila Reilly describes Louise Leidner – or is it Katherine Woolley? Whatever – it is a brilliant description:

> *"She's the kind of woman who's never had a row with anyone in her life - but rows always happen where she is! She makes them happen. She's a kind of female Iago."*

SWIGATHA RATING 6/10

The narration, characterisations and descriptions flow well, and it is clear that Agatha Christie put a lot of herself into them. The revelations at the end, however, strain the reader's credulity to the utmost.

WHAT HAPPENED NEXT

After Mesopotamia, Poirot travels to Syria to work for the French delegation there, and on his way home takes a ride on the Orient Express (the events described by Nurse Leatheran's narration had taken place a few years before).

Agatha Christie was spending more time in the Middle East and so was Poirot: in 1937 she placed him in Egypt (*Death on the Nile*) and the following year in Petra (*Appointment with Death*).

ADAPTATIONS

The production by ITV 'embellishes' the original by introducing Hastings as the uncle of one of the people on the expedition and reducing Nurse Leatheran to a walk-on part. It also adds a sub-plot involving Countess Rossakoff of *The Big Four* fame and a drug-related murder and suicide. It does, however, contrive to make the Leidner marriage slightly more credible.

NOTES

[1] Agatha Christie, *An Autobiography:* pages 403-405 and elsewhere (Fontana 1977 edition)

Dumb Witness (1937)

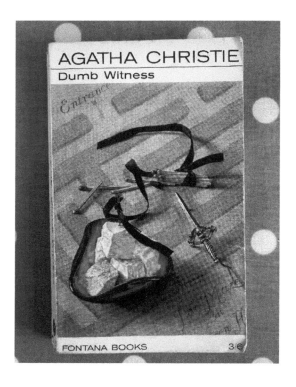 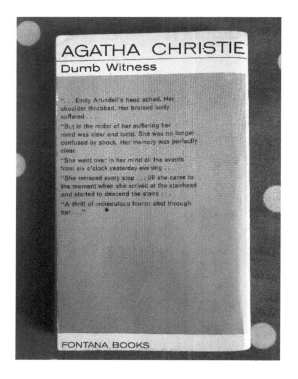

THE BOOK Fontana, 1967 pp 255

The cover is one of Ian Robinson's. The matches are a reference to phosphorous poisoning but the relevance of the bowl of sweets, the maze at Littlegreen House and the pin escape me.

At 255 pages, this is Agatha Christie's longest detective story.

THE STORY

Emily Arundell falls down the stairs and, as she recovers in bed, begins to think it was not an accident. She writes to Hercule Poirot asking for help, but her reasons are not clearly specified. The letter is not delivered until a couple of months after it was written, and when Poirot and Hastings go to call on her they find that she has died.

Poirot decides to act as though she was still his client, and delves into the past, initially presenting himself in a number of different roles to gain access to the characters involved.

Unusually, the opening chapters, which deal with the accident and its aftermath, are not narrated by Hastings, and are much the better for it. This book reads like a play to me, with limited settings and many, many long conversations and interrogations. Also, unusually, no murder actually takes place, although one is assumed.

CHARACTERS AND ATTITUDES

Emily Arundell is a snob of the first water, but fair-minded and fiercely proud of the family name. Her unscrupulous blood-relatives, on the other hand, have each considered killing her for her money; and her companion, having learnt that she inherits all of Miss Arundell's fortune, fraudulently prevents the old lady from changing her will before she dies.

The only straight character is Dr Tanios, and he is widely derided by everyone else for being Greek: a Dago, no less! In this case, however, I think the author is (gently) mocking the "insular prejudices" of her characters. Note that Dr Tanios' forename is Jacob: by 1937 Agatha Christie was becoming a bit more careful about giving her characters anti-semitic sentiments to intone, and there are none here, but you get the impression there would be a few in the narrator's absence.

Apart from Emily Arundell herself, the characters are hollow. The most excruciating member of this excruciating household is the terrier, Bob.

Hastings has no role in the story. Poirot's pointless role-playing came across as padding to me; his application of 'psychology' is laughable, his means of obtaining a confession is hugely unconvincing, and his collusion with the culprit, to allow her to take their own way out, is criminal. Not his finest hour.

Dumb Witness grew out of an unpublished 14-page short story, *The Incident of the Dog's Ball* [1]. The extra 241 pages have very little to recommend them.

QUOTES

Here is Dr Tanios, as seen by the other characters:

> *For Bella had married a foreigner - and not only a foreigner - but a Greek. In Miss Arundell's prejudiced mind a Greek was almost as bad as an Argentine or a Turk* (Emily Arundell)

> *"And anyway, it isn't Bella - it's Tanios. I bet he's got a nose for money all right! Trust a Greek for that!"* (Charles Arundell)

> *"Made a fool of herself though. Married some Dago who was over at the University. A Greek doctor."* (Miss Peabody)

> *"What can he have been doing to her? I believe Turks are frightfully cruel sometimes."*
>
> *"Dr Tanios is a Greek."*
>
> *"Yes, of course, that's the other way about - they're usually the ones who get massacred by the Turks - or am I thinking of Armenians?"* (Miss Lawson)

And finally, Arthur Hastings:

> *"And yet you liked Tanios, did you not? You found him an agreeable man, open-hearted, good-natured, genial. Attractive in spite of your insular prejudice against the Argentines, the Portuguese and the Greeks - a thoroughly congenial personality?"* *"Yes," I admitted. "I did."*

Hastings 'admits' to liking the Dago when prompted by Poirot. It is remarkable that his 'insular prejudice against the Argentines' had survived 14 years of living amongst them.

Apart from the Greek element, there are few points of interest in the writing, but here are a couple. I love Miss Peabody's description of Mrs Tanios' mother:

> *Then came Arabella. Plain girl. Face like a scone.*

And here is Poirot on Britain as self-perceived haven of liberty:

> *"After all, this is a free country - "*
>
> *"English people seem to labour under that misapprehension," murmured Poirot.*

That is an extraordinary statement from a man who had come to the country as a refugee twenty years earlier and stayed.

SWIGATHA RATING 4/10

The main clue to the perpetrator of the first murder attempt is sign-posted in letters three feet high.

There is never any confirmation that Miss Arundell was murdered, there is no police involvement, and no direct evidence of either an accusation by Poirot or a confession by the culprit.

These factors all combine to make it one of the more unusual, bloodless Christies. That should make it interesting, but unfortunately, there is no flow to it; all seems forced and humourless, and it becomes boring.

WHAT HAPPENED NEXT

Hastings is (not surprisingly, for Agatha Christie had clearly tired of the pairing) despatched back to the Argentine and does not re-appear in published form until 1975 (in *Curtain*). He takes the dog with him.

ADAPTATIONS

The ITV adaptation struggled with a flimsy and unexciting plot and therefore added some bits of its own:

- Charles Arundell's failed attempt to break the water-speed record on Lake Coniston

- the mediumistic Tripps' ability to foresee tragedy

- a love affair between Dr Grainger and Miss Lawson

- the murder of the doctor

… and so on. The finest performance is by the dog. The incidental wind music is, however, lovely.

NOTES

[1] First published in 2009 as the coda to *Agatha Christie's Secret Notebooks* (John Curran)

Death on the Nile (1937)

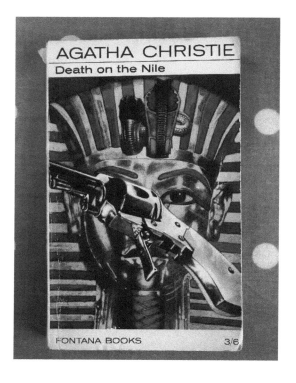

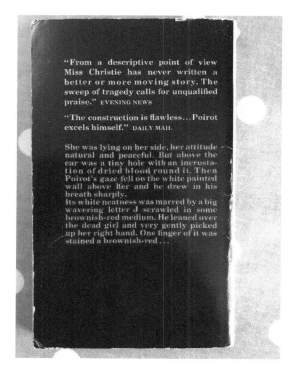

THE BOOK   Fontana, 1968 pp 222

Tom Adams' iconic cover painting depicts (exactly) the pearl-handled revolver featured in the story and shrieks "Egypt".

It would have shrieked it even more loudly when the phenomenal Tutankhamun exhibition came to London four years later, which may explain why he only did one cover for this book (in many other cases, his 1960s covers were superseded in the 1970s editions).

THE STORY

Simon and Linnet Doyle arrive in Egypt on their honeymoon tour. Their tour had thus far been frequently disturbed by appearances on the scene of Jacqueline de Bellefort, Simon's ex-fiancée. Hercule Poirot joins the three of them, plus a colourful group of passengers, on a trip up the Nile.

Jacqueline confides to Poirot that she would like to shoot Linnet in the temple with her pearl-handled pistol, and soon enough Linnet is found shot in the head by a pearl-handled pistol ...

CHARACTERS AND ATTITUDES - spoiler!

There is a great variety of characters on board the *SS Karnak*: Salome Otterbourne, a dipsomaniac writer of lurid sex fiction; Mrs van Schuyler, a kleptomaniac New York millionaire; Ferguson, an aristocrat dedicated to ridding the world of the aristocracy; a German physician, an Italian archaeologist-cum-terrorist, a young man (Tim Allerton) a bit too much in admiration of his mother ... and so on.

The most interesting character is the tragic Jacqueline de Bellefort, bright and intelligent and full of life when the book begins and suicidal at the end. When Poirot first meets her, he takes an instant liking to her and feels a great sympathy for her situation, whilst worrying what it might lead her to do. Time and again he tries to persuade her to think again, but she cannot: she realises that, without her intelligence and planning, the moronic brute Simon, for whom she is willing to sacrifice everything, would go ahead without her and make a total hash of things.

Poirot's compassion for her allows Jackie to take the easy way out: suicide, rather than trial, conviction and the hangman's rope or life in prison. Agatha Christie deemed incarceration for the rest of one's life to be a worse fate than immediate death. Poirot shows no compassion towards Miss de Bellefort's three victims.

QUOTES

More than in any other of these stories, Poirot thinks aloud, but in French; someone wishing to know 'who-dun-it' would do well to pause and consider what he is actually saying. Here is one example. Poirot and Colonel Race are examining the dead woman's bedroom, when Poirot says:

> *"On ne prend pas les mouches avec le vinaigre."*

Poirot is examining two bottles of nail varnish, one full and one empty. His reaction after sniffing them made little sense to me when first I read it: "You don't put vinegar on your moustaches" was my ill-informed guess. The actual translation is "You don't catch flies with vinegar", but even that does not tell us much. What I think he is saying is that Linnet presumably used make-up to make herself look attractive to herself and others, so she would hardly have been applying something that had should have such a bitter smell. He has no intention of explaining himself to Race, but it proves to be a vital clue.

Here are some examples of Agatha Christie's narrative style, with its dry humour and flow ('as though in supreme enquiry' Is perfect):

"There's no reason why women shouldn't behave like rational human beings," Simon asserted stolidly.

Poirot said dryly: "Quite frequently they do. That is even more upsetting!"

"Mrs Doyle!" exclaimed Ferguson with deep contempt. "She's the sort of woman who should be shot as an example."

Cornelia looked at him anxiously.

"I believe it's your digestion," she said kindly.

"What a poisonous woman! Whew! Why didn't someone murder her!"

"It may yet happen," Poirot consoled him.

And it does... Poirot and Race have just survived a visit from Salome Otterbourne. On her next visit:

Bang! The noise of the explosion filled the cabin. There was an acrid sour smell of smoke. Mrs Otterbourne turned slowly sideways, as though in supreme enquiry, then her body slumped forward and she fell to the ground with a crash.

SWIGATHA RATING 9/10

This is one of the best of her books: terrific story, well-written, great setting (and one, like the Orient Express, that she knew very well), interesting characters and twists that surprise.

Unusually, we are given more than the usual number of indications of what Poirot is thinking, and, even more unusually, feeling. He warns Jackie again and again not to do it, to turn back before it is too late, so it should come as no surprise to learn that she is the brains behind the crime ... yet it does!

WHAT HAPPENED NEXT

After Mesopotamia and the Nile, Poirot's middle-eastern odyssey next takes him to Jordan for an *Appointment with Death*. He goes to visit the British authorities in Amman, armed with a letter of introduction from Colonel Race. After that case, Agatha Christie packed him off back to England for good ...

ADAPTATIONS

A British film was made in 1978, with Peter Ustinov as Poirot and a firmament of stars, including Angela Lansbury in brilliant form as Mrs Otterbourne (capturing the 'supreme enquiry' beautifully),

David Niven as the definitive Colonel Race and Bette Davis as Mrs van Schuyler. Mia Farrow gives a fine performance as Jacqueline de Bellefort, and Simon McCorkindale is suitably wooden as her lover. The characters of the Allertons, Cornelia Robson and Fanthorp have been ditched, and an awful Indian stereotype boat-manager inserted, but otherwise it is quite faithful to the original.

Although an enjoyable film, it is rather too full of Ustinov going around to each character and saying "YOU could have done it, by ..." If nothing else that is a dead give-away, because the only people he does not accuse in this way are, of course, the ones who did do it.

ITV's adaptation for its *Poirot* series plays it fairly straight, apart from making Tim Allerton gay. It is one of the better full-length films in the series, and is unusually faithful to the original dialogue.

The Murder in the Mews (1937)

 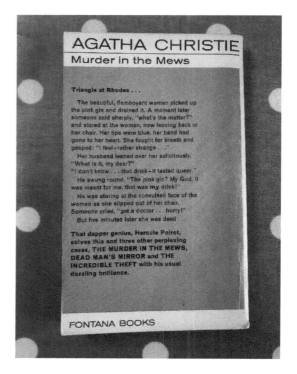

THE BOOK   Fontana, 1967 pp 191

Murder in The Mews is a collection of four long (for Agatha Christie) short stories. Tom Adams' cover, not one of his favourites, depicts the shattered glass that is one of the clues in *Dead Man's Mirror* (the title of the collection in the US). The dog-headed figure is Anubis, the Egyptian God of the Dead. I cannot think of any reason for its inclusion, although one of the characters claims to be a 'reincarnation of Hatshepsut'.

THE STORIES

Murder in the Mews

Poirot and Japp are called in to investigate an apparent suicide that took place on Fireworks Night. A good example of double-bluff, and another example of the author gently exploring the affection between two women living together. A re-working of *The Market Basing Mystery*, one of *Poirot's Early Cases*.

The Incredible Theft

Lord Mayfield is persuaded, against his better judgement, to call in Poirot to investigate the disappearance from his home of secret plans for a bomber aircraft. A re-working of *The Submarine Plans*: once again, from *Poirot's Early Cases*.

Dead Man's Mirror

Arch-snob Gervaise Chevenix-Gore writes to Poirot, summoning him to investigate some double-dealing close to home. Poirot consults his friend Mr Satterthwaite about the character of the writer. When Poirot arrives at the Chevenix-Gore abode, he discovers that his summoner is dead (another apparent suicide).

Triangle at Rhodes

Poirot is on holiday on the island of Rhodes. In the company of Miss Pamela Lyall, he observes the behaviour of fellow guests at their seaside hotel. He finds it lamentably predictable, and is totally unsurprised at the later demise of one of them. As should the reader be: variations on the triangle depicted in this story were also evident in *Evil Under the Sun*, *Death on The Nile* and *The Thirteen Problems*.

CHARACTERS, ATTITUDES AND QUOTES

Although these stories are longer than her usual, indeed *Dead Man's Mirror* qualifies as a novella, they still do not permit their characters to emerge fully-formed. In most examples, we are permitted but one sentence to visualise a character; sometimes that sentence is very directional.

Here are two 'give-away' examples from *Murder in the Mews* (I think we can assume that Laverton-West is ok if unremarkable, and that Eustace is up to no good):

Charles Laverton-West

> *He was clean-shaven, with the mobile mouth of an actor, and the slightly prominent eyes that so often go with the gift of oratory. He was good-looking in a quiet, well-bred way.*

Major Eustace

> *... was a tall man, good-looking in a somewhat coarse fashion. There was a puffiness about his eyes - small crafty eyes that belied the geniality of his manner.*

Major Eustace is yet another example in Christie of a retired army officer gone to seed. Here are some examples from *The Incredible Theft* that are slightly less judgmental:

Mrs Vanderlyn

> *... an extremely good-looking blonde. Her voice had a soupçon of an American accent, just enough to be pleasant without undue exaggeration ...*

Mr Carlile

> *... a pale young man with pince nez and an air of intelligent reserve. He talked little*

Air-Marshall Carrington

> *... his career had begun in the Navy, and he still retained the bluff breeziness of the ex-Naval man*

Julia Carrington

> *She was very thin but still beautiful. Her hands and feet, in particular, were exquisite. Her manner was abrupt and restless, that of a woman who lived on her nerves*

Mrs Macatta

> *... barked out short sentences rather than spoke them, and was generally of somewhat alarming aspect*

Reggie Carrington

> *... 21, weak mouth, charming smile, indecisive chin, eyes set far apart with rather a narrow head*

Lord Mayfield

> *... a big man, square-shouldered with thick silvery hair, a big straight nose and a slightly prominent chin*

It feels like the reader has been given access to the parade ring at Ascot.

In *Triangle at Rhodes*, Pamela Lyall and her friend Sarah try to persuade Hercule Poirot of the fascination of human nature and the unexpected actions of which a human being is capable. Poirot is having none of it:

> *"It is most rare that anyone does an action that is not* dans son caractère. *It is in the end monotonous... (human) nature repeats itself more than one would imagine. The sea," he added thoughtfully, "has infinitely more variety."*

Sarah turned her head sideways and asked: "You think that human beings tend to reproduce certain patterns? Stereotyped patterns?"

"Précisément," said Poirot.

SWIGATHA RATING 6/10

These are four decent stories, each very different from the other, and enjoyable to read. They are far superior to the Hastings-narrated short stories of the 1920s, but with each of them one gets the feeling that one has read it before (and in two cases, one just about had!). For a new reader, of course, that would not matter.

Ruth Rendell once said that calling Agatha Christie characters 'cardboard cut-outs' was an offence to cardboard cut-outs; in that context, it is quite interesting to hear Poirot (often the mouthpiece of the author) imply that human beings are indeed little more than that.

WHERE IT LED

The *Dead Man's Mirror* story allows Agatha Christie the opportunity to include a favourite quote from Tennyson's *Lady of Shalott*, one that she used far more effectively 30 years later for *The Mirror Crack'd from Side to Side* ('Out flew the web and floated wide ...').

Poirot's next set of short stories were his last - collected under the title *The Labours of Hercules* in 1947. In the opinion of many critics, but not in mine, this was the best short story collection that Agatha Christie produced.

ADAPTATIONS

Each of these stories was adapted for the ITV *Poirot* series. A few liberties were taken, especially with *Dead Man's Mirror*, but the productions of the first and fourth stories are huge fun, and very typical examples of what made the series such a huge global phenomenon.

Appointment with Death (1938)

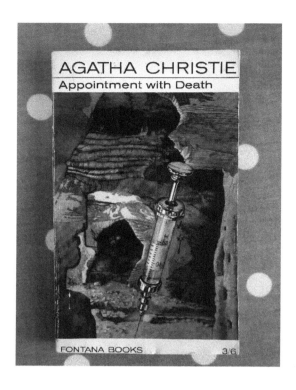

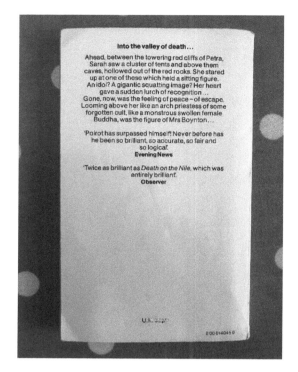

THE BOOK Fontana, 1972 pp 160

Tom Adams cover shows the 'monstrous, swollen female Buddha' of Mrs Boynton amid the red caves of Petra, as well as the cause of her death.

The Observer quote on the back of a later edition is not *quite* what Torquemada wrote in 1938, but it's a great line[1].

THE STORY

The book, one of Agatha Christie's shortest, is in two parts. In the first, the Boyntons, an American family totally dominated by a tyrannical, sadistic matriarch, are on a holiday in the Middle East. Himself on holiday in Jerusalem, Poirot overhears one member of the family telling another that Mrs Boynton has to be killed. The Boynton's move on to Jordan, and Mrs Boynton duly dies during a visit to Petra.

In the second half, Poirot is visiting a local British official, Colonel Carbury. Carbury is not convinced that Mrs Boynton's was a natural death and asks Poirot to investigate. He gives him 24 hours to report back, and the rest of the book consists of Poirot's interrogations of members of the touring party.

CHARACTERS AND ATTITUDES

In the character of the sadistic Mrs Boynton, Agatha Christie has created a wholly believable monster, and the total control that she exercises over her three step-children and her own daughter is utterly convincing. The supporting cast also convince: the hopeless Lennox Boynton, the evanescent Ginevra, the newly-qualified, emergent Dr Sarah King and the suggestible Miss Pierce. The story could have been written a hundred years ago, or a hundred days ago; it is truly timeless.

QUOTES

What an opening line:

> *"You do see, don't you, that she's got to be killed?"*

Here, Agatha Christie's gentle mockery of Anglo-Saxon attitudes (evident throughout her golden period) continues:

> *"Heard of a Frenchman called Gerard? Theodore Gerard?"*
> *"Certainly, a very distinguished man in his own line."*
> *"Loony bins," confirmed Colonel Carbury. "Passion for a charwoman at the age of four makes you insist you're the Archbishop of Canterbury when you're thirty-eight. Can't see why and never have, but these chaps explain it all very convincingly."*

Dr Gerard's thoughts here echo those of Poirot in *Dumb Witness* (to the effect that those who believe that England is a free country are deluding themselves):

> *Mr Cope rose. "In America," he said, "we're great believers in absolute freedom."*
> *Dr Gerard rose also. He was unimpressed by the remark. He had heard it made before by people of many different nationalities. The illusion that freedom is the prerogative of one's own particular race is fairly widespread. Dr Gerard was wiser. He knew that no race, no country and no individual could be described as free. But he also knew that there were different types of bondage. He went to bed thoughtful and interested.*

The most interesting quotation in the book is taken from Shakespeare, when, at its end, Ginevra sings a lament (from *Cymbeline*) for her murdered mother:

119

Fear no more the heat o' the sun

Nor the furious winter's rages;

Thou thy worldly task hast done,

Home art gone, and ta'en thy wages ...

Ginevra's mother had been mentally abusive towards her all her life, and her step-siblings worried for her mental health. This show of pity for her mother indicates that she has finally broken free from her, and now stands a chance in life.

SWIGATHA RATING 8/10

This is a very interesting and enjoyable book to re-read. It always helps when the author has expert knowledge of a setting. The characters are convincing, too, and the first half of the book is as good as anything Agatha Christie wrote, in my opinion; the second half of it at least eschews the temptation to add another murder to string it out a bit (which is why it is 30 pages shorter than the usual 192 pages of these editions).

The solution is a surprise, but really anyone could have done it; it feels like the author got three-quarters of the way through, stopped, picked out the least likely suspect, and took it from there, so it's not quite top-drawer.

But what a great read for an eleven-year-old.

WHAT HAPPENED NEXT

Poirot's various trips to the Middle East, following *Death on the Nile* and *Murder in Mesopotamia*, come to an end, and he is despatched back to Blighty for good.

ADAPTATIONS

Agatha Christie adapted this story for the stage in her 'theatrical decade' of the 1950s. As with most of her plays, the character of Hercule Poirot does not appear, and the identity of the murderer is changed.

A dire version of the story was filmed in 1988 with Peter Ustinov as Poirot. It dispenses with the psychological hold that their mother has over the children, and if I say that it was directed by Michael Winner and was a Golum-Globus production, I need say little else.

ITV pulled off the rare feat of sinking even lower into the mire of mediocrity with their 2008 version, which dispenses with the brilliance of Christie's plot altogether and substitutes one involving white slave-trading nuns and the head of John the Baptist. By some way this was the worst of the Suchet *Poirots*.

NOTES

[1] *"Death on the Nile was entirely brilliant; Appointment with Death, while lacking the single stroke of murderer's genius which provided the alibi in the former story, must be counted mathematically nearly twice as brilliant, since the number of suspects is reduced by nearly half ... "*

Torquemada, *The Observer*, June 1938.

Hercule Poirot's Christmas (1938)

THE BOOK   PAN, 1967 pp 204

One of PAN's striking photographic covers depicting key elements of the plot - the diamonds, sheet music for the Dead March, blood, the bedroom door key, a cinema ticket and what must be a passport. I love the font used and also the image of Agatha Christie (wearing what I saw at the time as her all-the-better-to-eat-you-with-my-dear smile).

The title alone would have been guaranteed to make this a best-seller in the run up to December 25th, 1938.

THE STORY

Pilar Estravados makes her way from civil-war-torn Spain to the home of the patriarchal Simeon Lee, who has invited his only grand-child for Christmas. She arrives to find a house full of his sons and their wives, and a poisonous atmosphere deliberately stimulated by old Simeon himself. All around her, she sees strange men stroking their jaws or throwing back their heads and laughing; within two days a bloody murder has occurred in a locked room. Pilar had hoped to experience a typical English Christmas (and maybe she did!), but instead she finds that her sharp eyes hold the key to the mystery.

CHARACTERS AND ATTITUDES - spoiler!

Heredity is a key element in this story. Simeon Lee's family is divided between those who take after their mother, and those their father. Adelaide Lee is dead, and so only appears in the story as a portrait, but Mr Lee is very much alive, as jaw-strokingly unscrupulous as ever. The three sons who take after him are each also unscrupulous in their own ways. One is a cheat, one a liar and one a murderer, with each constantly giving away their true nature by their physical mannerisms.

Take away the jaw-stroking and the throwing back of the heads (see Quotes, below) and this is a classic type of Christie family group - a prodigal son and his stay-at-home brother, a sensitive artist son and his pompous MP brother, the cheating wife and so on: similar Alfreds, Georges, Harolds and Lydias may also be found at Enderby Hall (*After the Funeral*), Yewtree Lodge (*A Pocket Full of Rye*) or Rutherford Hall (*4:50 from Paddington*).

QUOTES

Pilar admires Stephen Farr (another example of Agatha Christie disparaging her own race, which she frequently does):

> She wondered if he was an Englishman and decided he was not. "He is too alive, too real to be English," Pilar decided.

Pilar gets philosophical:

> "Everyone must die! That is so, is it not? If it comes quickly from the sky - bouff - like that, it is as well as any other way. One is alive for a time - yes, and then one is dead. That is what happens in this world."

Hilda here is trying to mitigate the shadows obsessing her husband:

> "I believe the present matters - not the past! The past must go. If we seek to keep the past alive, we end, I think, by distorting it. We see it in exaggerated terms - a false perspective."

... and Agatha Christie was the wife of an archaeologist! One of the minor themes in this book, increasingly developed in her later ones, was that 'old sins have long shadows'.

Here is Simeon Lee on heredity:

"I'll say this for you, Lydia, you're a well-bred woman. Breeding tells. I know that well
enough. A funny thing, though, heredity. There's only one of you who's taken after me - only
one out of all the litter."

Little did Simeon realise that there were at least three ... Ironically, the character most like him
(Pilar) is not one of his family, but an impostor. Likeness and mannerisms are well to the fore in the
plot, and Agatha Christie does lay it on with a trowel somewhat:

Harry threw up his head. He drew the finger along the line of his jaw. It was a gesture that
was habitual with him ...
The Superintendent stroked his jaw ...
Harry lifted up his chin and laughed ...
For a moment he (Colonel Johnson) took the entering figure to be that of Harry Lee, but as
Stephen Farr advanced into the room he saw his error ...
"Mr Harry Lee seemed in very good spirits, sir. Throwing back his head and laughing a great
deal" ...
Pilar was easily recognisable as one of the figures, and he (Poirot) thought the other was
Stephen Farr, then he saw that the man with Pilar was Harry Lee ...
Superintendent Sugden drew a doubtful finger along his jawbone ...
Superintendent Sugden threw back his head and laughed ...
Harry laughed, throwing his head back ...
"Who's that out there in the garden? Superintendent Sugden or Mr Farr?"...
Superintendent Sugden stroked his jaw cautiously ...

SWIGATHA RATING 9/10

This is a classic curl-up-at-the-fire-for-Christmas book, and judged as a swigatha it is one of the very
best. On just about every page, Agatha Christie repeats the vital clue, but I bet that 99% of her
readers are still surprised by the conclusion: *A Talent to Deceive*[1] indeed! The locked room element,
however, is a bit ridiculous, and the attempted murder of Pilar through the use of a large concrete
ball placed on top of her bedroom door even more so. Good fun, though.

WHAT HAPPENED NEXT

Agatha Christie moved on to sleuth-less serial killing in 1939 (*Murder is Easy, And Then There Were*
None). The character of Pilar Estravados obviously made an impression on Kenneth Branagh,

because he decided to use her name for one of the characters aboard the Orient Express in his 2017 film.

ADAPTATIONS

ITV, 1994. The producers must have felt that the viewing audience would be too easily confused by the issues of heredity and the wider family, so they ditched the characters of David, Hilda and Stephen Farr, and the jaw-stroking was kept to a minimum. I suppose a household full of people throwing back their heads and laughing would have looked rather odd on screen.

NOTES

[1] The title of an excellent appreciation of Agatha Christie by Robert Barnard.

Murder is Easy (1939)

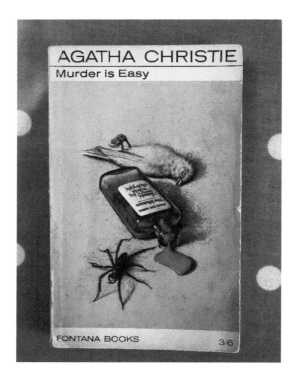

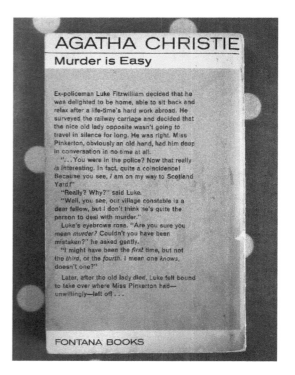

THE BOOK Fontana, 1968 pp 190

A typical Tom Adams cover, with two clues - the mixture and the dead canary - augmented by yet another of his creepy-crawlies. The wording on the back is brilliantly enticing to a casual bookshop browser.

THE STORY

Luke Fitzwilliam returns to England having retired from the colonial police force. On the train into London, he shares a carriage with Miss Lavinia Pinkerton. When she discovers that he had been a policeman, the old lady tells him that she is on her way to Scotland Yard to report on a series of murders in Wychwood-under-Ashe, the small village where she lives. She also tells him who the next victim will be.

Luke dismisses her story as an old lady's fancy, but when he hears of her death in a hit-and-run, and then sees the name she gave him in the Births and Deaths column of The Times, he decides to go down and investigate for himself ...

126

THE SETTING

Wychwood-under-Ashe is a classic Christie village setting, with its two tribes of Masters and Servants augmented by a swarm of old ladies. It is named after a historic forest in Oxfordshire, and there is a village there (Ascott-under-Wychwood) which could serve as a setting for an adaptation of this story even today.

There are hints of pagan village rituals, and when Luke meets his supposed cousin, Bridget Conway, he thinks she looks like a witch (the supposed modern version of 'wych') and imagines her flying on a broomstick. Luke keeps getting the feeling that he has been bewitched.

CHARACTERS

Most of the victims of the serial killer are culled from what might be termed the servant class: the maid Amy Gibbs, the newsagent's son Tommy Pearce, Carter the publican and Rivers the chauffeur. It is only when the life of Dr Humbleby is threatened that Miss Pinkerton decides to act!

Luke is staying with Lord Whitfield, who is engaged to Bridget Conway. His Lordship manages the feat of being both the self-proclaimed squire of the village and its village idiot at the same time. He is beautifully drawn - completely self-centred, and convinced that everything that is happening is designed for his own convenience. As such, there is something of the Donald Trump about him. There are few Establishment figures in Agatha Christie stories that are not portrayed as either ill-tempered, gormless or murderous.

Lord Whitfield's father had been a cobbler, whereas his ex-fiancée Honoria Waynflete has come upon greatly reduced circumstances, having been a member of the principal family in the district. She enters the story as a Marple-esque figure but departs it as something quite different.

These people dominate the story, but there is also a range of stock village characters comprising the suspects - doctor, solicitor, antique-shop owner, barmaid, garage-hand, newsagent - with a particularly nasty turn from Amy Gibbs' aunt, who hopes to make money from her niece's demise.

Superintendent Battle, a veteran of plots involving feisty young women, appears for the last couple of pages to tidy things up.

ATTITUDES AND QUOTES

Luke Fitzwilliam's first thoughts on returning to his native country are not flattering:[1]

127

England! England on a June day, with a grey sky and a sharp biting wind. Nothing welcoming about her on a day like this! And the people! Heavens, the people! Crowds of them, all with grey faces like the sky - anxious worried faces. The houses, too, springing up everywhere like mushrooms. Nasty little houses! Revolting little houses!

Luke meets Miss Pinkerton:

Luke's eyebrows rose. "Murder?"

The old lady nodded vigorously. "Yes, murder. You're surprised, I can see. I was myself at first... I really couldn't believe it. I thought I must be imagining things."

"Are you quite sure you weren't?" Luke asked gently.

"Oh, no." She shook her head positively. "I might have been the first time, but not the second, or the third or the fourth. After that, one knows."

(What a brilliant start to a swigatha that is.)

Here is a comment from Miss Waynflete that encapsulates upper-class social attitudes of the time:

"Mr Ellsworthy - he keeps the new antique shop but he is actually a gentleman ... "

The two may have been incompatible in 1939, but the imminent World War II was about to effect quite a shuffling of the social scales.

"Major Horton never disguises his curiosity very well," said Bridget. "He did stare rather."

"He's the sort of man you could tell was a major anywhere," said Luke rather viciously.

Why 'viciously'? Agatha Christie rarely has anything good to say about retired colonels and majors either. Her feisty young women, on the other hand, usually outshine their male counterparts where brains are concerned.[2]

"I cramped your style," said Bridget. "I saw that. It rather amused me, I'm afraid."

"Women with brains are usually cold-bloodedly cruel."

Bridget murmured: "One has to take one's pleasures as one can in this life."

They can be also unsentimental; one wonders how much of the author is in this exchange:

Luke drew a deep breath. Then he exploded. "What the hell do you mean by marrying that absurd little man? Why are you doing it?"

"Because as his secretary I get six pounds a week, and as his wife I shall get a hundred

thousand settled on me, a jewel case full of pearls and diamonds, a handsome allowance and various perquisites of the married state."

"But for somewhat different duties!"

Bridget said coldly: "Must we have this melodramatic attitude towards every single thing in life...?"

Luke, by contrast, is somewhat bone-headed. Here, he is astonished that Lord Whitfield could be his prime suspect (Amy Gibbs' boyfriend Jim is the 'mere garage mechanic' who had been a previous prime suspect):

It was not a case of the butcher, the baker, the candlestick maker. It was not a case of a mere garage mechanic. The person in question was one against whom an accusation of murder was a fantastic, and, moreover, a serious matter.

Luke's thought processes here are very unusual for a Christie detective. In almost all of her stories the most important element of an investigation is to clear the innocent, no matter who they were. Miss Marple and Hercule Poirot would have considered it just as important to clear Jim as any of the others involved - maybe even more so.

And, finally:

Bridget said: "Liking is more important than loving. It lasts."

Voice of the author!

SWIGATHA RATING 7/10

The opening chapter is one of Agatha Christie's finest. The twist at the end is very satisfying, but it is one for which the reader has been fairly prepared. Bridget the witch is one of the best-drawn characters in any of the Christie novels, Lord Whitfield is a hoot and the character of the killer is terrifying. What keeps it out of the top-drawer is the character of Luke and his endless musings.

ADAPTATIONS

The first adaptation was for American TV. It updates the setting to the 1980s but the actual plot survives intact. Helen Hayes, who went on to play Miss Marple for American TV, plays Lavinia, and is very convincing. Olivia de Haviland played Honoria in one of her last major roles.

ITV's *Agatha Christie's Miss Marple* series (2008) parachuted Julia Mackenzie as Jane into the village of Wychewood-under-Ashe, but she fits in well with the setting. It has an absolutely stellar cast - Benedict Cumberbatch plays Luke and the wonderful Shirley Henderson is excellent as Honoria - but the underlying motive for the mayhem is changed into something ludicrous for an Agatha Christie story.

NOTES

[1] One cannot help but think that Luke's thoughts here are an echo of those of the author, when she returned from her world tour and her many trips to the Middle East. Similar sentiments are repeated in other books, such as *Hercule Poirot's Christmas* and *The Secret of Chimneys*.

[2] See also *The Sittaford Mystery*, *The Seven Dials Mystery*, *Sad Cypress*, *The Hollow*, the Tommy and Tuppence books and many more.

And Then There Were None (1939)

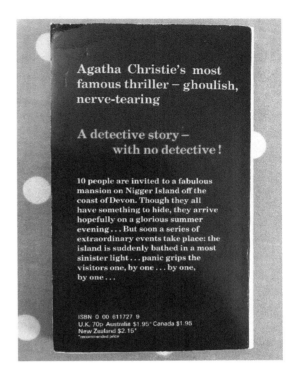

THE BOOK Fontana 1977 pp 190

Tom Adams apparently liked his 'gollywog' cover but I think it is horrible. My original version still had the original title of the book, but I censored it for obvious reasons.

THE STORY

Ten people are invited, on various pretexts, to a house on an otherwise uninhabited island off the coast of Devon; none of them will ever leave it.

After dinner on the day of their arrival, each of the ten characters is accused of 'getting away with murder' by a recording, and within minutes one of them is dead, soon to be followed by another, then another ...

CHARACTERS

The collection of characters is typical of Christie books at the time: young governess, purse-lipped spinster, alcoholic doctor, judge, man always to be found where trouble is brewing, police officer, thoughtless 'Greek God'. Cardboard cut-outs, one might imagine ...

Two of the ten are servants hired for the party, Mr and Mrs Rogers. We are never privy to their thoughts, but we certainly are to those of the other eight as they consider their guilty pasts and try to understand what is happening in the present. This adds flesh to the cardboard cut-out, and, unusually, the more we find out about them, the less we sympathise with them, the less we care about them.

As a result, there is no element of the 'Perils of Pauline' tension that one finds in many of the Christies that do not feature her usual detectives. To this first-time reader, the situation was so brilliantly established that I raced through the book wondering who was going to be next, and not actually caring who was doing it.

Reading it again 50 years later and taking a bit more time over it, I thought it should have been obvious who the culprit was and why - it was so perfectly in character: hidden in plain sight. But, as with all the best Christies, most people still won't see it.

ATTITUDES AND QUOTES

It might be thought unsurprising that a book originally entitled *Ten Little N*****s* contains a few comments that would now (and then, in fact) be considered offensive, but there is more to it than that. Here is Philip Lombard, deep in thought:

> *That little Jew had been damned mysterious ... He had fancied, though, that the little Jew had not been deceived - that was the damnable part about Jews, you couldn't deceive them about money ...*

I do not think that the author of these words was necessarily being anti-semitic. Agatha Christie never puts sentiments like the above into the mouths of her detectives or heroines; if they do crop up, it is almost always in connection with an unsavoury character or one she is satirising. And Lombard is a vile character, one who had been directly responsible for the deaths of 21 members of his regiment, but had never felt any remorse over it:

> *"And natives don't mind dying, you know. They don't feel about it as Europeans do."*

Lombard had taken the 'natives' food and abandoned them to their fate - a 'matter of self-preservation, you know.' Vera Claythorne sympathises with the action taken:

> *"Well, there is that Mr Lombard. He admits to having abandoned twenty men to their deaths."*

Vera said: "They were only natives ..."

Emily Brent said sharply: "Black or white, they are our brothers."

Vera thought: "Our black brothers - our black brothers. Oh, I'm going to laugh. I'm hysterical. I'm not myself ..."

Vera compares the dead 'natives' to the china figures that gave the book its original title. There is a heavy irony here, because Vera feels no sympathy or compassion whatsoever for any of the nine Europeans that pre-decease her on the island. There is an extra level of irony when she shoots Philip Lombard - a matter of self-preservation, you know ...

SWIGATHA RATING 9/10

This is Agatha Christie reaching the height of her powers, and I think she knew it. The idea for the plot was one of genius, yet again: ten murderers being picked off one by one, each knowing that any one of the others was perfectly capable of being responsible. The one thing lacking was the humour usually found in her books; I guess that she may have found it somewhat inappropriate!

WHERE IT LED

Only two years later, Agatha Christie used the same setting (based on Burgh Island, near her Torquay home) for *Evil Under The Sun*.

ADAPTATIONS

Unsurprisingly, there have been many, many adaptations for cinema and TV, in English, Indian, German, French, Russian ... and for the stage by the author herself. The most recent was shown over three nights on BBC TV in 2015, a successful production that gained a new audience for the book.

Sad Cypress (1940)

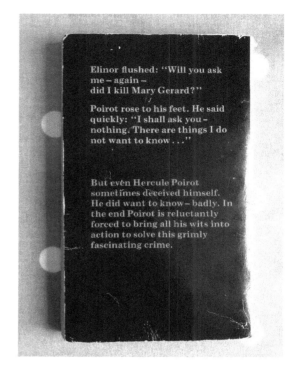

THE BOOK Fontana 1968 pp 191

Ian Robinson's cover refers to three key elements of the plot - a thornless rose, a hypodermic syringe and a tea-strainer. Taken together they give an alert reader a pretty hefty clue ...

The wording on the back cover intrigued me then - I could not understand the purpose of Elinor's question, nor Poirot's answer, and still cannot.

The book says that it was first published in 1935, whereas every other reference puts the date as 1940. Agatha Christie had begun work on the story in 1935[1] but it was not complete for another 4 years.

THE STORY

The book opens with Elinor Carlisle on trial for the murder of her late aunt' s ward, Mary Gerrard, who had stolen the heart of her childhood sweetheart and fiancé, Roddy. While the counsels make their pitches to the court, Elinor casts her mind back to the events leading to the trial.

Poirot is called into the case by the local doctor, Peter Lord, after her arrest. Elinor is suspected of murdering both Mary and her aunt by everyone but him.

CHARACTERS

Elinor Carlisle is an intriguing character. She feels guilty, because she had desperately wished Mary out of the way. She is so drained by the criminal process that she almost confesses to the murder just to get it all over with (as such she is a fore-runner of both Supt Battle's daughter Sylvia and Audrey Strange in *Towards Zero*). Elinor totally dominates the book until Poirot comes along - and even then ...

I get the impression that the author was for once interested in all of her characters, with the exception of Poirot. He hovers over the case, rather than being at the heart of it. Dr Lord is that staple Christie character - the young man with the "pleasant, ugly face" to whom people should always turn in times of trouble. The invalid aunt and her two nurses are very distinctive, and there are no ciphers amongst the servants.

ATTITUDES

Mary Gerrard's parents were (apparently) estate workers for Elinor's aunt. Laura Welman had taken her in hand and made sure she had an expensive education, much to Old Gerrard's disgust, and that of many in the village, none of whom are great believers in social mobility:

> Roddy said irritably: "People never dream what harm they may do by 'educating' someone. Often it's cruelty, not kindness!"

Here is an extract from a touching scene between Mary and her mechanic boyfriend Ted Bigland:

> "You're almost a lady, Mary."
> Mary said, with sudden bitterness: "Almost isn't good enough, is it?"
> "No, I reckon it isn't."

The irony is that, unbeknownst to everyone, Mary is actually Lady Welman's next-of-kin.

The moral dilemma of euthanasia dominates the early part of the book. Lady Welman has had enough of pain and makes sure Mary (and her doctor) knows it:

> "Soon it will be over... If they went the proper way about things, my life could be ended here and now - none of this long-drawn-out tomfoolery with doctors and nurses.... I told him (Dr

135

Lord) the other day that in a decently civilised state, all there would be to do would be for me
to intimate that I wished to end it, and he'd finish me off painlessly with some nice drug."

In the event, of course, someone does just that. And there is no shortage of possibilities for the role of killer-through-kindness, including both Elinor and Roddy:

"One does feel, Roddy, that people ought to be set free - if they themselves really want it."
Roddy said: "I agree. It's the only civilised thing to do. You put animals out of their pain."

Agatha Christie's obsession with Jewish features, which had seemingly vanished in the years approaching the Second World War as stories emerged of the persecution in Nazi Germany, unexpectedly returns (which makes me believe that the trial scene was one of the earliest written). Here is a line from Elinor's internal commentary on the trial:

Over now. The horrible man with the Jewish nose was sitting down.

This little exchange from the cross-examination that had touched on Roddy's honest and chivalrous nature is not quite what it seems:

"Where did you go to school, Mr Welman?"
"Eton."
Sir Samuel said with a quiet smile:
"That is all."

... the implication being that an Old Etonian always plays with a straight bat. Agatha Christie, however, has made it very clear that Roderick Welman is a shiftless character, and a liar, overwhelmed by Mary while she was alive but crawling back to Elinor afterwards.

SWIGATHA RATING 9/10

This is still a good read and an excellent 'swigatha'. The revelation of the truth through the cross-examinations during the trial works very well, and Agatha Christie was probably relieved not to have to write a *"Mesdames et Messieurs"* chapter for once.

Agatha Christie is so clever at 'hiding in plain sight' - all the clues are fairly placed before the reader, and really there is only one person other than Elinor who could have done it - and yet, once again, 99% of her readers will be surprised by the ending.

The only slight quibble is that the author gets a bit carried away by Pharma again - no wonder her Poirot is becoming an expert on the subject.

This book made a huge impression on me when I first read it. I was 13 (an impressionable age!) and I took it with me when I travelled, alone for the first time, to stay with my French cousins for the whole of the 1969 Easter holidays. I remember reading it as slowly as I could, to drag things out - I guess it was a comfort read.

TITLE QUOTE

The title of this book is a quote from one of the clown Feste's songs in *Twelfth Night*, one that 'dallies with the innocence of love'. Maybe it is referring in some way to Elinor's childhood crush on Roddy, or Mary Gerrard's relative innocence; maybe it has no meaning, but it is somehow a perfect title for the book.

There is another quote from a poem that is also superbly apposite:

> *But she is in her grave, and oh!*
> *The difference to me*

It is taken from *She Dwelt Among the Untrodden Ways*, a poem by William Wordsworth (surely the finest surname possible for a poet). The rest of the poem deals with an innocent, unknown Venus, and as such is very germane to the story of Mary Gerrard. These, the last two lines, are drily quoted by Hercule Poirot to Roddy after her death as a summary of his reaction to it, which was more one of relief than sorrow.

WHERE IT LED [2]

For Agatha Christie, this was the beginning of what many critics consider her peak period. It provided her with a template for later books such as *Five Little Pigs* and *The Hollow*, with the main focus being on the revelation of the characters caught up in the drama, and far less of a focus than usual on the participation and mannerisms of Hercule Poirot.

ADAPTATIONS

The ITV *Agatha Christie's Poirot* adaptation in 2003 is quite faithful to the plot, although it is plain that the adaptor has little truck with the character of Roddy, who says to a dismayed Poirot that "those Nazis could teach us a thing or two" (Poirot was a refugee from the First World War).

The main character of Elinor Carlisle is beautifully captured by Elizabeth Dermot Walsh.

NOTES

[1] John Curran *Agatha Christie's Secret Notebooks*

[2] For me, what happened next was that I learnt both Feste's song and Wordsworth's poem by heart, because they had made such an impression on me in the context of the book. From that time on, it became a habit to remember lines that stood out from whatever the texts that we were studying at school or college, and I recall them still.

A couple of years later, I started hankering after a young girl who had a dog named Feste ...

... and much, much later, I was honoured to organise a memorial concert for the conductor Vernon Handley, and one of the settings of Feste's song, by Gerald Finzi, was part of the programme.

One, Two, Buckle My Shoe (1940)

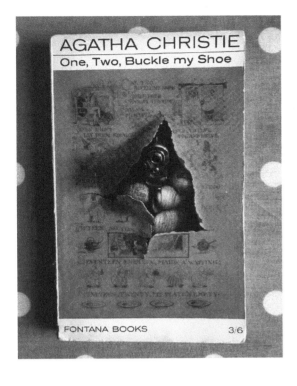 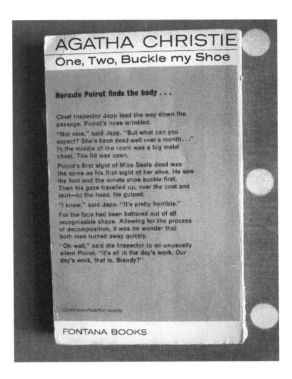

THE BOOK Fontana, 1981 pp 191

This brilliant Tom Adams painting depicts the murder weapon bursting through wallpaper featuring a traditional nursery rhyme – thereby illustrating the disturbance of a seemingly cosy world by violent reality (the story was written during the build up to World War II).

This was the first swigatha that I ever bought, and re-reading the extract on the back was hugely evocative, especially when It came to Japp's offer at the end. What a cover that Is.

THE STORY

Hercule Poirot nervously visits his dentist Mr Morley for a routine appointment. He observes in the waiting room some other patients, also nervously awaiting their appointment with the dentist's chair.

Poirot's relief when he gets home afterwards is disturbed by a call from Inspector Japp, telling him that Morley has been shot, probably by one of his patients and probably around the time of Poirot's appointment.

Not for the first time (but it was for the last)[1], Japp asks Poirot to 'help him with his enquiries ...'

CHARACTERS - spoiler!

This story was written in 1939, in the lead-up to the Second World War. There was civil war in Spain, the right-wing extremes of Fascism were spreading across mainland Europe and North Africa, and what was seen as the threat of the spread of Communism was being championed by an increasingly militaristic Soviet Union.

Accordingly, among the suspects in this story are two radical young men of the Far Left (Howard Raikes) and Far Right (Frank Carter), both anxious to sweep away the old order, and neither the remotest bit concerned by the death of a 'miserable little dentist'.

Ranged against these hotheads is the solid, unruffled character of Alastair Blunt, self-proclaimed figurehead for the stability that would keep Britain from suffering the same fate as the rest of Europe.

Except, of course, that the real menace and threat to the nation's stability is in fact Blunt: a man so desperate to preserve his status that he does not bat an eyelid at the murder of anyone who gets in his way, a man far more dangerous than any of those opposing him.

The true moral figurehead for what Britain required is, of course, Poirot himself. Frank Carter, a racist bullying thug, stands for everything he despises and fears. Poirot is sorely tempted not to disclose his conviction that Carter was incapable of murder, but resists it.

Alastair Blunt, on the other hand, has many qualities that he admires. Poirot realises, however, that there is one aspect to him that is far more frightening than anything found in the Carters of this world: on mainland Europe in the 1930s there were other tyrants who had started out by believing that they stood between their countries and chaos.

It has been often said that Agatha Christie rarely gives away much of herself in her books, but I think there are at least a couple of elements of her in this one - her concern for the rights of the innocent, even an ugly fascist like Frank Carter, and her instinctive mistrust of the 'great and good'.

ATTITUDES AND QUOTES

Some of the descriptions of foreigners, and especially Jews, in early Agatha Christie are shocking to readers today, but they are often deliberately given to particular characters to mislead the reader. She saves her most withering comments for the English as seen through Poirot's eyes. Here he is observing the patients sitting in a dentist's waiting-room:

In one of them sat a military-looking gentleman with a fierce moustache and a yellow complexion. He looked at Poirot with an air of one considering some noxious insect. It was not so much his gun he looked as though he wished he had with him, as his Flit spray. Poirot, eyeing him with distaste, said to himself, "In verity there are some Englishmen who are altogether so unpleasing and ridiculous that they should have been put out of their misery at birth."

The final exchanges between Poirot and Blunt could have come out of an episode of *Foyle's War*[2]. Here are a couple of examples:

"You have said that Mabelle Sainsbury Seale was a foolish human being and Amberiotis an evil one, and Frank Carter a wastrel - and Morley - Morley was only a dentist and there are other dentists. That is where you and I, M. Blunt, do not see alike. For me the lives of these four people are just as important as your life."

"Don't you realise, Poirot, that the safety and happiness of the whole nation depends on me?"
"I am not concerned with nations, Monsieur. I am concerned with the lives of private individuals who have the right not to have their lives taken from them."

SWIGATHA RATING 8/10

This is a classic mid-era swigatha – never boring, plenty of murders to keep the thing flowing and very much a reflection of the time it was written.

Poirot is very human in this book - frightened of the dentist, sick of the prejudices held against him, and totally unimpressed by people with no empathy for their fellows.

The solution is a classic example of Agatha Christie toying with a perception that might have been widely-shared by her readership and turning it on its head. Experienced readers should by now be very wary of any character who keeps escaping murder attempts, as Blunt does, but the vast majority will be fooled yet again. How she does it ...!

Where the book fails to convince is in trying to structure the story to fit the nursery rhyme, to the extent of describing Blunt's sister-in-law as 'fat' simply to fit in with '9, 10 The Big Fat Hen'.

The use of nursery rhymes as a theme had begun with *And Then There Were None* the previous year, and had worked brilliantly. Not so this time.

WHERE IT LED

Agatha Christie continued to employ the nursery rhyme device for a few years. In some cases it worked well - *Mrs McGinty's Dead*, *Crooked House* - and some it most certainly did not (*Hickory Dickory Dock* being the worst example, and, thankfully, the last).

ADAPTATIONS

The ITV adaptation for their long-running *Poirot* series (1989 - 2013) was one of the early ones. It dispensed with the character of the Communist hothead Raikes, but otherwise sticks closely to the plot, giving away perhaps more about Blunt's actual marital status than the book does.

NOTES

[1] This was Inspector James Japp's final appearance (chronologically) in an Agatha Christie story.

[2] *Foyle's War* was a TV series set in England during WW2. It was created by Anthony Horowitz (who adapted some episodes of ITV's *Poirot* series) and concerns the eponymous Inspector's efforts at preserving the rule of law at a time when it was close to breaking down. He often finds himself confronting members of the establishment and army hierarchies who justify their lawbreaking as being essential to the ultimate success of the campaign against Nazism, and try to persuade him to cover it up.

Evil under the Sun (1941)

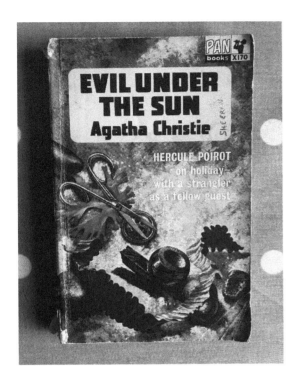 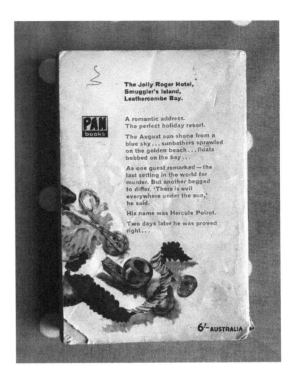

THE BOOK PAN, 1964 pp 218

This is one of the original second-hand copies we bought as kids in Brighton in 1966, and it is still In good (i.e. readable-without-half-the-pages-falling-out) condition. The cover painting depicts some of the items found on the beach where the murder took place.

THE STORY

Hercule Poirot is on holiday on Smugglers' Island, off the coast of Devon. As he sits with fellow-guests on the terrace looking down on the people sunbathing on the beach below, he comments that all their bodies look the same, arranged on slabs like butcher's meat. When one of the guests comments that at least nothing untoward was likely to occur on the island, Poirot retorts that a holiday location provides an excellent opportunity for a murderer, that there is evil everywhere under the sun ...

He soon finds himself investigating the murder of Arlena Marshall as she sunbathed alone in one of the island's coves.

CHARACTERS AND ATTITUDES

The island setting (based on Burgh Island, which Agatha Christie had visited) isolates all the characters from the outside world: the hotel is the only building on the island. There is no suggestion of its *time* about the narrative: the events could just as easily have taken place at any time in the 1930's or 50's, and World War 2 is not even mentioned.

There is quite a variety of people staying at the island hotel - almost too much variety. Some of the more interesting ones are not developed much: Arlena the vamp, her mild-mannered husband Kenneth and hate-filled sixteen-year-old step-daughter Linda; the husband's childhood sweetheart Rosamund Darnley; the brash smuggler Horace Blatt; the Gardeners, a comic American couple; the mannish Miss Brewster; the India-bore Major Blore; and the Redferns: one a handsome, well-built extrovert, the other a mousey introvert who has to stay out of the sun and is frightened of heights.

This story is all about plot and interrogation, and the affairs of the wider world do not intrude.

QUOTES

There are some amusing passages in this book, many of them featuring the American couple. Poirot has just scandalised Mrs Gardener by comparing the sight of the people sunbathing on the beach to the Morgue in Paris:

> *"All the same," Mrs Gardener knitted with energy, "I'm inclined to agree with you on one point. These girls that lie out like that in the sun will grow hair on their legs and arms. I've said so to Irene - that's my daughter, M. Poirot. Irene, I said to her, if you lie out like that in the sun, you'll have hair all over you, hair on your arms and hair on your legs and hair on your bosom, and what will you look like then? I said to her. Didn't I, Odell?"*
> *"Yes, darling," said Mr Gardener.*
> *Everyone was silent, perhaps making a mental picture of Irene when the worst had happened.*

Poirot interrogates Rosamund Darnley:

> *"When you came in to change for tennis that morning, did you have a bath?"*
> *Rosamund stared at him.*
> *"A bath - what do you mean?"*
> *"That is what I mean. A bath! The receptacle of porcelain, one turns the tap and fills it, one*

gets in, one gets out and ghoosh - ghoosh - ghoosh, the water goes down the waste pipe!"

"M. Poirot, are you quite mad?"

SWIGATHA RATING   7/10

This is a typical mid-era swigatha - an ingenious plot, written with such verve and confidence that there is no need for further murders to keep it running. It is a great read for an 11-year-old, but on re-reading it I found it all a bit soulless; it wasn't obvious to me what the logic behind Arlena Marshall's murder was, and the narcotics sub-plot fizzles out completely, with the perpetrator last encountered taking photos at a picnic.

WHERE IT LED

This was to be just about the last novel in which Poirot is present in the build-up to a crime. Henceforth he is usually brought in after the event - often many years after the event - as a consulting detective. Agatha Christie was trying to escape from her Poirot strait-jacket, and succeeded magnificently in her next Poirot story - *Five Little Pigs*.

ADAPTATIONS

In 1981, a film version of *Evil Under the Sun*, featuring Peter Ustinov once again as Poirot, was produced in the wake of the success of *Death on the Nile*. It had the usual star-studded cast - James Mason, Maggie Smith, Diana Rigg - but was over-stylised in an Art Deco way, and the hamming of the main characters, especially Ustinov's turn as Poirot, doesn't work as well as it had done in the previous film.

The ITV adaptation for its *Poirot* series (2000) was far superior, even if it decided to add Hastings, Japp and Miss Lemon to the plot to cheer it up. It benefits from actually being filmed on Burgh Island, with David Suchet playing it straight as Poirot and the clues fairly placed. For no obvious reason, Linda Marshall in this version becomes Lionel Marshall (played by a young Russell Tovey).

N or M? (1941)

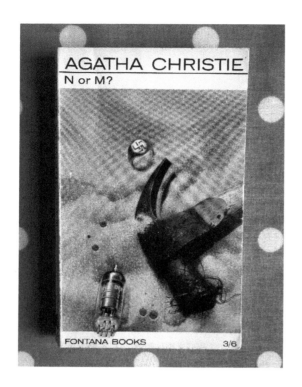
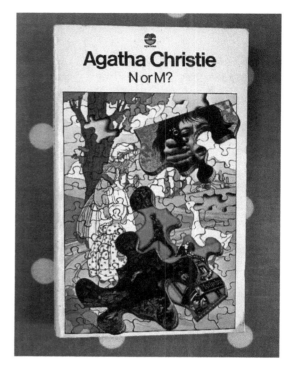

THE BOOK Fontana, 1964 pp 192

The book I originally read has a simple Tom Adams cover: the sand evokes the seaside setting, the transmitter and ring reference the Fifth Column element and the hammer is the one used in an assault. His later jigsaw-puzzle cover might be thought to give away too much of the plot.

The title is another example of excellent judgement by the author: for some reason, the more obvious *M or N?*, or *X or Y?*, would not sound right; *N or M* does[1].

THE STORY

Early in WWII, Tommy Beresford is sent (via a roundabout route) to investigate a German Fifth Column cell based in the seaside town of Leahampton. A Nazi agent, either known by the code-name N (for a male) or M (female), is believed to be co-ordinating preparations for a German invasion of Britain from a boarding house (the *Sans Souci*) in the town.

When Tommy arrives at *Sans Souci* he is surprised to find his wife Tuppence already in residence there under an alias ...

Agatha Christie wrote this story during 1940, and unlike many of her others it is very much set in its time (the spring of that year), with many references to the fall of France, then the Dunkirk evacuation, and, finally, a hint of the Battle of Britain that was about to come.

CHARACTERS AND ATTITUDES

Agatha Christie manages to create a cast of characters at *Sans Souci* that appear both innocuous and threatening at the same time. By the end, therefore, it is no surprise to find that, of the twelve residents, there are two members of the IRA, three agents working on behalf of the British secret service and one Nazi agent.

This is the second full-length title to feature Tommy and Tuppence and there is an element of *déjà-vu* to it; as in the previous novel, *The Secret Adversary*, Tommy has his head bashed in and is taken prisoner, for example. Possibly because of the circumstances under which the story was written, however, the two of them are far less flippant than previously: this is no light-hearted thriller.

The atmosphere of suspicion, unhappiness and a moaning acceptance of difficult times is well drawn and one can almost smell the dreadful cabbage that passes for rations. The residents are individually drawn, and their opinions are surprisingly diverse considering the peculiar circumstances of the time. It is tempting to read into these opinions some of the author's own[2].

QUOTES

Mrs Sprot is considering taking her baby back with her to London (because 'everyone's going back, aren't they?') and is shouted down by the others:

> *"What I say is one mustn't risk anything with children. Your sweet little Betty! You'd never forgive yourself, and you know that Hitler said the Blitzkrieg on England is coming quite soon now - and quite a new kind of gas, I believe."*
> *Major Bletchley cut in sharply:*
> *"Lot of nonsense talked about gas. The fellows won't waste their time fiddling about with gas. High explosive and incendiary bombs. That's what was done in Spain."*

Tuppence (in the role of Mrs Blenkensop) tries to listen in on a conversation between Carl von Deinem and the landlady's daughter:

> *Unobtrusively she turned and again passed the two.*
> *"Smug, detestable English ..."*

The eyebrows of Mrs Blenkensop rose ever so slightly. Carl von Deinem was a refugee from Nazi persecution, given asylum and shelter by England. Neither wise nor grateful to listen assentingly to such words.

Mr Cayley proves to be remarkably prescient:

> *"What's that you're saying?"*
>
> *"We're saying," said Miss Minton, "that it will all be over by autumn."*
>
> *"Nonsense," said Mr Cayley. "This war is going to last at least six years."*

And, as far as Britain was concerned, it did (1939-1945). Major Bletchley (ret'd) takes a modern view of the refugee crisis of the time:

> *"You take my word for it, this refugee business is dangerous. If I had my way I'd intern the lot of them. Safety first."*
>
> *"A bit drastic, perhaps."*
>
> *"Not at all. And I've got my suspicions of Master Carl. For one thing, he's clearly not a Jew."*

Sheila Perenna on 'the last refuge of a scoundrel':

> *"I hate patriotism, do you understand? All this country, country, country! Betraying your country - dying for your country - serving your country. Why should one's country mean anything at all?"*

Tuppence in a conflict of emotion about the likely fate of a possible spy:

> *"Oh, damn, damn, damn the Irish!" thought Tuppence in a fury of mixed feelings. "Why have they got the power of twisting things until you don't know where you are? If Carl von Deinem's a spy, he deserves to be shot. I must hang on to that, not let that girl with her Irish voice bewitch me into thinking it's the tragedy of a hero and a martyr."*

The landlady of Sans Souci snaps:

> *"I'm sick of the cruelty, the unfairness of this world. I'd like to smash it and break it - and let us all start again near to the earth and without these rules and laws and the tyranny of nation over nation ..."*

Mr Grant trying to explain why people might betray their country:

"You do not know the force of German propaganda. It appeals to something in man, some desire for lust or power. These people were prepared to betray their country not for money, but in a kind of megalomaniacal pride in what they, they themselves, were going to achieve for that country. In every land it has been the same. It is the Cult of Lucifer - Lucifer, Son of the Morning. Pride and a desire for personal glory!"

SWIGATHA RATING 7/10

The revelation at the end will come as a surprise to most readers, which is quite an achievement because the killer is, once again, hidden in plain sight. The thing that most distinguishes this story is the light it sheds on the people and the attitudes they held at a particular time in history, by contrast with how their history has since been written.

This is the best of Tommy and Tuppence. It is a good flowing read, requiring no extra crimes to pad it out to the usual 192 pages, although the revelation about the 'German refugee' at the end is a bit unnecessary.

WHERE IT LED

Tommy and Tuppence disappeared for another quarter of a century until a comeback in *By the Pricking of My Thumbs* in 1968; this time it is Tuppence's turn to be smashed on the head.

Agatha Christie returns to the idea of the 'Cult of Lucifer' in *They Came to Baghdad*, and somewhat similar sentiments are at the heart of the plot of *Passenger to Frankfurt*.

Unlike Mrs Sprot, Christie *did* go back to London in 1940, after Greenway, her house in Devon, had been requisitioned to house refugees fleeing London. The house in London was indeed damaged during the Blitz, though she was not there at the time.

ADAPTATIONS

The BBC produced a version as part of its (now-abandoned) *Partners in Crime* series, with David Wallians as both executive producer and playing the part of Tommy. It bears little resemblance to the book. There is therefore room for a version which plays straight with the original and evokes the period in which it is set - between the end of the 'Phoney War' and the start of the Battle of Britain.

NOTES

[1] For the origins of this title see Appendix A, 'Title Quotes'

[2] Agatha Christie has a reputation for 'casual racism' in her writings but she often reserves her most withering and sarcastic comments for the 'smug, detestable' English. No matter how many sinister foreigners there are in a story, the real bastards and culprits are, as in this one, almost certain to be English (or, at a pinch, Americans). She was, I am sure, reasonably patriotic, but, like Samuel Johnson (and Edith Cavell), would not have seen patriotism as an excuse.

The Body in the Library (1942)

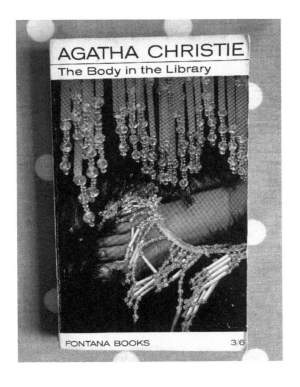

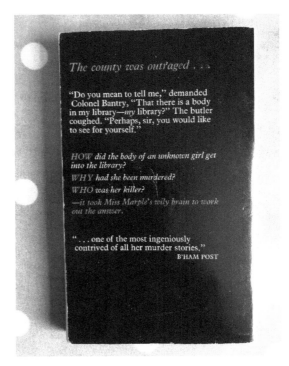

THE BOOK   Fontana, 1967 pp 191

Tom Adams' painting hints at, rather than points to, some of the elements of the plot: a dead girl's made-up nails, a rug like the one used to wrap and transport her to the library and the spangled dress she may have worn while dancing that evening. It also contains an insect very similar to the ones adorning his cover of *The Murder of Roger Ackroyd*.

THE STORY

Early one morning, Colonel and Mrs Bantry are woken by their maid, who tells them that she has found a young girl's body in their library. Tongues begin to wag in St Mary Mead when no explanation can be found for its presence there. Mrs Bantry enlists the aid of her neighbour Jane Marple in her efforts to find one.

The idea of a dead body being found in the library of a mansion or country house such as Gossington Hall was already as big a cliché in the 1930s as that of the butler being the guilty party. Agatha Christie had been toying with the idea of the library-as-scene-of-the-crime for a while, and settled on making the body's presence as incongruous as possible.

CHARACTERS

The characters who inhabit St Mary Mead and its environs are colourfully drawn - the Bantrys, the Blakes and the local gossips. The members of the party staying at the seaside hotel where the dead girl worked, on the other hand, are mostly unmemorable and not very likeable; in particular Conway Jefferson, a dirty old rich man wanting to adopt an 18-year-old dancer who flattered him.

My favourite character is that of the tennis-pro-cum-gigolo, Raymond Starr, who is desperate to break free of his role. He re-invents himself as "one of the Devonshire Starrs" in an attempt to attract Jefferson's son's widow.

ATTITUDES

No-one seems to have any pity or sympathy for an 18-year-old girl who has been murdered far from home, with the exception of Miss Marple. Nor does anyone seem outraged that a drunken man, on finding the dead body of what proves to be a 16-year-old girl guide, should pile it into his car and dump it in someone else's house, not even that house's owner.

QUOTES

Miss Marple is on great form; here are some classic quotes, variations of which appear in many of the stories featuring her. The strange thing is, one never tires of reading them, or indeed hearing them (when intoned by Joan Hickson):

> *"I must say," said Sir Henry ruefully, "that I resent the way you reduce us all to a general common denominator."*
> *Miss Marple shook her head sadly. "Human nature is much the same anywhere, Sir Henry."*

> *Miss Marple made a contribution to the conversation. "Gentlemen," she said, with her old-maid's way of referring to the opposite sex as though it were a species of wild animal, "are frequently not as level-headed as they seem."*

> *"Married people, I have noticed, quite enjoy their battles and the - er - appropriate reconciliations." She paused, twinkling benignly.*
> *"Well, I – " Dinah stopped and laughed. She sat down and lit a cigarette. "You're absolutely marvellous!" she said.*

Elsewhere the level of callousness shown by everyone else but Miss Marple to the murder of two young girls is almost breathtaking. Here, Mark Gaskell quotes Wordsworth's lament for 'Lucy' as he reacts delightedly to the death of Ruby Keene:

But she is in her grave and oh! the difference to me![1]

Colonel Melchett slaps down his Inspector when they are trying to work out whose body is in the library and Slack is telling him that there is a 16-year-old girl missing:

"Don't go on reading idiotic details, Slack. This wasn't a schoolgirl."

Well, actually, Colonel, it was. When Mrs Bantry and Miss Marple view the body, Miss Marple has to point out to her friend that the body had belonged to a real person:

She said at last in a gentle voice: "She's very young."
"Yes - yes - I suppose she is."

Another reaction, one from Mrs Bantry's husband, the principal magistrate of the district, to the discovery, removal and dumping of a young girl's dead body is singular:

"Bottled, was he?" said Colonel Bantry, with an Englishman's sympathy for alcoholic excess.
"Oh well, can't judge a fellow by what he does when he's drunk."

SWIGATHA RATING 7/10

The book has an excellent beginning (the author considered it her best)[2]. It is sometimes difficult to appreciate nowadays how original her plotting was; this is in part because she herself kept re-using bits of it![3]

Because Miss Marple arrives at her solution, as usual, through pure reasoning rather than any actual evidence, she stages a drama to 'smoke 'em out'. This became something of a hallmark of the stories featuring her.

WHAT HAPPENED NEXT

This was the first Marple novel for twelve years. It was a huge success, establishing her as one of the great characters of detective fiction. Fans didn't have long to wait for the next one - *The Moving Finger*, in 1943.

Colonel and Mrs Bantry continued to live happily at Gossington Hall until the Colonel's death, whereupon she sold the house to a famous Hollywood actress (although she continued to live in the grounds).

ADAPTATIONS

BBC, 1984: this was the first film to be produced of the Hickson *Marples*, and a good start, if rather a bit too heavy with the isn't-she-marvellous stuff. I suppose that was necessary to underline the fluffy old lady's status as master-detective to a new audience. A good cast includes Moray Watson, excellent as Bantry, and the wonderful David Horovitch as Slack.

There was also a somewhat lamentable version made by ITV in 2004, also the first in a series, featuring Geraldine McEwan. This laid responsibility for the murders at the door of two lesbians, and implied that Miss Marple had never got over the death of her lover on the field of battle in WW1.

This series was entitled '*Agatha Christie's Miss Marple*', though I doubt the author would have recognised her.

NOTES

[1] Christie had already used exactly the same quote, and the relief that it expresses, a couple of years earlier (in *Sad Cypress*).

[2] *Agatha Christie's Murder in the Making* John Curran

[3] In *Nemesis*, for example, two young girls are also murdered: one disfigured and deliberately mis-identified by her killer, and the other the object of inappropriate attention from someone much older.

Five Little Pigs (1943)

THE BOOK Fontana, 1968 pp 189

This cover refers to the scene of the crime - the battery at Avonbury - and the pipette used to introduce the fatal poison. I am not sure what the ball of wool refers to! A well-used paperback but still in good condition 50 years on.

The book on the right, on the other hand, was picked from a second-hand book shop recently and is in incredible condition for a fifty-year-old paperback.

THE STORY

Poirot is commissioned by Carla Lemarchant to investigate the murder of her father, Amyas Crale, 16 years previously. The original police investigation and trial had found her mother, Caroline Crale, guilty of the murder. Caroline was sent to prison for life ('extenuating circumstances') but died there soon afterwards. Carla was 5 at the time, but when she came of age she was shown a letter from her mother, protesting her innocence.

Poirot talks to representatives of the prosecution, defence and police, all of whom are convinced of Caroline's guilt. Unabashed, he sets out to interview the five other people present at the time of the tragedy. Each of them agrees, reluctantly, to write down their recollections of the events during those days in September 16 years before.

Poirot works out what happened and who was responsible, but there is no evidence and the murderer walks free.

CONTEXT AND STRUCTURE

Again and again, one finds that Agatha Christie is at her best when she incorporates what she knows best into the fabric of her stories, whether it be archaeology, travelling, poisons or people. This book is awash with references to *her*.

For example, the murder took place at Avonbury, a country house based on Greenway, Agatha Christie's country home in Devon. You can visit Greenway today and walk down the same paths to the battery, the murder scene, with its view out over the river Dart.

Across that river is the village of Dittisham; Elsa Greer is married to Lord Dittisham when Poirot meets her. And so on.

The story was written in 1942-3, 16 years after Christie's mother had died and husband Archie had walked out on her for a younger woman[1], leaving her alone with a 5-year-old daughter, Rosalind; Amyas Crale bears the same initials as Archie Christie. And so on ...

This is possibly a bit fanciful, but the fact is that the main characters are treated with far more care and understanding than usual, and Poirot (and we) end up feeling sympathy for just about all of them.

Equally unusually, the book is structured carefully. After a prologue, there are four sets of five chapters each:

- 5 chapters of interviews with the forces of the law
- 5 interviews with the Little Pigs
- 5 written statements from the Little Pigs
- 5 chapters of dénouement

Details of the same story are thus described fifteen times, each time from a slightly different angle, and each time it becomes more intriguing. It is Agatha Christie at her very best.

CHARACTERS AND ATTITUDES - spoiler!

The characters that dominate the story do not appear in it, except in retrospect. Amyas Crale is an artist for whom the need to create overwhelms not only all other emotions, but also anyone or anything that gets in the way of that need. Caroline has a multi-plex character (as evinced by the 'little pigs' five different assessments of it). She loves her family, and her actions are driven by the guilt she feels over an event from the past Involving one of them.

The little pigs pale in comparison, but are by no means ciphers: their written statements especially expose their characters.

Each of them is still haunted by the events of sixteen years ago. In most Agatha Christie books, once the murderer is uncovered, everyone else is able to go back home and carry on as normal. Not in this one.

Sympathy is shown to every character - even to the murderer, who is perceived as having been treated cruelly. This book is mercifully free of attitudes that characterise the era of its setting, possibly because there is a lack of humour within it: the death of Carla's parents is a real tragedy.

QUOTES

Caroline Crale's letter to her sister from prison before she dies is almost Sydney Carton-esque:

> *I have never told you lies and I don't now when I say that I am actually happy - that I feel an essential rightness and a peace that I have never known before.*

She does not quote Dickens, but it is there between the lines[2].

Poirot looks at the painting that Amyas had been working on when he died:

> *Yes, here was life. All there was, all there could be of life, of youth, of sheer blazing vitality. The face was alive and the eyes ... What were the eyes of Elsa Greer like now? He went out of the room with one last look. He thought: 'She was too much alive.'*

The descriptions of the paintings throughout indicate that Agatha Christie had a good pair of eyes herself.

Caroline Crale is sentenced to life in gaol, but it is to the killer that fate has handed the real life sentence (something which the author considered the cruellest outcome for any criminal):

> *"She and Amyas both escaped - they went somewhere where I couldn't get at them. But they didn't die. I died."*

By dying in prison, Caroline Crale escaped it; Elsa Greer, on the other hand, considered herself '*too much alive*' and was stuck with it.

SWIGATHA RATING 10/10

Five Little Pigs has little of the overt drama and plot twists that characterise Agatha Christie's more famous stories but, from beginning to end, this is the most satisfying of her novels. Nothing is wasted. All of the characters have substance, and the ending for once holds much more than just a surprise.

WHERE IT LED

This was the first (and best) of the 'murder in the past' stories that became a common feature of Agatha Christie's output in the second half of her career. It was a device that enabled her to dispense with a narrator, and explain Poirot's presence in the story as a consulting detective.

The nursery rhyme titles were packed away for ten years, re-emerging with *Mrs McGinty's Dead* in 1952.

ADAPTATIONS

The only adaptation I have seen was by ITV for its *Agatha Christie's Poirot* series in 2003.

This adaptation was exceptional. I consider it the finest *Poirot* episode, maybe even the best adaptation anywhere of a story involving him, and much credit for that should go to its producer, Margaret Mitchell. She had to work with a riot of executive producers and came through in triumph (later series would not be so successful).

The casting is perfect, the music haunting and the screenplay (with a couple of unnecessary exceptions) does full justice to a book that is not particularly 'telegenic'. The relative simplicity of the story gives just the framework needed for the talents of those involved to flourish.

Agatha Christie adapted this story for the stage: *Go Back for Murder*. As with all her stage adaptations of her own novels, Poirot does not appear in it.

NOTES

[1] Suggested by Robert Barnard In *A Talent to Deceive*

[2] from *A Tale of Two Cities*:

> It is a far, far better thing that I do, than I have ever done; it is a far better rest to go to, than I have ever known.

The Moving Finger (1943)

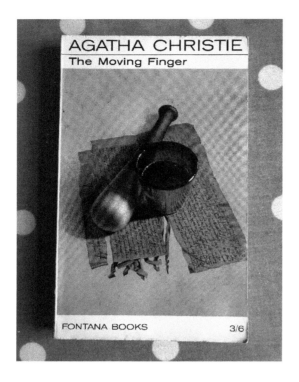
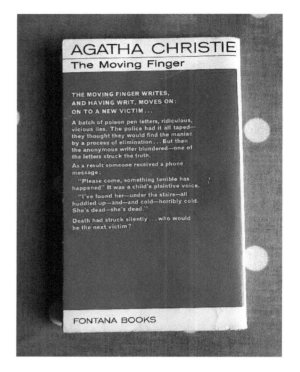

THE BOOK Fontana 1969 pp 160

In my opinion, this is Tom Adams' finest cover, and I am the proud owner of a signed print of it. The pestle and glass refer to two of the means used during the murders of Mrs Symington and her maid, but the beautifully produced parchment - some kind of legal document - does not directly refer to anything in the book.

Adams said[1] that the painting actually contains an extra clue, but did not reveal it; my guess is that it would be the parchment's hint of the involvement of a solicitor and maybe the tear in it. A torn piece of paper is all Miss Marple needs to work out who the culprit was.

Agatha Christie's peak period Fontana books usually amounted to around 192 pages in these editions, so this is one of her shortest ones.

THE STORY

A wounded WWII pilot and his sister move to the village of Lymstock in a bid to speed his recovery. They soon receive an anonymous letter accusing them of not being siblings, and discover that many other people in the village have also received poison pen letters. Death follows.

160

The vicar's wife calls in Miss Marple ...

THE TITLE

It is taken from the first English translation of *The Rubaiyyat of Omar Khayyam*:

> *The moving finger writes, and, having writ, moves on;*
>
> *Nor all thy Piety nor Wit*
>
> *Shall lure it back to cancel half a Line,*
>
> *Nor all thy Tears wash out a Word of it*

The implication is that, once an accusation has been made, it will stick no matter what you do (a constant expression used throughout the story is "no smoke without fire"). The twist here is that all the accusations are false. Maybe Agatha Christie was anticipating the calumnies of today's social media, which also can never be fully cancelled.

CHARACTERS - spoiler!

Although it has a typical village setting, there is quite a variety of character on display in this book: the fierce Maud Dane Calthrop and her remote husband Caleb; the 'extremely lady-like plump little Mr Pye'; the bland Miss Holland; the frustrated feminist Miss Griffith; the distrait Megan and the disapproving Partridge. Some very interesting ideas are expressed. The only person without any real character traits is the murderer.

ATTITUDES AND QUOTES

Many of the opinions expressed by the characters are, I suspect, close to those of Agatha Christie herself (see the quotes below). When she re-read some of her books some 20 years later, she found that this was one that she was very pleased with - maybe because there was more of her in it than usual.

Here is one of her ideas from the mouth of the somewhat camp Mr Pye:

> *"I do believe in atmosphere, you know. People's thoughts and feelings. They give their impression to the walls and the furniture."*

And another from James Burton, the narrator:

> *I have never been able to accept that education is the panacea for every ill.*

One wonders what Mr Burton would have made of the Education Act, guaranteeing education for all in the UK up to the age of 14, which was introduced the following year (1944). He does share one interesting idea:

> "It is a theory of mine," I said, warming to my theme, "that we owe most of our great inventions and most of the achievements of genius to idleness - whether enforced or voluntary. The human mind prefers to be spoon-fed with the thoughts of others, but deprived of such nourishment it will reluctantly begin to think for itself ..."

Aimée Griffith, her brother's receptionist, rightly feels frustrated:

> "It is incredible to you that women should want a career. It was incredible to my parents. I was anxious to study for a doctor. They would not hear of paying the fees. But they paid them readily for Owen. Yet I should have made a better doctor than my brother."

Miss Marple is severe:

> "Yes, it was dangerous, but we are not put into this world, Mr Burton, to avoid danger when an innocent fellow-creature's life is at stake. You understand me?"

SWIGATHA RATING 7/10

It scores well for the excellent simplicity of its plot: a series of poison-pen letters providing a smoke-screen to hide what would otherwise have been pretty obvious.

And it really is obvious: a solicitor lives with a neurotic wife and a beautiful governess; the two people murdered are killed in his house; the typewriter used for the envelopes had been owned by him and donated to the Women's Institute ... and so on. And yet I would bet that most people would not fix on him as the killer. Very clever.

Miss Marple appears to have been brought in as an after-thought, however, and the ploy used to trap the killer is as ridiculous as the somewhat similar ones used in *The Murder at the Vicarage*, *The Body in the Library*, *A Murder is Announced* and *A Caribbean Mystery*.

WHAT HAPPENED NEXT

Miss Marple disappeared for seven years, before making a triumphant return in *A Murder is Announced*. In 1961, Mr and Mrs Dane Calthrop re-appeared, strangely, in *The Pale Horse*, as part of a detective super-group, alongside Rhoda and Colonel Despard and the author's *alter ego* Ariadne Oliver (all three of whom met in *Cards on the Table*).

ADAPTATIONS

BBC, 1985: another of the *Hickson Marples*. This is a faithful adaptation, apart from giving Miss Marple a much greater role than she has in the book.

There was also an ITV production starring Geraldine McEwan ...

NOTES

[1] *Tom Adams' Agatha Christie Cover Story*

Towards Zero (1944)

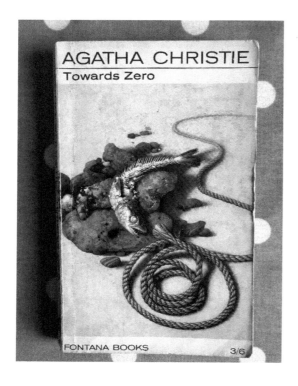 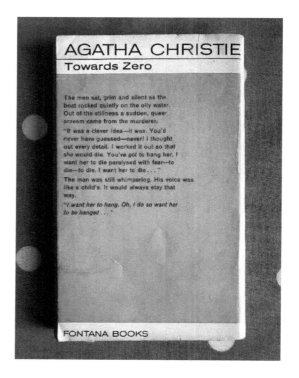

THE BOOK Fontana, 1966 pp 192

Another cover by Tom Adams: very distinctive, and the reader will wonder what it represents until almost the end of the book. The wording on the back is very atmospheric; whoever put together potted extracts such as these for Fontana did a terrific job.

The dedicatee is the English poet and author Robert Graves[1].

THE STORY

A year after a failed attempt to thrown himself off its cliffs, Angus MacWhirter returns to Stark Head, in Devon. He is just in time to prevent a woman in white from throwing herself off the same cliffs, a woman involved in a murder investigation.

Later, during an altercation in a dry-cleaners, he demands that they return his suit (unwashed). The one he's given turns out not to be his, whereupon he smells something fishy ...

A meticulously planned murder attempt reaches its climax at the end, rather than the beginning, of this story.

CHARACTERS

The characters are all given time and space (over 100 pages) to establish themselves before the main events of the story and subsequent interrogations take place. All-round sportsman Neville Strange has invited his ex-wife Audrey and current wife Kay to stay with him at a house-party given by Lady Tressilian, his ex-guardian's wife. Other members of the party include Thomas Royde, in love with Audrey since childhood, and Mary Aldin, Lady Tressilian's companion. During the fortnight of their stay, each character feels a growing tension within the house without being able to put a finger on its root cause.

Then Lady Tressilian is killed. Superintendent Battle, holidaying in the area, is called in (by his nephew) to investigate a seemingly senseless murder.

The psychotic character of the killer is quite convincingly drawn, but many of the other characters seem to be from the author's stock list: the taciturn Royde, back from the colonies, reads like Hector Blunt (from *Roger Ackroyd*); the calm, intelligent, 30-ish Mary Aldin is an echo or foreshadow of Midge from *The Hollow*; Kay Strange is an echo of Elsa Greer in *Five Little Pigs* ... and so on.

One of the more interesting cameos is that of MacWhirter's nurse as he recovers in hospital at the beginning of the book; I suspect that, for this scene, Agatha Christie drew on her own experience nursing wounded soldiers coming back from the Western Front during WW1.

QUOTES

Here are a couple of extracts from a pivotal scene, very early on, between MacWhirter and the red-haired hospital nurse. MacWhirter does not take part in events until the end of the story, but his re-appearance proves the nurse to be prescient:

> *"My dear girl, what use am I to anybody?"*
> *She said confusedly: "You don't know. You may be - someday - "*
> *"Someday? There won't be any someday. Next time I'll make sure."*
> *She shook her head decidedly. "Oh, no," she said. "You won't kill yourself now."*
> *"Why not?"*
> *"They never do ..."*
>
> *" ... it may be just by being somewhere - not doing anything - just by being at a certain place at a certain time - oh, I can't say what I mean, but you might just - walk along a street*

someday and just by doing that accomplish something terribly important - perhaps even without knowing what it was."

The uncomfortable subject of breeding, heredity and eugenics appears yet again (Agatha Christie seems inordinately interested in it - at least, she keeps introducing it). Thus, Mary Aldin:

She had a good figure, an air of breeding, and dark hair to which one lock of white across the front gave a touch of individuality.

And Kay Strange:

"I do not like her - she's quite the wrong wife for Neville - no background, no roots!"
"She's quite well born," said Mary placatingly.
"Bad stock!" said Lady Tressilian.

TITLES

The four main chapter titles are quotations or references, and more pertinent than was often the case:

Open the Door and Here are the People

From the children's rhyme 'Here is the Church, here is the Steeple...' In this chapter, all of the main characters are introduced.

Snow White and Red Rose

Referring to the characters projected by Audrey Strange and Kay Strange. 'Snow White and Rose-Red' is a German fairy-tale (nothing to do with the Brothers Grimm / Disney Snow White); in it the two girls marry a prince and his brother rather than, as here, the same person.

A Fine Italian Hand

A phrase used by Battle as he begins to suspect a devious cunning behind what seems to be thuddingly obvious. This phrase began to be used when Italian script (and later Roman type-faces) started to be used instead of the heavy Gothic script in England in the 18th Century.

Zero Hour

This refers to the time at which a 'usually significant or notable event is scheduled to take place'. It is particularly relevant because what most readers would have assumed was the notable event - the murder of Lady Tressilian - had already taken place. The definition of Zero Hour, as far as the murderer is concerned, is the arrest (to be followed by trial and hanging) of Audrey Strange for her murder; he had for a long time been planning the events leading up "towards zero".

SWIGATHA RATING 7/10

This story is a superb example of what Robert Graves wrote about its author.[1] It also has the added attraction of being different from the usual structure of a work of crime fiction. She was so original.

As a *swigatha*, however, I don't think it quite makes the top bracket - this is one of those that feels more like a romantic play than a whodunit. MacWhirter's leap of the imagination - from a fishy smell on a jacket to someone swimming across a bay, climbing up a cliff via a rope, banging an old lady on the head, swimming back, changing clothes in a cave and going off to play billiards - takes a bit of swallowing.

WHERE IT LED

Retirement for Superintendent Battle! Both he and Captain Hastings were pensioned off in the early 1940s. I have wondered whether Battle and Hastings were named deliberately or whether the name Battle came to her subliminally.

ADAPTATIONS

ITV produced a version of the story for its *Agatha Christie's Miss Marple* series in 2007, Superintendent Battle being replaced (obviously) by Miss Marple.[2]

There was also a French version in 2007 featuring Commissaire Bataille ...!

NOTES

[1] Graves was a near-neighbour in Devon at the time. He had written, also in 1944:

> *Agatha's best work is, like P.G. Wodehouse and Noel Coward's best work, the most characteristic pleasure-writing of this epoch and will appear one day in all decent literary histories. As writing it is not distinguished, but as story it is superb.*

(Quoted in *Talking about Detective Fiction*, by PD James).

[2] Poor Battle might feel a bit harshly treated by posterity! He was also replaced by Marple in adaptations of *The Secret of Chimneys* and *Murder is Easy*, and he didn't even get to make an appearance in the ITV *Poirot* production of *Cards on the Table*.

There's definitely an opportunity for some bright spark to propose a new series: *Agatha Christie's Superintendent Battle*, which could be given the license to shoe-horn him into just about any story Agatha Christie wrote (apart from *Death Comes as the End*).

Sparkling Cyanide (1945)

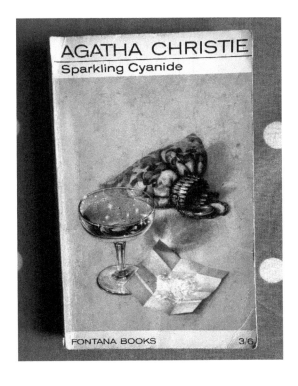 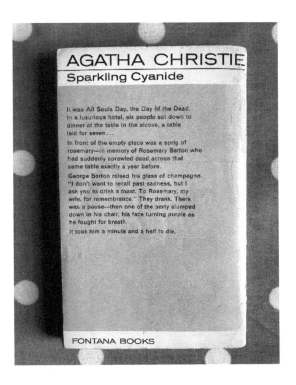

THE BOOK Fontana, 1964 pp 189

Another cover by Tom Adams - an excellent, clear image that deals with three key elements of the plot: the drink, the poison and where it was found.

This was the first Agatha Christie book that I read. It was bought by my eldest brother Jim at a second-hand bookshop In Brighton, for the equivalent of 5p, when I was 11. We were soon looking for more of the same, and with covers as distinctive as this one they were not hard to spot.

THE STORY

Rosemary Barton dies suddenly at a birthday dinner in her honour. One year later, her husband George, having received anonymous letters stating that Rosemary had been murdered, organises a re-union dinner, at the same restaurant, for the guests that had been present the previous time. The inevitable happens ...

The story is divided into three parts. The first section is entitled *Rosemary*, and consists of the guests at the fateful dinner recalling her and their attitudes toward her; the second section (*All Souls Night*) describes the night of the remembrance dinner, and the third (*Iris*) the investigation that follows, led by Inspector Kemp and Colonel Race.

Sparkling Cyanide is an extended version of *Yellow Iris*, which had originally been written as a radio play in the 1920s.

CHARACTERS - spoiler!

The characters do not leap off the page but there are some very descriptive names for the three main females:

> *Rosemary*, whose ghost dominates most of the story: the herb rosemary is a symbol of remembrance;

> *Iris* is the flower of wisdom and hope; Iris Marle is the one dinner-guest who ends the book with the promise of happier times to come;

> *Ruth* is a name that means 'friend', but her surname is Lessing, giving a very unsubtle clue as to her true nature.

In the original story, Hercule Poirot investigated the crime. He is replaced here by Colonel Race, who first appeared in *The Man in the Brown Suit* in 1924, and had appeared with Poirot in *Cards on the Table* and *Death on the Nile*. Race is usually to be found in 'some part of the Empire where trouble is brewing', but in this book he is a friend of Barton's who counsels him against trying to re-create the dinner.

Inspector Kemp is a protegé of Superintendent Battle, another of the *Cards on the Table* detective super-group.

QUOTES

There is a nice little exchange between Kemp and Race[1] :

> *"Do you think she is the type to slip incriminating evidence into a girl's handbag? A perfectly innocent girl, mind, who has never harmed her in any way? Is that in the Kidderminster tradition?"*
>
> *Inspector Kemp squirmed uneasily in his seat and peered into his teacup. "Women don't play cricket," he said. "If that's what you mean."*
>
> *"Actually, a lot of them do," said Race smiling.*

SWIGATHA RATING 6/10

Having been totally mesmerised by this book at the age of eleven, I now consider it a very average swigatha on re-reading it. The identity of the murderer is almost spelt out in Chapter Two, which is, however, a convincing portrayal of hatred (an unusual motive for murder for Agatha Christie). There really is not much else to say. It's ok.

WHERE IT LED

This was the last of four outings for Colonel Race. *Yellow Iris* was finally published as a short story in 1991 in the collection *Problem at Pollensa Bay*.

On a personal level, this book created an appetite for these paperback editions that persists to this day.

ADAPTATIONS

There have been two TV films - one starring Anthony Andrews from 1983 and one featuring Pauline Collins from 2003. The first was co-scripted by Sue Grafton, now a famous crime writer, and is very much of the time that it was made (rather than written): it feels a bit like *Columbo* meets *Dynasty*. The second transplants the characters and action to a football club. Avoid.

Yellow Iris was included as an episode in the ITV *Poirot* series.

NOTES

[1] Agatha Christie knew and loved her cricket; she was a regular spectator of her local team, and used to arrange games on her lawn at Greenway; in her will she specified funds for overseas tours by young cricketers.

Death Comes as the End (1945)

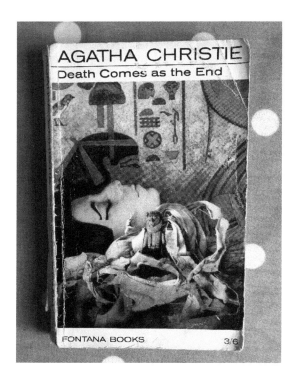 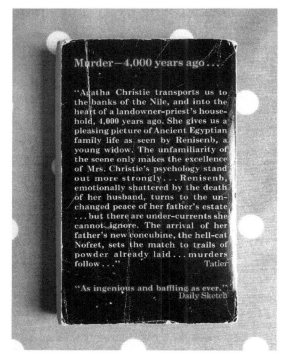

THE BOOK Fontana, 1968 pp 191

Tom Adams' cover depicts the embalmed body of Nofret, amongst burial wrappings and the toy lion that Hori repaired for Renisenb when she was a child. The artist's model bears a strong resemblance to the image on the mural behind her.

The dedication is to Stephen Glanville, who had persuaded Agatha Christie during the Second World War years to write a story based in Ancient Egypt.

THE STORY

The story is set in Thebes around 2000BC. The recently-widowed Renisenb returns with her young daughter Teti to her family home, and all seems to her very much unchanged from when she had left it as a girl.

When her father brings home a concubine, Nofret, undercurrents are stimulated that indicate that all was far from well within Renisenb's extended family. The murder of Nofret follows, and not many of them survive its chaotic aftermath.

Given the setting, and the lack of an investigative force after the murders occur, there are none of the usual interrogations and no physical evidence. Suspicion is based on superstition, until the murderer is lured out into the open by the one character who trusts the evidence of his own eyes.

CHARACTERS AND ATTITUDES

All the main characters are based on the contents of letters that Agatha Christie researched from the 11th Dynasty (2134-1991 BC). Egypt was at the time disunited, and the power lay in the hands of local rulers. This historical background is a key element of the story, evident in the local mistrust of the characters who arrive from the North (Nofret and Kameni) and Hori's yearning for a re-united Egypt.

Unlike most historical novels, this one does not involve actual characters from the time, which Agatha Christie saw as 'phoney':

> ... but you can place a character of your own creation in those times and as long as you know enough of the local colour and the general feeling of the period it would be all right. [1]

So, in from central casting she places the hen-pecked brother always out to please his father (Yahmose), the squandering ne'er-do-well younger brother (Sobek), the shrewd grandmother (Esa), the young woman trying to make her way in the world (Renisenb), with all of them under the roof of a patriarch who keeps all the power to himself (Imhotep) and brings home a concubine much younger than himself (Nofret)[2].

Many of these character types have appeared before (in *Hercule Poirot's Christmas*) and would appear again (in *A Pocketful of Rye*). The one totally original character is that of Henet, poor relation and self-proclaimed drudge, but with eyes like a snake ...

Unsurprisingly, Agatha Christie deals very sympathetically with Renisenb, a woman alone in the world with a six-year-old daughter (she knew what it was like!). By the end, similarly to Lucy Eylesbarrow in *4:50 from Paddington*, Renisenb has to make a choice for her future life - either with someone attractive and exciting but unreliable, or someone disconcerting but comforting and seemingly reliable; unlike Lucy, she makes a choice and we find out what it is.

QUOTES

As well as the bones of the descriptions of everyday living, Agatha Christie uses conversation, usually between Renisenb and Hori, to put a bit of meat on her setting.

"You know that in all tombs there is always a false door?"

Renisenb stared. "Yes, of course."

"Well, people are like that too. They create a false door - to deceive. If they are conscious of weakness, of inefficiency, they make an imposing door of self-assertion, of bluster, of overwhelming authority - and after a time, they get to believe in it themselves. They think, and everyone thinks, that they ARE like that. But behind that door, Renisenb, is bare rock ..."

"Fear is only incomplete knowledge," said Hori.

Hori said with sudden bitterness: "All of Egypt is obsessed by death! And do you know why, Renisenb? Because we have eyes in our bodies, but none in our minds."

"Look, Renisenb. Look out from here across the valley to the River and beyond. That is Egypt, our land. Broken by war and strife for many long years, divided into petty kingdoms, but now - very soon - to come together and form once more a united land - Upper and Lower Egypt once again welded into one - I hope and believe to recover her former greatness!"

SWIGATHA RATING 7/10

It was brave to set a murder mystery 4000 years in the past, and brilliant to use superstition to such effect: everyone thinks they know what is happening, so no-one tries to seriously investigate it until after the first few murders have taken place.

The surprise rating of the ending is not huge, because practically all the suspects are dead by the end! Also, anyone surviving a murder attempt in a swigatha is automatically suspect to an experienced reader of them.

Agatha Christie said[1] that she was persuaded to change her own preferred ending by Stephen Glanville, and regrets it. It would be fascinating to know whom she originally had in mind for the murderer: based on the extracts from her secret notebooks, I would plump for Hori[3].

WHERE IT LED

Agatha Christie never again attempted to set a crime story in the distant past, but many other writers have! She was the first. Again.

ADAPTATIONS

None so far, although the BBC has announced its intention to produce one. It will be interesting to see who they choose as the murderer ...

NOTES

[1] Agatha Christie *An Autobiography*

[2] In the *Neues Museum* in Berlin there are floors dedicated to Ancient Egypt, including the famous bust of Nefertiti - which in German is Nofret-ete. There are also carved figurines with names such as Sobek and Imhotep; Agatha Christie may not have used famous historical figures, but she did use names held by people of some substance.

[3] John Curran, *Agatha Christie's Secret Notebooks* pp 230-236.

The Hollow (1946)

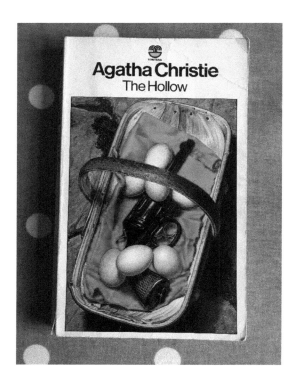 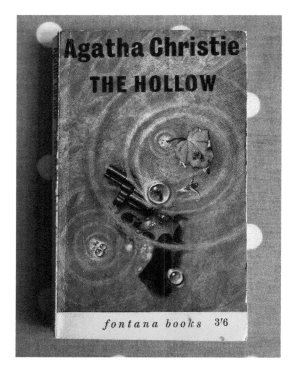

THE BOOK Fontana, 1980 pp 189

The book I first read is a fairly straightforward representation of a plot-line concerning the murder weapon, one of a collection of fire-arms housed at The Hollow, and the basket of eggs carried by Lady Angkatell. I prefer the version I later found with Tom Adams' painting on the front. That is a brilliant cover, depicting another of the guns, one that was deliberately dropped into the swimming pool on a fine autumnal day.

Dedication: 'For Larry and Danae, with apologies for using their swimming pool as the location'. Larry was Francis L Sullivan, who had portrayed Poirot on the London stage in *Black Coffee* (in 1930, at the age of 27!), one of the rare Christie plays to feature her main detective.

The title is the name of a house, but also a reference to a poem by Tennyson which Poirot quotes half-way through[1].

THE STORY

Hercule Poirot is staying at his house in the country and is invited to The Hollow for lunch by his neighbours, Sir Henry and Lucy Angkatell. When he arrives, he is shown outside by Gudgeon, the butler, and finds other members of the house-party standing around a swimming-pool - all apart from one, who is lying beside it, having been shot in the chest. His wife is standing over him, gun in hand.

Although Poirot is asked by the family to help with the investigation, he finds his path impeded by some of them, seemingly intent on preventing him discovering the truth.

CHARACTERS

Hercule Poirot is hardly in the story at all, and very un-Poirot-esque when he is in it (no strange exclamations in French, *par exemple*). It is difficult to envisage him as the owner of a house out in the country, moreover in a countryside that he has always professed to abominate, so one comes to the conclusion that he has been shoe-horned into it by the author (or publisher).

The other characters, on the other hand, are drawn much more strongly than usual for the cast of a whodunit: the delightfully vague and outrageous Lucy Angkatell, the fiercely independent Midge, the wan, listless, almost useless Edward, the super-intelligent if somewhat amoral sculptress Henrietta, the seemingly inadequate but sly Gerda Christow and her dominant, life-embracing husband John.

This is more like a romantic novel by Mary Westmacott (her *alter ego*) than one by Agatha Christie, and it works well in its own right until the somewhat bonkers ending, which has one character trying to shove their head into a gas oven, and then Poirot sitting at a tea-table watching approvingly as someone take a fatal dose of poison.

The rest of the story is all about relationships: between Edward and Midge; between Lady Angkatell and the servants; between Henrietta and John Christow; and between John Christow and just about everybody else, including a charming old cockney lady named Crabtree who is dying of a disease that Christow is researching.

The point is often made in the book that Christow is more alive than anyone else, even after he has died; the other characters are but echoes, and

> *Echo there, whatever is ask'd her, answers 'Death'...*[1]

I think that is a bit unfair on Lucy and co, but certainly Poirot is but an echo of his earlier self when he visits The Hollow.

QUOTES AND ATTITUDES

The two strongest characters in this story are Mrs Crabtree and Lady Angkatell. The author was clearly very fond of both. Here, Dr Christow is thinking about Mrs Crabtree, a patient dying of a disease for which he is trying to find a cure:

> But she wanted to live - she enjoyed life - just as he enjoyed life! It wasn't the circumstances of life they enjoyed, it was life itself - the zest of existence. Curious, a thing one couldn't explain.

This is the author talking! She certainly had her share of ups and downs during her life but never lost 'the zest for life', and was proud of it. Mrs Crabtree consents to Christow trying out different treatments for her incurable disease:

> "'Ad me 'air permed, I did, when I was a kid. It wasn't 'alf a difficult business then. Looked like a n*****, I did. Couldn't get a comb through it. But there - I enjoyed the fun. You can 'ave your fun with me. I can stand it."

Now Sir Henry describes Lucy Angkatell, who really does believe she can get away with murder (even if it was committed by someone else). She certainly 'runs riot' over every other question.

> "She's put deadly enemies next to each other at the dinner table, and run riot over the colour question ... I'm damned if she hasn't got away with it!"

Here, Lucy expresses her own unique take on the ramifications of the Beveridge Report: education for all and a future Welfare State throughout the UK. *The Hollow* was published between the publication of the report in 1944 and the establishment of the NHS in 1948:

> "I must have a talk with you, David, and learn all the new ideas. As far as I can see, one must hate everybody, but at the same time give them free medical attention and a lot of extra education (poor things, all those helpless little children herded into schoolhouses every day) ... "

Now she considers the man who has been murdered in her home:

> "Poor devil!"
>
> "Why? Oh, you mean because he's dead? Oh well, everyone has to die sometime. I never worry over people dying ..."
>
> He looked at her curiously. "I always thought you liked Christow, Lucy?"

"I found him amusing. And he had charm. But I never think one ought to attach too much importance to anybody."

Lucy tells Inspector Grange that he is making far too much fuss over the murder, and considers the possible fate of one of his suspects (one that that suspect is allowed to avoid, because Poirot evidently shares Lucy's opinion):

"And if you go and put her in prison and hang her, what on earth is going to happen to the children? If she did shoot John, she's probably dreadfully sorry about it now. It's bad enough for children to have a father who's been murdered - but it will make it infinitely worse for them to have their mother hanged for it. Sometimes I don't think you policemen think of these things."

Finally, Lucy offers to tell Poirot who did it, and how, if he will drop the case:

"If you were to know the truth - if you were to be told the truth, I think - I think perhaps that might satisfy you? Would it satisfy you, M Poirot?"

Whatever all the others may think about John Christow, she is the dominant character in the book.

SWIGATHA RATING 6/10

The first half of the story is totally engaging - and then Poirot arrives, and it seems to tail off! All of the characters have more than one dimension on display. And the end is a surprise, but it feels to me like here was an author who had set out to write something different; for some reason, she felt obliged to introduce one or two incongruous elements (including Poirot) and so ends up turning out more of the same.

It's still very clever, though.

WHERE IT LED

This had been the first 'Poirot' story for three years, but even so, when Agatha Christie adapted it as a play, his character was dropped. To satisfy her readers' insatiable appetite for Poirot, *The Labours of Hercules*, a collection of short stories that had appeared in The Strand magazine the previous decade, was published in book form the following year.

ADAPTATIONS

The ITV adaptation for their *Poirot* series had a very strong cast, with Edward Fox as Gudgeon and Sarah Miles in excellent form as Lucy. It is a pretty faithful version, although Poirot is given somewhat more prominence in it, unsurprisingly. It was directed by Margaret Mitchell, who was also responsible for the peerless *Five Little Pigs* episode for the same company.

NOTES

[1] The quote is another one to be taken from Tennyson's 'Maud':

> *I hate the dreadful hollow behind the little wood*
> *Its lips in the field above are dappled with blood-red heath*
> *The red-rib'ed ledges drip with a silent horror of blood*
> *And Echo there, whatever is ask'd her, answers 'Death'.*

A different quote from the same piece was used in *Sparkling Cyanide*.

The Labours of Hercules (1947)

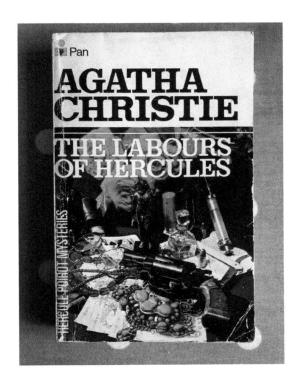 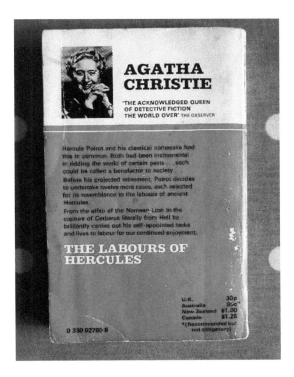

THE BOOK   Fontana, 1969 pp 256

The Labours of Hercules is a collection of twelve stories featuring Hercule Poirot, each of which echoes one of the twelve Labours of Hercules from Ancient Greek Mythology.

The PAN image is a bit of a mish-mash, and it is not totally clear what some of the articles allude to, but at least it has the naked figure of Hercules at its heart.

THE STORIES AND QUOTES

Poirot is inspired by a conversation about classical myths with his friend Dr Burton, Fellow of All Souls, to take a final series of cases before his retirement, based on one criterion: he would choose only cases that had a connection with the Labours of his namesake.

The Nemean Lion

Inspired by Miss Lemon, Poirot investigates the disappearance of Pekinese dogs in London. The principal protagonist is a dog with the heart of a lion; during his investigations Poirot encounters the organisational genius of Amy Carnaby. An excellent, gentle introduction to his Labours.

The Lernean Hydra

Dr Oldfield is the subject of rumours that he poisoned his wife. As soon as one rumour is quashed, another two spring in its place. An example of the eternal triangle that feels familiar from other short stories: man, difficult wife, plus third person who is not what they seem.

The Arcadian Deer

A garage mechanic asks Poirot to find a girl 'with hair like wings of gold'. Another example in a swigatha of people impersonating their servants, but unusual in that the main protagonists are from what used to be called 'rude stock'. Poirot, as ever, is class-less.

I am sot certain but I think Agatha Christie is being a bit saucy in this extract:

> There was a knock at the door and the chambermaid appeared.
> "Please sir, the man from the garage is here and would like to see you."
> Hercule Poirot replied amiably: "Let him mount."
> The girl giggled and retired.

The Erymanthian Boar

Poirot is enlisted to help trap a beast of a man in a hideout in the Alps. Not great: the whole scenario and plot seem ludicrous.

The Augean Stables

The new British Prime Minister asks Poirot to clear up the mess left by his predecessor and father-in-law, a man revered during his lifetime but now revealed to be a dishonest rascal. Poirot achieves this through devious means, thereby keeping the ex-Prime Minister's reputation intact: cover-ups a speciality (see also short stories such as *The Theft of the Royal Ruby*, *The Submarine Plans* etc).

The Stymphalean Birds

Poirot intervenes when he sees a young man being preyed upon by a pair of bloodsuckers. The two most enjoyable characters never say a word. Set in Herzoslovakia[1], the scam revolves to a degree around the supposed bribability of Balkan locals and the police. However, as Poirot later reveals:

> "The police of a country are not so easily bribed - certainly not when it is a question of murder! These women trade on the average Englishman's ignorance ..."

The ignorance of An Englishman Abroad ... and 'these women' are also English, so they should know.

The Cretan Bull

Poirot is asked to help when a 'magnificent specimen' of a young man is suspected of behaving like a deranged maniac. An(other) example of Agatha Christie's grasp of genetics supplying her with her twist. There is an enjoyable flow to the dialogue.

> Diane Maberly: *"Everyone is a little mad."*
> *"It has been said so," said Poirot cautiously.*
> Diane: *"It's only when you begin to think you're a poached egg or something that they have to shut you up."*
>
> *He quoted derisively: "'Canst thou minister to a mind disturbed?'"*
> *Hercule Poirot said dryly: "I am trying to."*

The Horses of Diomedes

A cocaine ring is preying on the smart set in London: vampires preying on flesh and blood. It has a decent twist, a typical Christie twist that relies on the reader's imagined innate prejudices to succeed.

The Girdle of Hippolyta

Poirot is hired to investigate the disappearance of a Rubens painting. Inspector Japp asks him to look into the case of a kidnapped schoolgirl while he is at it. Uses a similar plotline to *The Kidnapped Prime Minister*. Presumably set around 1936 (the time of the Jarrow March):

> *It was at the time when the unemployed were pursuing their tactics of lying down on street crossings and penetrating into the Ritz.*

The Flock of Geryon

The head of a religious cult is preying on his flock. Miss Amy Carnaby, mastermind behind the Nemean Lion scam, agrees to help Poirot's investigation by becoming one of the members of the cult. Agatha Christie's knowledge of the effects of drugs is again put to good use. Miss Carnaby is an appealing character, one that this reader would have liked Agatha Christie to have explored more.

The Apples of the Hesperides

An American collector asks Poirot to track down a Cellini goblet, the poison chalice of the Borgias. His enquiries (via something of a leap of imagination) take him to the West Coast of Ireland. This is one of the best stories, and certainly the most moving, in the collection, even if it somewhat bizarrely manages to incorporate a horse-racing reporter named 'Atlas' coming to Hercules' aid.

Emery Power said: "When I really want a thing, I am willing to pay for it, M. Poirot."

Hercule Poirot said softly: "You have no doubt heard the Spanish proverb[2]: 'Take what you want - and pay for it, says God.'"

This story has quite an interesting ending in an Irish convent chapel:

"He needs your prayers."

"Is he then an unhappy man?"

Poirot said: "So unhappy that he has forgotten what happiness means. So unhappy that he does not know he is unhappy."

The nun said softly: "Ah, a rich man ..."

Hercule Poirot is a rich man ...

The Capture of Cerberus

Poirot is invited to the nightclub 'Hell', where he meets again with Countess Vera Rossakoff. Miss Lemon excels herself once more, and Japp chips in. It is clear that Agatha Christie enjoyed writing this:

"We have all kinds here," said the Countess. "That is as it should be, is it not? The gates of Hell are open to all?"

"Except, possibly, to the poor?" Poirot suggested.

The Countess laughed. "Are we not told that it is difficult for a rich man to enter the Kingdom of Heaven? Naturally, then, he should have priority in Hell."

SWIGATHA RATING 7/10

Some of these short stories are among the best Agatha Christie wrote, and the underlying idea is, once more, brilliant. It is not quite top-drawer for me, because, as is often the case with her shorter stories, I kept thinking I had come across some of the plot devices before.

WHAT HAPPENED NEXT

Miss Lemon and Japp had never appeared in the same story before (and never would again). *The Capture of Cerberus* was also the swansong of Countess Rossakoff.

ADAPTATIONS

ITV, having previously adapted individual Poirot short stories masterfully in 50-minute episodes for the early series of *Agatha Christie's Poirot*, decided to squeeze this set into one two-hour episode. They may have had to; maybe the cast had had enough and could not face another 12 episodes.

Even so, the result is a travesty of this collection: the 'Labours' are paintings, the supposed 'Erymanthian Boar' Marrascaud turns out to be Countess Rossakoff's daughter, and the film ends in farce, with everyone pulling guns on each other. David Suchet overdoes his Poirot-in-pain act but at least he seems to be taking it seriously, unlike the rest of the cast.

The two best stories in the collection do not even get a look in. I would love to see individual episodes of those stories (*The Nemean Lion* and *The Apples of the Hesperides*), maybe as animations.

NOTES

[1] Herzoslovakia was the country which had offered its throne to Anthony Cade and Virginia Revel in *The Secret of Chimneys*.

[2] The readers certainly *will* have heard this old Spanish proverb, pronounced by both Pilar Estravados in *Hercule Poirot's Christmas* and Elsa Greer in *Five Little Pigs*.

Taken at the Flood (1948)

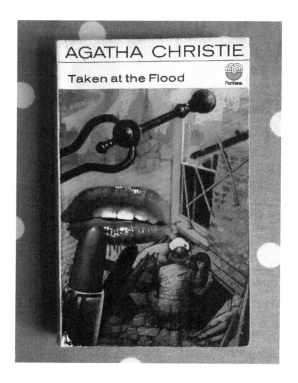
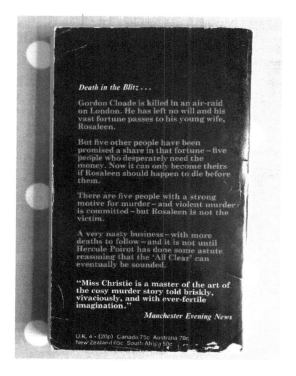

THE BOOK Fontana, 1970 pp 192

Tom Adam's cover suggests the background to the story (the London Blitz) and two items found in a later crime scene (the tongs and the lipstick).

THE STORY

It is 1944, and Hercule Poirot is sheltering from an air-raid in his club. He is happy to be distracted from the mayhem outside by the club bore, Major Porter. Porter recounts the story of the death of Gordon Cloade in the Blitz, and the survival of his young widow, Rosaleen, who had thereby inherited a considerable fortune at the expense of Cloade's family.

Major Porter had known Rosaleen's first husband, Robert Underhay, reported dead in Africa, and hints darkly that Underhay might still be alive and living under the name of Enoch Arden.

Soon afterwards, aware of Porter's story, a member of the Cloade family consults Poirot and asks him to find Underhay. Poirot refuses.

Two years later, a man named Enoch Arden is found dead in a pub in Warmsley Vale, home to most of the Cloades ...

CHARACTERS AND ATTITUDES

This story is very much of its time - the period immediately after the end of the Second World War. Lynn Marchmont has returned home after six years with the WRNS in the Middle East; David Hunter, ex-commando, and Rosaleen Cloade have moved to Warmsley Vale having recovered from the bomb that destroyed the hotel where they had been staying; Rowley Cloade, having, as a farmer, been in an exempt occupation, had sat out the War and resents it, while the remaining Cloades have all seen their incomes greatly diminished due to raised taxes and War Damage Insurance payments.

Everything has, naturally, been changed by the experience of the War and its aftermath. 'Life isn't Safe' is one of the themes of the book; Warmsley Vale certainly is no longer safe, and without Gordon Cloade's millions to bail them out, neither are the Cloades.

Lynn doesn't actually want to be safe, nor does she wish to go back to her pre-War lifestyle. She is unhappy at coming down from the excitements of wartime to the boredom of a grim, grey ration-book Britain. Fortunately, she ends up in the arms of a lying, conniving person whom she knows is complicit in the deaths of two people, and is therefore happy.

There is one tragic character in this story - Major Porter, the retired Army Officer, who perjures himself because he needs the money and then cannot live with the consequences ... yet another example in Christie of a retired senior officer gone to seed.

QUOTES

Agatha Christie once again mocks the insularity of the British:

> *"Her first husband (poor child, such a grief to her) was reported dead in Africa. A mysterious country, Africa."*
> *"A mysterious continent," Poirot corrected her.*

Lynn is shocked at what she finds when she returns home:

> *It's the aftermath war has left. Ill will. Ill feeling. It's everywhere. On railways and buses and in shops and amongst workers and clerks and even agricultural labourers. And I suppose even worse in mines and factories. Ill will.*

This is not a side to the War and its aftermath that one often comes across in the journals of the time, but it rings true: Lynn was clearly not alone in not wishing things return to the pre-war 'normal'.[1]

Here is an interesting thought that occurs to Lynn, one that might also occur to one during a pandemic:

> *Was that what, ultimately, war did to you? It was not the physical dangers - the mines at sea, the bombs from the air, the crisp ping! of a rifle bullet as you drove over a desert track. No, it was the spiritual danger of learning how much easier life was if you ceased to think ...*

Lynn cannot help but think now that she has returned home. Here is David Hunter's take on coming back:

> *"Back to safety! Back to tameness! Back to where we were when the whole bloody show started! Creep into our rotten little holes and play safe again."*

There are many slighting references to foreigners in Christie's canon of work, and some readers have ascribed these attitudes to the author herself. Others have excused her on the grounds that this was how things were at the time she wrote them. That excuse is unnecessary; almost always, the words are spoken by unsympathetic characters, and there is a classic example in this book:

> *"You're a foreigner."*
> *"Yes," said Hercule Poirot.*
> *"In my opinion," said the old lady, "you should all Go Back."*
> *"Go back where?" inquired Poirot.*
> *"To where you came from," said the old lady firmly. She added as a kind of rider,* sotto voce*: "Foreigners!" and snorted.*
> *"That," said Poirot mildly, "would be difficult."*
> *"Nonsense," said the old lady. "That's what we fought the war for, isn't it? So that people could go back to their proper places and stay there."*

To be fair to her, the old lady is not the only person in this book wondering what the war was fought for.

SWIGATHA RATING 9/10

Agatha Christie was at the absolute peak of her powers in the 1940s, seemingly inspired by World War II and the years following it. The sensationally original plotting of the previous decade had given way to stories where her characters were more to the fore (but the twists just as brilliantly concealed).

In this story, one presumed murder turns out to be manslaughter, another turns out to be suicide and a presumed suicide turns out to be murder. The deception at the heart of the plot is referred to again and again in conversations between the main protagonists, but it would be a rare reader who would realise what they meant. When the book is re-read, on the other hand, it is staggeringly obvious. This is brilliant deception.

WHERE IT LED

Poirot disappeared off the radar for four years. Agatha Christie finished off the 1940s in real style with *Crooked House* and *A Murder is Announced*, but thereafter the quality of her books was more mixed. This may not be unconnected to the flowering of her dramatic genius in the 1950s, as she became the most successful living writer for the English-speaking theatre.

ADAPTATIONS

ITV's *Poirot* series insisted on setting almost all the adaptations of the Poirot stories in 1936, even though they were written any time between 1916 and 1972. This often does not matter, because many of her stories were not date-stamped, but it does in this case. The events of WW2 and the privations afterwards are core to the plot of *Taken at the Flood*. By ignoring them, they have had to change the characters to an extent that they are rendered uninteresting and almost ridiculous.

NOTES

[1] And things didn't return to normal: within five years of WWII, the UK had introduced free Education for all, a National Health Service and a Welfare State.

Crooked House (1949)

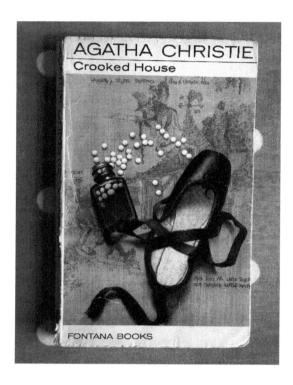 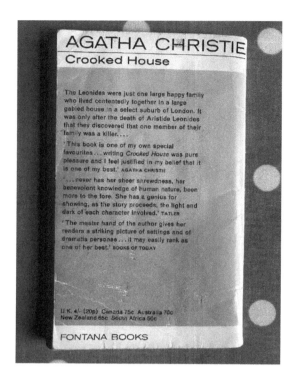

THE BOOK Fontana, 1969 pp 160

The Tom Adams cover gives prominence to the murder method and the motive, and the nursery rhyme wallpaper is reminiscent of that used for his cover of *One, Two Buckle My Shoe*.

THE STORY

Aristide Leonides, an immensely rich, but 'fantastically ugly' Greek restaurateur, is poisoned by a member of his family. Charles Hayward, back from war-time Special Branch duties and in love with Leonides' grand-daughter Sophia, joins the police investigation into which of the family is responsible.

This unlikely opportunity is explained by the fact that Charles' father is the Assistant Commissioner of Scotland Yard.

CHARACTERS - spoiler!

Three Gables, the Crooked House of the title, is home to various generations of Aristide Leonides' family: his three grandchildren, Sophie, Eustace and Josephine; their step-grandmother Brenda; their great-aunt Edith; their parents Philip and Magda, and Uncle Roger and Aunt Clemency. Most of them are quite lack-lustre characters, with the exception of Edith de Haviland and her adored Josephine.

The eleven-year-old Josephine is not, however, adorable: she is a clever but vain show-off, she spies on people and gathers secrets about them, she has no empathy with anyone else in the house and despises the lot of them, apart from a grudging respect for her Great-Aunt Edith.

But that is not a surprise when you consider the way that this youngest member of the household is routinely treated. Her dysfunctional parents take no interest in her and refer to her as a 'changeling'. Her step-grandmother Brenda says that Josephine 'gives me the shivers'. She is described by her sister's boyfriend as being 'a fantastically ugly child'. Her only dream, of learning to be a ballet dancer, is dismissed by her grandfather, who says, bluntly, that she'd be 'no good' and refuses to even let her have a trial lesson. She has been farmed out to a nanny and a tutor and has no friends. No-one pays her any attention until after her grandfather dies, and even then it is only because she claims to know what happened.

Josephine is (literally!) a car-crash waiting to happen. When it does, there is a trace of somewhat belated sympathy for her, 'the pathetic little monster, born with a kink', but little evidence of regret from anyone at the way that they treated her.

In a 'nature v nurture' debate, Agatha Christie would come down on the side of the former - heredity plays a part in many of her plots. Unwittingly or not, however, she gives the latter an airing here, as the Leonides give a master-class in how not to raise an eleven-year-old girl.

ATTITUDES AND QUOTES

Miss de Haviland tells Charles about their host:

> "Came here when my sister died. He asked me to. Seven children - and the youngest only a year old... Couldn't leave 'em to be brought up by a dago, could I? An impossible marriage, of course. I always felt Marcia must have been - well - bewitched. Ugly common little foreigner!"

Whatever her opinion, the speaker stayed with the common little foreigner for 40 years.

The Assistant Commissioner of Scotland Yard explains children to his son:

> "A child, you know, translates desire into action without compunction. A child is angry with a kitten, says 'I'll kill you' and hits it on the head with a hammer - and then breaks its heart

because the kitten doesn't come alive again! Lots of kids try to take a baby out of a pram and 'drown it' because it usurps attention - or interferes with their pleasures."

Agatha Christie doesn't include many children in her books, but when she does they are certainly not portrayed as 'born innocent'[1]. And now the Assistant Commander explains heredity:

"Interesting thing, heredity. Take the de Haviland ruthlessness, and what we might call the Leonides unscrupulousness - the de Havilands are all right because they're not unscrupulous, and the Leonides are all right because, though unscrupulous, they are kindly - but get a descendant who inherited both these traits - see what I mean?"

AC as A.C.?

Agatha Christie also allows Sophie to voice a nightmare that the author recognised only too well: [2]

*"I don't know, Charles," she whispered. "I only know that I'm back - back in the nightmare -"
"I know. Those were the very words I used to myself as I drove down with Taverner."
"Because this is just what a nightmare is. Walking about among people you know, looking in their faces - and suddenly the faces change - and it's not someone you know any longer - it's a stranger - a cruel stranger..."*

Here is the infamous entry in Josephine's diary:

Today I killed Grandfather. Grandfather wouldn't let me do bally dancing so I made up my mind I would kill him.

And here her great-aunt explains why she has driven both of them to their deaths:

"I do not want the child to suffer as I believe she would suffer if called to earthly account for what she has done. There is often one of the litter who is not quite right."

There were quite a few of that particular litter who are not quite right. Anyway, the upshot is that, once again, a murderer is not brought to trial to be sentenced to a lifetime of confinement. Time and again, Agatha Christie allows characters to take their own way out rather than face that prospect (which Josephine surely would have done).

SWIGATHA RATING 8/10

This may have been Agatha Christie's favourite book to write, but (for me) it is not quite up there with her very best: it feels like a story built around a single (brilliant) idea, with everything else forced to fit in around it.

There are hints throughout the book that Josephine is the culprit. For example, Charles' father advises him that the murderer is vain and will want to talk about their cleverness; that he should talk to Josephine, who won't be able to resist showing off what she knows; that children are natural killers who have to have it punished out of them; that some children, however, are born with the Mark of Cain and will not feel that murder is wrong, and that the wrong combination of de Haviland and Leonides genes could produce a monster ...

There are also the physical clues for the supposed attempt on Josephine's life that are fairly on display; for example, the mud on a chair that point to the culprit being someone not tall enough to reach the top of a low door, and so on.

Even so, the ending is shocking. Agatha Christie was not the first person to have a child as the killer[3], but surely only in a swigatha could you have a grandfather and a nanny murdered by an eleven-year-old girl, or indeed an eleven-year-old girl murdered by her great aunt, and then have everyone else seemingly set to live happily ever after.

WHERE IT LED

This was the last Agatha Christie novel to be published in the 1940s, but she still proved capable of coming up with the goods as she entered her 60s: her next book featured the return of Miss Marple, after a gap of eight years, in the excellent *A Murder is Announced*.

ADAPTATIONS

The first adaptation I have come across was hidden away on Channel 5 during Christmas 2017. There had been a radio version for BBC, and previous attempts to adapt the book for the screen had been mooted. It is possible that these were scuppered by the sensitivities engendered in the aftermath of real-life murder cases in the UK involving 10-11 year olds occurring around the same time that they were being discussed (Mary Bell in the 1960s, Jon Thompson and Robert Venables in the 1990s)[4].

Channel 5's film was screen-played by Julian Fellowes, and he makes an excellent job of it without taking too many liberties with the plot. The cast is well-chosen. Glenn Close is excellent as Edith de

Haviland and Honor Kneafsey is perfect for Josephine - but then, they did have the two best parts! The ending is genuinely horrifying and moving.

NOTES

[1] A kitten-killing child also features in *Curtain*. For an even more shocking example of a killer-child, read the opening chapters of *Towards Zero*.

[2] When she was a very little girl, Agatha Christie had a recurring nightmare about "The Gunman". She and her family would be sitting down to tea, everyone chatting normally, when all at once one of them would morph into the Gunman - and only Agatha could see it. (Agatha Christie, *An Autobiography* p 36)

[3] For example, Ellery Queen and Margery Allingham (*Agatha Christie's Secret Notebooks* John Curran)

[4] *Agatha Christie on Screen* Mark Aldridge

A Murder is Announced (1950)

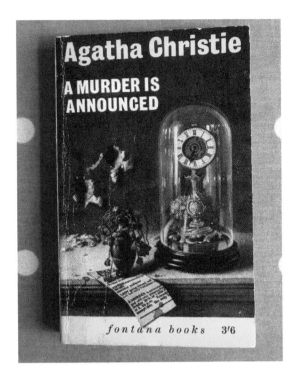

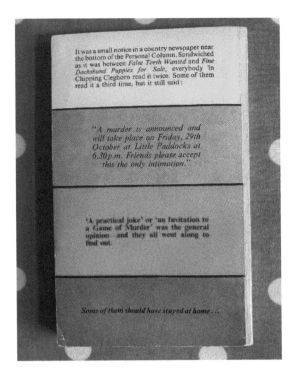

THE BOOK Fontana, 1964 pp 192

The cover features the first painting created by Tom Adams for Fontana. It depicts the immediate aftermath of the murder announced for 6:30pm - bullet-holes, dead violets and blood. There are the usual 192 pages in this book - a very standard Christie length! Some might say that it would have benefitted from being ten pages shorter, but Agatha Christie was very meticulous about the number of words that constituted her novels: for her the 'right length' of a detective story was 50,000 words.

THE STORY

An announcement in the Chipping Cleghorn Gazette proclaims that a murder will take place at the home of Miss Blacklock. Curious villagers gather there at the appointed time expecting some kind of parlour game but a murder duly takes place.

Miss Marple had been staying at the hotel where the victim (Rudi Scherz, a receptionist) worked, and she contacts the police to tell them what she suspects about him. She then invites herself to the vicarage at Chipping Cleghorn, the home of Bunch Harmon, vicar's wife and her own god-daughter, to investigate for herself.

CHARACTERS - spoiler!

The book was published in 1950, and the writing clearly reflects post-war realities in Britain: shortages, rationing, the black market, displaced persons and people reduced to slender means.

This story has an unusually rich cast of characters (or suspects). Miss Blacklock's home provides a haven for a variety of 'refugees' – either genuine ones, such as Mitzi the cook, or economic ones, including Dora Bunner, Patrick and Julia Simmons, and Mrs Haymes. Miss Blacklock herself proves to be in hiding, and the police grow (justifiably) suspicious that no-one in the house, or village, is who they proclaim themselves to be[1].

The character of the murderer is most unusual for a swigatha, in that she is hugely upset at the enormity of what she has done, especially the murder of her only friend. We are not told what happens to her afterwards but can only presume that her remorse will not save her from being hanged.

Also unusual in this context are the characters of Miss Hinchcliffe and Miss Murgatroyd, two ladies living together in a loving relationship. Both are sympathetically, even movingly, treated.

QUOTES

Here is Miss Marple on the medical profession:

> *"I always feel that the young doctors are only too anxious to experiment. After they've whipped out all our teeth, and administered quantities of very peculiar glands, and removed bits of our insides, they then confess that nothing can be done for us. I really prefer the old-fashioned remedy of big black bottles of medicine. After all, one can always pour them down the sink."*

Agatha Christie was also unconvinced: doctors do not get a good press in many of her books.

And here Miss Marple explains the character of the murderer, an echo in some ways of Caroline Sheppard's analysis of her brother's character in *The Murder of Roger Ackroyd*:

> *"Weak and kindly people are very often treacherous. And if they've got a grudge against life it saps the little moral strength that they may possess."*

Here's an interesting take on post-war Britain, not one we have often heard – the local view on the death at Miss Blacklock's:

> *"An' that sort of thing wouldn't 'ave 'appened afore the war. Deserters, that's what it is. Desperate men roaming the countryside …"*

Miss Blacklock defends Mitzi, displaying the kindly instincts that were later to betray her:

> *"Please don't be too prejudiced against the poor thing because she's a liar. I do really believe that, like so many liars, there is a real substratum of truth behind her lies. I mean that though, to take an instance, her atrocity stories have grown and grown until every kind of unpleasant story that has ever appeared in print has happened to her or her relations personally, she did have a bad shock initially and did see one, at least, of her relations killed. I think a lot of these displaced persons feel, perhaps justly, that their claim to our notice and sympathy lies in their atrocity value and so they exaggerate and invent."*

SWIGATHA RATING 8/10

On re-reading it, I realised that this is one of the more impressive Christie books. It is well-set, and the original idea (to invite all the neighbours round when you're planning to kill someone) is a great way to kick it off. The knock-on effects of WWII on village life are well-integrated into the story and there are genuine elements of tragedy in it.

The villagers who take up the invitation to the murder are not quite sure if they have actually been invited or not, and in their awkwardness each of them makes the same inane observations. One of these is that it is unusual for the central heating to be on. This proves to be a crucial clue, and Agatha Christie manages to repeat it three times on the same page, and yet still hide it in plain sight by virtue of including it in a comic passage.

Unfortunately, there is a fatuous passage towards the end of the book, leading to the attempted murder of Mitzi, which detracts from the quality of the rest of it.

The author must have been 3,000 or so words short!

WHAT HAPPENED NEXT

Bunch Harmon re-appears in a later short story (*Sanctuary*) set in her parish church. Dermot Craddock, the investigating officer and godson of Sir Henry Clithering, Assistant Commissioner of Scotland Yard, re-appears in later Marple stories such as *4:50 from Paddington* and *The Mirror Crack'd from Side to Side*. By the latter, he is referring to Marple as 'Aunt Jane', an assumption also made by others with no actual blood connection to her.

ADAPTATIONS

There was a superb, brilliantly cast BBC version from 1984 featuring Joan Hickson as Miss Marple. It stays very true to the book, and the pivotal scene with Marple and Dora Bunner in the café is so atmospheric – the actors play off one another brilliantly. John Altman's musical arrangements are also, as ever, excellent.

A later adaptation for ITV's *Agatha Christie's Miss Marple*, featuring Geraldine McEwan, is also well-cast and one of the best in the series (admittedly that is not saying a great deal).

NOTES

[1] See also Appendix C: 'Who's Who in Chipping Cleghorn'.

They Came to Baghdad (1951)

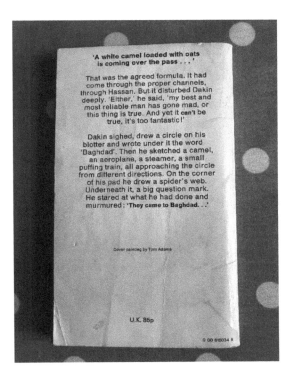

THE BOOK   Fontana 1980, pp 192

Tom Adams' cover is based on a simple sketch found in one of Agatha Christie's notebooks. He has added one of his insects (which feature on many of his cover paintings), some drops of blood and a spider's web entangling the name of one of the main characters in the story. Strangely, this well-known cover appears in neither of his books *Agatha Christie Cover Story* or *Tom Adams Uncovered*, so maybe he didn't like it much.

THE STORY

Down on her luck and out of work, having talked herself out of a job by impersonating her boss in front of her work-mates, young Victoria Jones meets Edward, seemingly her dream man, in a London park. He tells her he is about to take up a position in Baghdad, and a smitten Victoria determines by hook or crook to follow him. She finds work as companion to an American travelling there, passing herself off as the niece of Pauncefoot Jones, an archaeologist on a dig at a local Tell. Once there, she meets up with Edward and he finds her a job in a local mission, The Olive Branch.

Within no time, Victoria finds herself harbouring a dying man in her hotel room, and is then herself kidnapped. Once she has escaped, Victoria realises that she will be needing to put her capacity to tell stories and impersonate others to the ultimate test ...

CHARACTERS

There are two groups of characters in this story.

On the one hand, Agatha Christie gives us members of British Intelligence in the Middle East and its adversaries. The latter includes a group-hellbent-on-world-domination that is preparing to disrupt a Baghdad peace conference between the super-powers of the time (the US and USSR), thereby provoking them into global conflict.

These individual characters are essentially cardboard cut-outs that could have been lifted directly from Christie's world-domination thrillers of the 1920s, and which are also slotted into later books such as *Passenger to Frankfurt* and *Destination Unknown*: stiff upper lip Colonel Race types ranged against self-proclaimed supermen and women seemingly happy to slaughter millions to achieve their goals.

On the other hand, we have the members of the dig at the Tell, whom Victoria joins after her escape. Unsurprisingly, given the author's increasing interest and participation in the subject, the archaeological party and their Arab workers and assistants are drawn with great affection and humour.

Victoria Jones herself is but the latest in a line of plucky, resourceful, unencumbered young women happy to embark on dangerous solo adventures, a line that began with Anne Beddingfeld in *The Man in the Brown Suit* in 1924. I think that, wittingly or unwittingly, Agatha Christie put a great deal of her (idealised) self into these characters, so by the end of the book it is no great surprise from which group of protagonists Victoria will be choosing her future mate.

ATTITUDES AND QUOTES

At the time this book was written, Britain's Mandates in Middle Eastern countries such as Iraq, Jordan and Syria maintained its dominant position in the area, which explains its policing role in both this book and others set there, such as *Appointment with Death* and *Murder in Mesopotamia*.

> *Captain Crosbie came out of the Bank with the pleased air of a man who has cashed a cheque and discovered that there is just a little more in his account than he thought there*

was. Captain Crosbie often looked pleased with himself. He was that kind of man ... nothing remarkable about him. There are heaps of Crosbies in the East.

A mere five years after the end of the Second World War, people were convinced that another was on the way:[1]

"I know everyone says there's going to be another war sooner or later," said Victoria.
"Exactly," said Dakin. "And why does everyone say so, Victoria?"
She frowned. "Why, because Russia - the Communists - America –" she stopped.
"You see," said Dakin. "Those aren't your own opinions or words ..."

Here Victoria has her eyes opened to a different culture *en route* to the Exhibition House at the dig:

"Arabs find our Western impatience for doing things quickly extraordinarily hard to understand, and our habit of coming straight to the point in conversation strikes them as extremely ill-mannered. You should always sit around and offer general observations for about an hour - or if you prefer it you need not speak at all."
"Rather odd if we did that in offices in London. One would waste a lot of time."
"Yes, but we're back at the question: What is time? And what is waste?"

The bent-on-world-domination theme, last encountered in *The Big Four* in 1927, comes back with a vengeance:

There must be total war - total destruction. And then - the new Heaven and the new Earth. The small chosen band of higher beings, the scientists, the agricultural experts, the administrators - the young men like Edward - the young Siegfrieds of the New World. All young, all believing in their destiny as Supermen. When destruction had run its course, they would step in and take over.

This soon-to-be-repeated plot makes one wonder what use Agatha Christie might have made of the companies in Silicon Valley today, and the attempts at mass brainwashing by the protagonists of cyber warfare that they have facilitated.

Finally, Victoria compares her crush on Edward with earlier adolescent ones for two interestingly-juxtaposed heartthrobs of the 1940s:

It had been the same feeling that she had experienced some years earlier for Humphrey Bogart, and later for the Duke of Edinburgh. It had been glamour.

SWIGATHA RATING 5/10

As with most of Agatha Christie's writing, this story is a very easy and enjoyable read, especially the parts set in the dig and those describing the Arab communities, but the story does not hang together like usual and the end feels very rushed. Even after a second reading, I still have no idea what happened to Edward, one of its main protagonists.

I think that both this story and *Destination Unknown* struggled for air because of the sheer volume of work that the author was taking on at the time they were being written (1950-53). As well as five other (pretty good) works of detective fiction and one romance written as 'Mary Westmacott', she was becoming increasingly involved in works for the stage, adapting *The Hollow* (first performed in 1951), *The Mousetrap* (1952) and *Witness for the Prosecution* (1953).

WHERE IT LED

To *Destination Unknown*, three years later! Many of the notes and ideas rejected for this story re-emerged for the later one, and the characters and organisations involved seem just to be slightly different versions of each other.[2] The 'Young Siegfried' theme re-appears, in spades, in *Passenger to Frankfurt*.

ADAPTATIONS

None so far.

NOTES

[1] During the year the book came out, the US and USSR engaged in Korea in the first of a series of proxy wars that would continue elsewhere in Asia, Africa, Central and Southern America throughout the following 30 years and indeed still continue in the Middle East today. But they have never (so far) declared war on each other.

[2] For more information about the preparation of the two books, read John Curran's analysis of *Agatha Christie's Secret Notebooks*.

Mrs McGinty's Dead (1952)

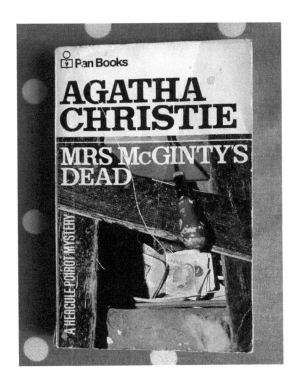
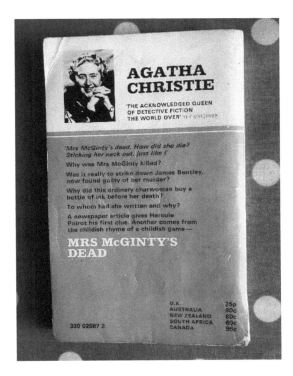

THE BOOK PAN, 1971 pp 191

PAN's rather plain cover matches the (seemingly) plain circumstances of Mrs McGinty's death - murdered for a few pounds that she was known to keep under her floorboards.

The novel is dedicated to Peter Saunders, who produced some of Agatha Christie's plays on the London stage in the 1950s.

THE STORY

James Bentley has been tried, convicted and sentenced to death for the murder of his landlady, Mrs McGinty. The police officer in charge of the investigation, Superintendent Spence, cannot convince himself that Bentley is a murderer. He consults Poirot and asks him to investigate and see if he can find further evidence that the police missed. Poirot leaps at the chance to relieve his boredom.

Mrs McGinty was charwoman to four homes in Broadhinny: the Upwards, the Carpenters, the Rendells and the Wetherbys, all 'very nice people'. Poirot visits each of them and finds that the cleaner had a reputation for snooping amongst their things, calling to mind the children's rhyme:

Mrs McGinty's dead

How did she die?

Sticking her neck out, just like I ...

At the Upwards' house, Poirot is re-united with crime novelist Ariadne Oliver, whom he last met in *Cards on the Table.*

CHARACTERS AND ATTITUDES

The plot revolves around a newspaper story about three young women and a girl involved in murders in the past. The article asks: *where are they now?*

A few of Agatha Christie's post-war novels share the same theme: no-one really knows who anyone else is anymore. This is particularly apparent in a village, where in the past everyone had known each other's backgrounds, sometimes only too well. In Broadhinny that is no longer the case, and any one or all of those girls could have been residing there at the time of Mrs McGinty's murder.

Another Christie theme resonates throughout the story: the importance of a happy (or indeed unhappy) childhood. References to the characters' childhoods abound. Thus, we have

- James Bentley, who has not recovered from the death of his domineering mother;
- Deirdre Henderson, all her life treated like a slave by her mother and her hated stepfather;
- Maude Williams, whose mother was murdered and father hanged;
- Maureen Summerhayes, handed over for adoption and haunted by her mother's rejection,
- and Robin Upward, also adopted (in fact, adopted twice).

QUOTES

As the story opens, Poirot is bored stiff, and realises how much he has been missing his only friend Hastings:

> *"I cannot, truly I cannot, sit in a chair all day reflecting how truly admirable I am. One needs the human touch. One needs – as they say nowadays – the* stooge.*"*

Poirot is unhappy, but there are also plenty of unhappy people in Broadhinny, including Deirdre Henderson:

> *"But of course nothing - anywhere - is like it used to be."*
> *"And do you mind that so much, mademoiselle?"*

"I? Oh, no." She seemed surprised. "But it's different for mother. She - she lives in the past a lot."

"You look forward, not back?"

Deirdre said slowly: "I don't know that I look anywhere ... I mean, today's usually enough, isn't it?"

Maureen Summerhayes is the most likeable character in the book, full of life, but nevertheless haunted by her past:

"I was an adopted child. My mother parted with me and I had every advantage, as they call it. And it's always hurt - always - always - to know that you weren't really wanted, that your mother could let you go."

"It was a sacrifice for your own good, perhaps," said Poirot.

Her clear eyes met his.

"I don't think that's ever true. It's the way they put it to themselves. But what it boils down to is that they can, really, get on without you ... And it hurts."

Many of Agatha Christie's wartime and post-war books cast a flickering background reflection on the times. The National Health Service, guaranteeing free healthcare for all, had come into being in 1948:

"Nowadays, even if you've got a chilblain you run to the doctor with it so as to get your money's worth out of the National Health. Too much of this health business we've got. Never did you any good thinking how bad you feel."

"I expect you're right," said Mrs Oliver.

The Education Act of 1944 had raised the school leaving age to 15 and guaranteed free education for all:

"Girls aren't trained nowadays, they're just educated, like Edna."

Both women looked at Edna, who leant against the post office counter, sucking a peppermint, and looking particularly vacant. As an example of education, she hardly did the education system credit.

Finally, here is Poirot showing a sense of humour as he gently mocks his tendency to indulge in *franglais* when trying to put people off their guard:

"For somewhere," said Poirot to himself, indulging in an absolute riot of mixed metaphors, "there is in the hay a needle, and among the sleeping dogs there is one on whom I shall put my foot, and by shooting the arrows into the air, one will come down and hit a glasshouse!"

SWIGATHA RATING 7/10

The clues are all there, meticulously and fairly laid.

WHERE IT LED

Ariadne Oliver, a self-penned pastiche of the author, having lain dormant for 16 years, returns in four of the following eight Poirot novels. The happy / unhappy childhood theme recurs in *A Pocket Full of Rye*, published the following year.

ADAPTATIONS

The story was adapted for ITV's *Poirot* series. It is reasonably faithful to the original, although it removes the Wetherbys, amalgamating them with other characters. Unfortunately, the humour of the original is missing: Poirot's tribulations in the Summerhayes' house and his affection for his landlady are beautifully written, but not represented on screen. On the other hand, the murderer's breakdown at the end is surprisingly moving.

They do it with Mirrors (1952)

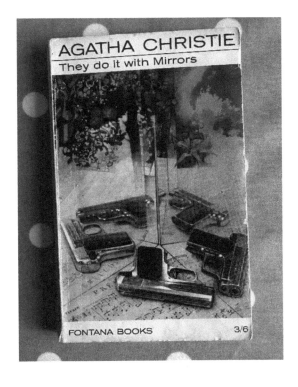 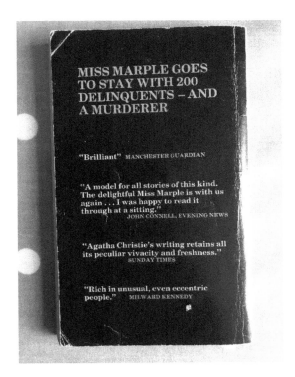

THE BOOK   Fontana, 1967 pp 188

Although there are no actual mirrors involved in the plot, Tom Adams cover is a clever one that suggests the piano that was being played while the guns were going off, and a hint of the importance of what was outside.

THE STORY

The sisters Ruth van Rydock and Carrie Louise Serrocold are very old friends of Jane Marple. Carrie Louise lives at Stonygates, a charitable young offenders' institution run by her latest husband, Lewis, and financed by the Gulbrandsen Trust that had been established by her first.

Ruth is convinced that there is something seriously wrong going on there and is worried for her sister's safety. She cannot put her finger on where the danger lies, and urges Miss Marple to go down and investigate.

While she is there, Carrie Louise's stepson, Christian Gulbrandsen, arrives unexpectedly to see Lewis on Trust business. The following day he is shot dead.

CHARACTERS

Stonygates is inhabited by 250 juvenile delinquents, plus a host of members or adopted members of Carrie Louise's somewhat chaotic family, including Walter and Gina Hudd, the Restarick brothers and Mildred Strete. There is also the splendidly-named juvenile psychologist Dr Maverick.

Walter Hudd is an American ex-serviceman, and it is noticeable that he is treated more sympathetically than Americans in previous swigathas. This may be because Agatha Christie's house, Greenway, had been requisitioned for use by the US Navy during World War II, and she was very impressed by the people who used it[1].

The two most interesting characters are Carrie Louise and her husband Lewis.

Lewis is a visionary, genuinely in love with his wife, who wants to do anything he can to give young offenders a new start in life. Apart from his wife, no-one in his extended family really believes in what he is trying to do. It emerges that his eventual plan is a somewhat fantastic one - raising enough money to set up an island colony where errant juveniles can be transported to establish and create a society of their own[2].

Carrie Louise is a very unusual character for these stories. She is seen by everyone (including Miss Marple) as someone with her head in the clouds, unaware of what is really going on, someone to be protected from the wickedness of the world. In reality, she has a very good idea of what is actually happening, and is oblivious to the conjuring tricks being perpetrated on everyone else. It is only when Miss Marple considers Carrie Louise's opinions seriously that she stumbles on the truth.

Everyone (bar Carrie Louise herself) is convinced that someone is trying to poison her. In most Agatha Christie books, it is a golden rule that characters who seem to keep having narrow escapes from death usually turn out to be the killer; not in her case.

QUOTES

Walter Hudd, US serviceman left over from the war, feels out of place and confides in Miss Marple:

> *"They're rich, these people. They don't need dough - they've got it.... They're rolling in dough." He paused and sat, deliberating. "I understand being poor. There's nothing much wrong with it, if you're young and strong and ready to work. I never had much money, but I was all set to get where I wanted. I was going to open a garage ... I talked to Gina about it. She listened. She seemed to understand. I didn't know much about her. All those girls in*

uniform, they look about the same. I mean, you can't tell from looking at them who's got dough and who hasn't."

Carrie Louise discusses her only child with her friend – definitely one for nature, not nurture:

"Perhaps," suggested Miss Marple, "Mildred had cause not to be happy?"
Carrie Louise said quietly:
"Because of being jealous? Yes, I daresay. But people don't really need a cause for feeling what they do feel. They're just made that way. Don't you think so, Jane?"

Lewis Serrocold disapproves of Walter Hudd; Miss Marple's reply is priceless (the author speaks?):

"He hasn't fitted in here - no. He's no interest or sympathy for what we're trying to do. But, after all, why should he? He's young, crude, and he comes from a country where a man is esteemed by the success he makes of life."
"Whilst here we are so very fond of failures," said Miss Marple.
Lewis Serrocold looked at her sharply and suspiciously.
"Foreigners can never understand why we're so proud of Dunkirk. It's the sort of thing they'd prefer not to mention themselves. But we always seem to be almost embarrassed by a victory - and treat it as though it weren't quite nice to boast about it. And look at all our poets! The Charge of the Light Brigade, *and the little* Revenge *went down in the Spanish Main. It's really a very odd characteristic when you come to think of it!"*
Miss Marple drew a fresh breath.
"What I really mean is that everything here must seem rather peculiar to Walter Hudd."

SWIGATHA RATING 6/10

This is a pretty average Christie, with rather more of her views about heredity intruding than is to my personal taste. The identity of the killer is pretty obvious if you read the pages dealing with the murder closely, and it does to a degree follow the golden rule!

WHAT HAPPENED NEXT

1952 was a busy year for Agatha Christie - apart from *They do it with Mirrors* and *Mrs McGinty's Dead*, it also saw the publication of one of her Mary Westmacott novels and the completion of the stage-play *The Mousetrap*. Maybe it was too busy - the attraction of writing plays for the theatre was such that, after 1953, she restricted herself to one crime novel per year for the rest of her career.

Thus, while the decade saw the appearance of 12 crime novels, she also completed no fewer than 9 stage plays and a radio play - some going for a woman in her 60s.

ADAPTATIONS

There have been 3 adaptations so far - one for American TV in the 80s, one for BBC in 1991 and one for ITV in 2009.

The BBC 'Hickson Marples' version struggles heroically with the holes in the plot (apart from the actual murder, nothing much happens for most of the book). Big names (Joss Ackland and Jean Simmons) take on the roles of the Serrocolds, and a greater emphasis is placed on the Hudds' relationship.

As ever, Joan Hickson shines throughout; it was to be her last performance as Miss Marple (well, she was 85!). All the Marple novels had by then been covered, and as for the short stories, she had read them as talking books.

NOTES

[1] Agatha Christie, *An Autobiography*:

> *I cannot speak too highly of the Americans, and the care they took of our house ... Ever since the war, relations of some officer or other who was at Greenway have come along to see where their son or cousin or whoever was stationed.*

[2] This fantastical idea echoes a passage, also from Agatha Christie's Autobiography, in which she considers what to do with the wicked:

> *The best answer we ever found, I suspect, was transportation. A vast land of emptiness, peopled only with primitive human beings, where man could live in simpler surroundings.*

A Pocket Full of Rye (1953)

 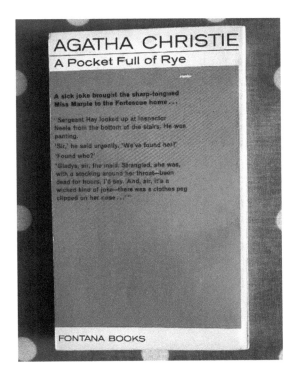

THE BOOK Fontana, 1968 pp 191

This is a typical Tom Adams cover of the earlier, sparer type, featuring a decomposing blackbird lying on the sheet music to *Sing a Song of Sixpence*[1]. The yew berries are used to create taxine, the poison used to kill 'the king'.

It is easy to take Tom Adams for granted, but his 1960s Fontana covers are the most distinctive paperback covers ever produced, anywhere, and they have not been bettered before or since.

The back covers are pretty good too, guaranteed to give any eleven-year-old pause. This is a classic example.

THE STORY

Rex Fortescue and a man named MacKenzie discover a potential goldmine in East Africa - the Blackbird mine. When Rex later returns to England, he announces that the mine is worthless, and that MacKenzie had died in Africa, having contracted a tropical disease.

Twenty years later, the by-now rich businessman Fortescue's peace of mind is disturbed by the repeated appearance of dead blackbirds around his house, Yewtree Lodge. Soon afterwards, he dies in his office, from a poison that had been administered to his breakfast. Some rye is discovered in his jacket pocket.

Within a day, there are two further deaths at Yewtree House - those of Adele, Rex's wife, poisoned whilst taking tea, and Gladys, the parlourmaid, strangled in the garden. A clothes peg is found clipped on to Gladys' nose. Gladys had been an orphan, trained in domestic service by Miss Jane Marple. When Miss Marple hears of her death, she travels to Yewtree Lodge to see if there is anything she can do about it ...

CHARACTERS

Yewtree Lodge is described by its housekeeper Mary Dove as a house without scruples; all the inhabitants are 'really quite odious'.

The Fortescue family are a typical group of Christie grotesques - the unscrupulous swindler Rex; his much younger, gold-digging second wife Adele; the sly goody-goody son Percival and his unhappy wife Jennifer; the ne'er-do-well son Lancelot and the defiant daughter Elaine. Making up this unhappy tribe is Rex's first wife's sister, a slightly demented old lady who never leaves her attic rooms but knows everything that is going on (and disapproves of all of it), and the two spineless suitors of Adele and Elaine (Vivien Dubois and Gerald Wright).

What is interesting about this story is that the person right at the heart of it is the parlourmaid Gladys. Servants are rarely important figures in Agatha Christie, still less suspects, but this somewhat gormless, adenoidal, unattractive girl provides the clue to the whole mystery. At the end, her story brings tears to Miss Marple's eyes (another extremely rare occurrence).

The greyness and snobbery of post-war austerity Britain is very much to the fore, and when Rex is taken ill there is an interesting sideline about how to access the new National Health Service (introduced five years before).

A NOTE ON THE NAMES

Rex's first wife had been a long-term (self-proclaimed) invalid with an obsession about Tennyson's poem *The Idylls of the King*. She had named her sons Percival and Lancelot after two of the most prominent knights of King Arthur's Round Table, and (strangely) her daughter after Elaine of Astolat, the un-requited lover of Lancelot.

Agatha Christie doesn't stop there - Percival is married to Jennifer (a modern form of Guinevere), and Vivien is the name of a character who betrays Guinevere. Her memory of Tennyson's poetry is reflected in a few of her later works[2].

ATTITUDES AND QUOTES

Rex Fortescue's office debates how to summon an ambulance for him under the new-fangled National Health Service system:

> *"It has to be the right hospital", Miss Somers insisted, "or else they won't come. Because of the National Health. I mean. It's got to be in the area."*
>
> *Someone suggested 999 but Miss Griffith was shocked at that and said it would mean the police and that would never do. For citizens of a country which enjoyed the benefits of Medical Service for all, a group of quite reasonably intelligent women showed incredible ignorance of correct procedure. Miss Bell started looking up ambulances under A ...*

The office staff relate to the police that Mr Fortescue had been behaving strangely:

> *"Most unlike his usual manner. Why, when the office boy had to go to his grandmother's funeral, Mr Fortescue called him in and gave him a five pound note, told him to put it on the second favourite and then roared with laughter."*

This is most unlike Agatha Christie's 'usual manner' too - an actual joke!

Miss Marple discusses the orphan Gladys:

> *"She was very keen on men, poor girl. But men didn't take much notice of her and other girls rather made use of her."*
>
> *"It sounds rather cruel," said Pat.*
>
> *"Yes, my dear," said Miss Marple, "life is cruel, I'm afraid."*

Miss Marple could not have cared less about the dead Rex and Adele Fortescue, but is absolutely determined to get justice for Gladys.

While many of her characters seem to come from central casting, Agatha Christie could write some splendid dialogue for them. Here is an extract from a quite insightful dialogue between Inspector Neele and the seemingly half-witted Mrs MacKenzie at a private sanatorium:

213

"Nobody knows where my husband died," said Mrs MacKenzie. "Nobody knows how he died or where he was buried ... All anyone knows is what Rex Fortescue said. And Rex Fortescue was a liar!"

"Do you think there may have been foul play?"

"Foul play, foul play, fowls lay eggs, don't they?"

"You think that Rex Fortescue was responsible for your husband's death?"

"I had an egg for breakfast this morning," said Mrs MacKenzie. "Quite fresh, too. Surprising, isn't it, when one thinks that it was thirty years ago?"

A foreign student of the history of social attitudes in (some parts of) England between 1920 and 1970 could do worse than starting with Agatha Christie's books. Here, Miss Marple finds a village parallel for Jennifer Fortescue in Mrs Emmett, the bank manager's wife:

She did not belong to the old guard of ladies in reduced circumstances who lived in neat houses round the church ... Mr Emmett, the bank manager, had undeniably married beneath him and the result was that his wife was in a position of great loneliness since she could not, of course, associate with the wives of trades people. Snobbery here raised its hideous head and marooned Mrs Emmett on a permanent island of loneliness.

A happy childhood was hugely important as far as Agatha Christie was concerned[3]. Here is Pat talking about hers:

"I had a lovely childhood in Ireland, riding, hunting and a great big, bare draughty house with lots and lots of sun in it. If you've had a happy childhood, nobody can take that away from you, can they?"

By contrast, the other members of the household had terribly unhappy childhoods[4]. Pat is about to face trials of her own, but Miss Marple knows that the resilience built into her by childhood experience would enable her to come through them.

The returning colonial Lance Fortescue rails against the Mother Country, as exemplified by his brother[5]:

"I'm sick of this country, and of the City. I'm sick of little men like you with their pin-stripe trousers and their black coats and their mincing voices and their mean, shoddy financial deals."

His wife Pat, however, gets to see another side of it as she sits with Miss Marple:

214

"With the fire and the lamps and you knitting things for babies... It all seems cosy and homely and how England should be." "It's like England is," said Miss Marple. "There are not so many Yewtree Lodges, my dear."

SWIGATHA RATING 7/10

An enjoyable romp - but it feels a bit churned out: the nursery rhyme series was beginning to pall, and we seem to have met many of the characters before. Still, the story offers some interest for those studying Britain around the time of the Coronation of its Queen, Elizabeth II, who is still on the throne as this is being written.

Miss Marple puts in a memorable, if extremely brief appearance; the scenes featuring her are wonderful. The suspects are uniformly dislikeable, so all the reader's sympathies are with Gladys (as they were meant to be). This was one of my most cherished swigathas when I was a boy, but one could not claim it as one of her very best.

There is also the first sign of decline. A scene between the Inspector and Lance (Chapter XXIII, scene II) seems to have been randomly inserted and is never followed up.

WHAT HAPPENED NEXT

1953 was the last year for which Agatha Christie produced more than one crime novel. She had become increasingly interested in writing for the stage following the successes of *Witness for the Prosecution* and *The Mousetrap*. She also turned increasingly to Miss Marple for her detective fiction: after just six appearances in the first 54 titles, Jane made a further six in the next 18.

ADAPTATIONS

There have been three - one for the BBC in 1984, one for ITV in 2009, and one for Russian TV, entitled 'The Secret of the Blackbirds'; *Sing a Song of Sixpence* is not a Russian rhyme, so heaven knows what Russian readers and viewers make of the plot. The BBC's 'Hickson Marple' is excellent: it has a very strong cast, including Timothy West as Rex and Tom Wilkinson as Inspector Neele, and a particularly moving performance by Annette Badland as Gladys.

NOTES

[1] The first three lines of this nursery rhyme provided Agatha Christie with three titles – see the Appendix chapter *Title Quotes*.

[2] For example, *The Hollow, Taken at the Flood, The Mirror Crack'd from Side to Side, While the Light Lasts*

[3] Agatha Christie, *An Autobiography*, opening line:

> *One of the luckiest things that can happen to you in life is to have a happy childhood. I had a very happy childhood.*

[4] See Appendix B: *Old Sins Have Long Shadows: Childhood and a Pocket Full of Rye*

[5] Other returning colonials who are similarly unimpressed include Anthony Cade in *The Secret of Chimneys*, Luke Fitzwilliam in *Murder is Easy*, Stephen Farr in *Hercule Poirot's Christmas* ...

After the Funeral (1953)

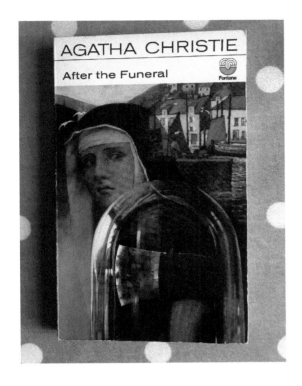

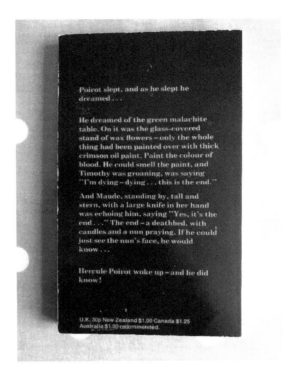

THE BOOK Fontana, 1971 pp 192

Tom Adams' cover features basic elements of the plot, including the murder weapon, the painting of the harbour and a particularly haunting image of an apprehensive nun. The blurb on the back is very enticing …

The novel was dedicated to 'James, in memory of happy days at Abney'[1].

THE STORY

The Abernethie family is gathered at Enderby Hall for the funeral of its patriarch Richard. After the ceremony is complete, and they are having lunch, one of their number proclaims that Richard had been murdered, and that everyone was well aware of the fact. The family's lawyer, Entwistle, there to read Richard's will, is perturbed; he becomes even more so when he hears later that the speaker has been axed to death.

He calls on Hercule Poirot to help; Poirot agrees, and, in the guise of 'M. Pontarlier', a representative of a fictional refugee organisation interested in buying Enderby, goes undercover to investigate.

CHARACTERS AND ATTITUDES

The story is (once again) very recognisably set in the post-war years of rationing, refugees and resentment. Some of the resentment is directed at the Education Acts of the previous decade, which, by making free education (and school meals) available to all, whilst raising both the minimum working age and school-leaving age, meant that the availability of cheap young labour to train in service and elsewhere was greatly compromised.

Another feature of the post-war era in the UK often referred to in this book is its lawlessness, which is also mentioned in a few other swigathas of the time.

The plot is dominated by members of the Abernethie family, a curious one in which female distaff members are addressed by the names of their husbands: so Helen is 'Mrs Leo', even though Leo is long dead, and Maude is 'Mrs Timothy'.

The younger generation of this family is not interested in keeping Enderby Hall going, even if there had been the servants around to look after it for them. Apart from Timothy, the only surviving one of Richard's eight children is Cora, widow of a French painter and something of a wild child, treated by the rest of the family with some bewilderment. In fact, she seems to be about the only one to have had any character at all.

Replacing the servant in Cora Lansquenet's house, and eventually in Timothy Abernethie's, is 'hired help' Miss Gilchrist, down on her luck after the failure of a tea-shop and dreaming of opening a new one.

Poirot's 'hired help', on the other hand, is the estimable Mr Goby, one of Agatha Christie's finest comic creations.

QUOTES

The grimness of post-war austerity is present throughout the book. The author was fond of her food, and clearly nostalgic here for the days before post-war rationing (and the lack of servants):

> *The large kitchen range of the days of Victorian grandeur stood cold and unused, like an altar to the past.*

Here's the cook Marjorie on the realities of post-war Britain:

"It was the night I made that chocolate soufflé that Mr Abernethie died. Six eggs I'd saved up for it. The dairyman he's a friend of mine. Got hold of some cream, too. Better not ask how."

Things were also hard for single independent women that ran tea-shops. Miss Gilchrist laments the collapse of her tea-shop which condemned her to a life of drudgery (and invisibility):

"Yes, I was doing really well and then the war came and supplies were cut down and I went bankrupt."

Her bitterness shines through:

"I ought to have seen it sooner – I felt in a vague kind of way I had seen you before somewhere – but of course one never looks much at – "
"No, one doesn't bother to look at a mere companion-help," said Miss Gilchrist. Her voice shook a little. "A drudge, a domestic drudge! Almost a servant!"

Inspector Morton's immediate reaction when he finds Cora beaten to death with a hatchet reveals something about the time that seems to have been forgotten since:

"Looks as though it's some chap with a screw loose - one of those adolescent criminals, perhaps - a lot of them about."

We are accustomed in the UK today to hear of the 'great generation' of WWII 'heroes' that gradually came home after 1945[2]. Agatha Christie's books of the time reflect a different perception. In *A Murder is Announced* (1950) there is talk of 'deserters roaming the countryside causing mayhem'; three years later, things don't seem to have improved. Here is Timothy Abernethie's judgment on some members of the 'great generation':

"The country's full of gangsters nowadays - thugs - left over from the war! Going about killing defenceless women."

At least he didn't blame the refugees:

Rosamund, however, had only said vaguely, "Oh! refugees all over again. I'm so tired of refugees." Thus voicing the unspoken reaction of many, who were usually too conventional to express themselves so frankly.

Ex-refugee Hercule Poirot's hired help, Mr Goby, considers the ramifications of the 1944 Education Act:

He shook his head sadly and shifted his gaze to an electric plug socket.

"It's the Government," he told it. "And all this education racket. It gives them ideas. They come back and tell us what they think. They can't think, most of them, anyway. All they know is things out of books."

And here's another great one-liner from him:

"Mr Abernethie enjoys ill-health and the emphasis is on the enjoyment."

SWIGATHA RATING 8/10

This book has a lot going for it. There is humour and pathos, and it is a hugely evocative reflection of its era; the book is definitely written in greyscale. Its basic plot had been used at least twice before, in short stories, but the motivation is very believable. One gets the feeling that this was an easy book for the author to write, possibly because of where she was when most of it was written[1].

WHERE IT LED

This is one of the last of the swigathas that deals with big country houses, old families, and faithful retainers. By the time that Poirot is next summoned to one (Nasse House, in *Dead Man's Folly*) the owner has seemingly sold up and retired to live in the entrance lodge.

The lawyer Entwistle, for reasons unknown, had changed his name to Endicott by the time Poirot is consulting him in a later novel (*Hickory Dickory Dock*).

ADAPTATIONS

There is a well-known MGM adaptation, *Murder at the Gallop*, which runs riot with the plot and replaces Poirot with Margaret Rutherford's Miss Marple (I would have kept to the original plot and cast Ms Rutherford in the role of Miss Gilchrist).

The Suchet *Poirot* version also takes quite a few unwarranted liberties with the plot. It is unable to evoke any of the atmosphere of the book, because, like the rest of the series, the adaptation is forcibly set in 1936. It does, however, boast a truly excellent performance by Monica Dolan, playing Miss Gilchrist.

Like all the rest, it chose to dispense with the character of Mr Goby. *Ca va sans dire!*

NOTES

[1] Agatha Christie's older sister, Madge, was married to James Watts, whose father (Sir James) built Abney Hall in Cheshire, later inherited by his son. AC visited it very many times, and it inspired many of the country houses in her stories. Much of *After the Funeral* was written there. Her nephew was also named James, but I think this story was dedicated to his father, who died in 1957. Maybe the name Abney was on her mind when she named the family who dominate the story.

Destination Unknown (1954)

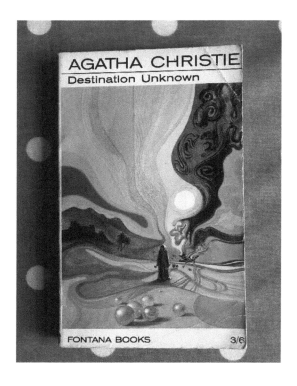

THE BOOK Fontana, 1967 pp 191

The Tom Adams cover from the 1960s was clearly influenced by the pop art of the time, and has the look of a psychedelic album cover. The images of the faked plane crash, a leper and broken necklace are all relevant to the story.

THE STORY

A glut of brilliant young research scientists has been disappearing without a trace, and British Intelligence suspects a conspiracy of the 'take-over-the-world' variety. They are on the trail of one scientist in particular, Thomas Betterton, and suspect that his wife Olive had been on her way to join him when her plane crashed *en route* to Casablanca.

Hilary Craven is intending to commit suicide - her own 'destination unknown'. She had been scheduled to be on the same flight as Olive Betterton and is somewhat rueful when she finds out what has happened. She determines to overdose on sleeping pills, but is prevented from doing so by the British agent Jessop, who persuades her that there are more interesting ways of killing oneself: one is to travel to Casablanca, posing as Olive Betterton, in an attempt to be taken to the enclave of scientists that is at the heart of the conspiracy. Jessop provides her with the means to advertise the route she has travelled, but by the time she meets her 'husband', she will be on her own ...

CHARACTERS

Many of the characters in this story are re-hashes of characters from *They Came to Baghdad*. Indeed, one could say that the story itself is:

> - a young woman with nothing to lose (Hilary Craven / Victoria Jones) is persuaded to impersonate someone else with whom they share a startling similarity (Olive Betterton / Anna Scheele);
> - she travels to the Middle East;
> - during her passage she is accompanied by a middle-aged American woman with a double barrelled name (Mrs Calvin Baker / Mrs Hamilton Clipp) who is not what she seems;
> - her activities are monitored by an officer from British Intelligence (Jessop / Dakin), who is on the trail of a mysterious cabal aimed at world domination that involves the disappearance of a group of brilliant young scientists ...

... and so on.

The character of Hilary Craven carries the whole book - if she were to be taken out of it there would be little point in reading it. The character of Hilary Craven also bears certain traits of her creator.

ATTITUDES AND QUOTES

The supposed sanctity of human life is not much to the fore in this book. Maybe for an author who had experienced the horrors of two world wars and a horrific pandemic in between them this is not surprising.

Hilary Craven's reasons for desiring oblivion are convincingly portrayed, possibly in part informed by the author's own experience:[1]

> *One could bear things, Hilary thought, as long as there was a reason for bearing them. She had borne her own long illness, she had borne Nigel's defection and the cruel and brutal circumstances in which it had operated. She had borne these things because there was Brenda. Then had come the long, slow losing fight for Brenda's life - the final defeat... Now there was nothing to live for any longer.*

She prepares to commit suicide:

She was once again a traveller as she had been at Heath Row, a traveller waiting to depart for an unknown destination, unencumbered by baggage, unaffected by farewells. For the first time in her life she was free, entirely free, to act as she wished to act ... Yes, light, free, unencumbered! Ready to start on her journey.

Jessop sweet-talks Hilary away from suicide and into a suicide mission:

She was thoughtful. "To you, I suppose I was just ..."
He finished the sentence for her. "A woman with a noticeable head of red hair and who hadn't the pluck to go on living."
She flushed. "That's a harsh judgement."
"It's a true one, isn't it? I don't go in for being sorry for people. For one thing, it's insulting. One is only sorry for people when they're sorry for themselves. Self-pity is one of the biggest stumbling-blocks in the world today."

Hilary is enchanted by Fez. The quote at the start is taken from the *Song of Solomon*:

'As a garden enclosed is my sister, my spouse....' This was what a garden was meant to be - a place of green and gold, shut away from the real world.

Hilary is almost persuaded by Dr Barron's dream of loosing a chemical plague across the globe just to see what happens: [2]

"It would be amazingly interesting to see the exact course, the exact progress." And he added with a deep half-sigh: "You see, there's so much more to know, so much more to find out." For a moment Hilary understood. For a moment she stood where he stood, impregnated with that single-hearted desire for knowledge which swept aside life and death for millions of human beings as essentially unimportant.

SWIGATHA RATING 5/10

As with a few of Agatha Christie's later books this one has a cracking premise at the start - a suicidal woman being offered a suicide mission - but it starts to drag once she has embarked on it. The writing flows, but there are a few tedious passages of travel and not many characters of interest, apart from the heroine. There are also too many echoes of *They Came to Baghdad*, published only three years before; this could easily have been titled *They Came to Somewhere Else*.

As ever with Agatha Christie, the North African countryside and the Arabs inhabiting it are drawn with knowledge and affection, but the mystery element of this book (the murder of a scientist in the US) is introduced at the end almost as an afterthought.

WHERE IT LED

There was a merciful hiatus in Agatha Christie's series of world-domination conspiracy novels until 1970 when the infinitely worse *Passenger to Frankfurt* emerged.

ADAPTATIONS

There have been none so far. Oddly enough, I think this book would work quite well on TV, with good character actors to flesh out the main and minor parts, as long as they keep the locations and time the same. It could be part of a World Domination trilogy, preceded by *They Came to Baghdad* and followed by *Passenger to Frankfurt*. Some of the best Christie adaptations have been of her less exalted works.

NOTES

[1] The 'brutal circumstances' of her own first husband's defection included the aftermath of the death of Agatha Christie's mother.

[2] Should Hilary still be alive today (in 2021) she would be able to track a plague of truly global proportions, thereby satisfying her 'single-hearted desire for knowledge'.

Hickory Dickory Dock (1955)

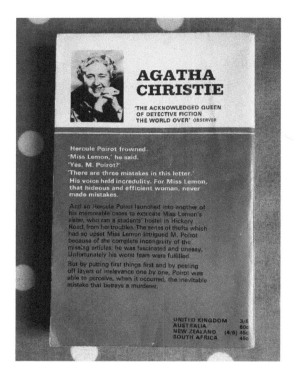

THE BOOK   PAN 1968   pp 189

PAN's cover is fairly straightforward: a clock. Which has absolutely nothing to do with the story.

The title of this book is possibly the most contrived yet - solely related to the name of the street in which a student hostel stands.

THE STORY

When Hercule Poirot finds three mistakes in a letter typed by his secretary, Miss Lemon, he is incredulous. For Miss Lemon had never before made a mistake. She has been distracted by worry for her sister, Mrs Hubbard, the manager of a student hostel which has experienced a series of petty thefts. Mrs Hubbard cannot make sense of the random collection of items taken and, in certain cases, destroyed.

Poirot agrees to visit the house on the pretext of giving a talk, and soon realises that Miss Lemon's sister is right to be concerned ...

CHARACTERS

This book has characters from many lands:

- A somewhat nasty-minded pair of French students, Genevieve and René

- An alcoholic Cypriot landlady, Mrs Nicoletis

- Italian staff Geronimo and Maria, dismissed as 'liars and thieves' by their employer

- Indian Chandra Lal, a medical student 'preoccupied with politics and persecution mania'

- West Indian Elizabeth Johnson, with 'the best brains in the hostel'

- Two Turks who cannot understand a word and keep disappearing

- The nervous American, Sally Finch

- The African Akibombo, genial but with appalling English

- A 'charming young Iraqi' (no surprises there!), an aggressive Egyptian, a stolid Dutchman...

On and on it goes, a bit like an episode of *Mind Your Language*[1]. The characters of the British inhabitants are not drawn in much greater depth, and one element of their interaction - that one of them persuades another to steal at random to draw the attention of the psychology student she loves - is somewhat unlikely.

The most realistic characters in this book are the 'hideous' Miss Lemon and her feet-on-the-ground sister.

ATTITUDES AND QUOTES

Poirot considers his confidential secretary, probably for the first time.

> *His voice held incredulity. For Miss Lemon, that hideous and efficient woman, never made mistakes.*

Poirot had never conceived of Miss Lemon having a sister. Or, for that matter, having a father, mother or even grandparents. Poirot is forced to concede that Miss Lemon is human. Later she considers the impact of what we would nowadays call the Windrush[2] generation:

> *"Half the nurses in our hospitals seem to be black nowadays,"* said Miss Lemon doubtfully, *"and I understand much pleasanter and more attentive than our English ones."*

Some of the language used by the characters would be deemed racist now. Jean Tomlinson explains why she thinks that Akibombo spoilt Miss Johnson's course-work:

"All these coloured people are very jealous of each other and very hysterical."

Elizabeth Johnson considers Sally Finch:

"They are all the same, these Americans, nervous, apprehensive, suspecting every kind of foolish thing! Look at the fools they make of themselves with their witch-hunts, their hysterical spy mania, their obsession over Communism."

This book was written at the time of the McCarthy witch-hunt of those suspected of 'un-American activities'.

Mrs Nicoletis' unique brand of man-management is to the fore as she upbraids the Italian kitchen staff:

"Liars and thieves," said Mrs Nicoletis, in a loud and triumphant voice. "All Italians are liars and thieves!"

SWIGATHA RATING 4/10

Evelyn Waugh's diary for July 18, 1955 contains an entry that begins:

The joys and sorrows of a simple life. Joys: A new Agatha Christie which began well ... Sorrows: The deterioration of Mrs Christie's novel a third of the way through into twaddle. [3]

Waugh was always a harsh critic, but many people might concur with his assessment. Robert Barnard considered it, if anything, an understatement.[4] As Waugh suggests, this book is typical of a few of the later swigathas, in that it begins with a great idea and then peters out.

There are some old Christie tricks in it - a letter from a dead person artfully used as a suicide note, the interrupted phone call - and the revelation comes as no real surprise at all. 'Foreigners' are never the culprits in her stories, so most of the suspects can be wiped off the list straightaway.

It gets a '4' solely because I remember enjoying it when I was 11. The re-read was another matter.

WHERE IT LED

This book heralds the start of a slow decline in the quality of the author's work (in my opinion, obviously). The next few books would wipe the floor with most of the opposition for readability and sales but, with a couple of notable exceptions, would not deserve to be mentioned in the same breath as her own classics.

228

ADAPTATIONS

The episode made by ITV's Poirot series is the only adaptation I have seen. It had a strong cast, including Damien Lewis as Len Bateson, and a strong writer in Anthony Horowitz, but it excluded all the foreign students, so it was even blander than the book.

NOTES

[1] An appalling UK sitcom from the 1970s that cast every racial stereotype it could.

[2] Named after the ship that brought the first wave of West Indian immigrants to Britain in response to an appeal made by the British Government. Following the devastation of WWII there was a serious shortage of manpower, in particular in factories and the recently-established National Health Service.

[3] *The Diaries of Evelyn Waugh*, ed Michael Davie

[4] Robert Barnard, *A Talent to Deceive*

Dead Man's Folly (1956)

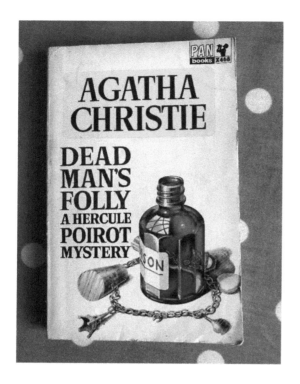

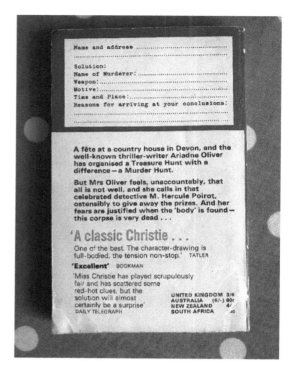

THE BOOK   PAN, 1968 pp 190

PAN's front cover is not especially inspired (although the blurb on the back is very enticing to a bookshop browser). This was the first swigatha that I ever bought which wasn't a second-hand copy (it came, commendably, from the school shop).

THE STORY

Hercule Poirot is invited by Ariadne Oliver, the well-known crime fiction writer, to hand out the prizes at a Murder Hunt that she is organising for a fête at Nasse House, in Devon.

He never gets to do so; Mrs Oliver's fabled female intuition had persuaded her that something was 'not quite right' at Nasse, and her fears prove to be justified when a 14-year-old girl guide is found strangled in its grounds.

CHARACTERS AND ATTITUDES

Agatha Christie might not have recognised herself as a feminist, but she was certainly a strong-willed, independent woman and her opinions of certain types of English male can be detected in many of her novels.

In this one, all the male characters (apart from Poirot and the gardener Merdell) are unsympathetically drawn: 'Sir' George Stubbs, 'Captain' Warburton, the eugenicist Alec Legge, the moaning Michael Weyman, the hen-pecked local MP Masterton, the chauvinistic de Sousa - even the two investigating police officers.

All the strong or sympathetic characters are female.

The main character in the book, however, is Nasse House itself and its grounds, which very obviously are based on Greenway, Agatha Christie's Devonshire home, and its surroundings. She even adds the Youth Hostel that used to neighbour Greenway into the plot.

The one locational element that she invents is the eponymous, out-of-place Folly. Whether sub-consciously or not, she also chooses the name Folliat for the family that had originally owned Nasse. Mrs Folliat has apparently sold it to Sir George Stubbs, but lives in its grounds, and acts for all the world as if she were still its châtelaine in the way she greets the locals arriving for the fête; unlike the Folly, Mrs Folliat is definitely in the right place.

This story could be seen as a lament for the fate of old families, forced to sell their ancestral homes to coarse businessmen made good. But, of course, being a swigatha, it isn't quite as simple as that.

People are not quite who they seem to be, which was a constant motif in Agatha Christie's books at the time: *how can we know, these days, that people are who they claim to be?*[1]

The two that we *can* trust are Mrs Oliver and Poirot, the author's main mouthpieces in this story.

QUOTES

Mrs Folliat laments the dearth of servants to order about:

> *"Life isn't like that in England these days. I wish it were." She sighed. "Nowadays one has to do nearly everything oneself."*

Captain Warburton discusses his hostess:

> *"But I believe she comes from the West Indies ... One of the old families there - a creole, I don't mean a half-caste. All very inter-married, I believe, on these islands. Accounts for the mental deficiency."*

The author speaks, via Hercule Poirot (as she often did):

"In the late war, during a severe air-raid, I was much less pre-occupied by the thought of death than of the pain from a corn on my little toe."

Here, Poirot responds with a brilliant put-down to someone possibly unaware of his own feeble-mindedness:

Alec Legge remained serious. "I should like to see every feeble-minded person put out - right out! Don't let them breed. If, for one generation, only the intelligent were allowed to breed, think what the result would be."

"A very large increase of patients in the psychiatric wards, perhaps," said Poirot dryly.

Sir George Stubbs is not what he claims to be:

"He isn't really Sir George - was christened it, I believe."

Jim Warburton is not what he claims to be:

"Silly the way he calls himself Captain. Not a regular soldier and never within miles of a German."

Etienne de Sousa's male chauvinism is at least at odds with Alec Legge's ideals.

"At fifteen Hattie was mentally undeveloped. Feeble-minded, do you not call it? She is still the same?"

"It would seem so - yes," said Poirot cautiously.

De Sousa shrugged his shoulders. "Ah, well! Why should one ask it of women - that they should be intelligent? It is not necessary."

The Devon Police approach to investigation takes its lead from the likes of de Sousa:

"Women," said the Inspector sententiously, "tell a lot of lies. Always remember that, Hoskins."

"Aah," said Constable Hoskins appreciatively.

And men don't ... well, they sure do in this book. Finally, Poirot and Mrs Folliat discuss 14-year-old Marlene Tucker's death:

"We old folks expect to die, but that child had her life before her."

"It might not have been a very interesting life."

"Not from our point of view, perhaps, but it might have been interesting to her."

SWIGATHA RATING 5/10

The story begins with the murder of Marlene Tucker, and it must be counted as somewhat unusual (for a whodunit) that, although we know what they *called* themself, we never find out the *actual* name of Marlene's killer. It is even more of an oversight when one considers that the Murder Hunt entries have 'Name of Murderer' on them, as shown by the above cover.

The three main clues are fairly, and cleverly, placed in the mouths of two people whom most people in the story would tend not to believe, but I think the book itself was put together hurriedly; maybe it was the work of a tired writer – she had so much else going on at the time.

WHAT HAPPENED NEXT

This story was based on a novella (*Greenshore's Folly*) that Agatha Christie had previously written to raise funds for a stained-glass window for her local church in Churston. That novella, incredibly, was rejected on the grounds of size, so she wrote a totally different Miss Marple short story for them instead called, confusingly, *Greenshaw's Folly*: maybe she was determined to get her tribute to Greenway House published somehow. Anyway, it did get published, and was included in the collection 'The Adventure of the Christmas Pudding'. The original *Greenshore's Folly* was finally published by Agatha Christie Ltd in 2014.

ADAPTATIONS

ITV's *Poirot* made a very decent fist of an average story. It was well-cast, and this adaptation played it very straight with the plot. The star of the cast played Nasse House - they were allowed to use Greenway itself, and it is perfect for it. This was the last Poirot episode to be made by ITV; they certainly went out on a high. Peter Ustinov also did one of his 1980s Poirot turns for US TV.

NOTES

[1] More examples of this can be found in *Taken at the Flood* (1948), *A Murder is Announced* (1950), *Mrs McGinty's Dead* (1952), *After the Funeral* (1953) and *Hickory Dickory Dock* (1955). The Second World War and its aftermath had hugely disrupted old societal certainties.

4.50 from Paddington (1957)

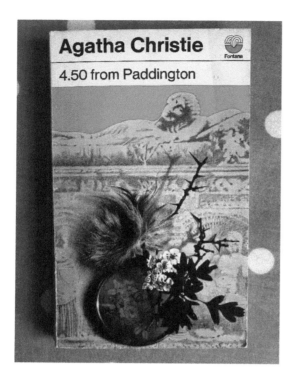

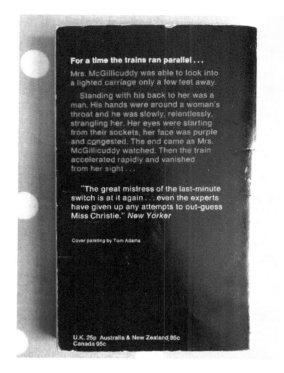

THE BOOK   Fontana, 1972 pp 189

Tom Adams' cover shows a couple of elements dropped from a body as it is being dragged to be placed in the sarcophagus depicted behind them.

THE STORY

Elspeth McGillicuddy is travelling on a train out of Paddington, on her way to stay with her friend Jane Marple, when she sees a woman being strangled on another train that briefly runs alongside hers.

She reports it to the police, but they can find no trace of a body either on a train or a railway line, and dismiss her unlikely story.

Miss Marple knows her friend, and so she knows she is telling the truth; she applies her mind chronotopically[1] to the problem of the missing body and finally realises how and where it must have been disposed of: in the huge grounds surrounding Rutherford Hall.

She persuades Lucy Eylesbarrow, a brilliant freelance purveyor of domestic labour, to apply for a post at the Hall and find the body ...

CHARACTERS - spoiler!

This is one of those large-family plots which Agatha Christie so enjoyed. There is quite a mix of characters.

The family patriarch is Luther Crackenthorpe, a completely self-centred monster, similar to Simeon Lee in *Hercule Poirot's Christmas*, who offers the hired help his hand in marriage. Luther is cared for by his daughter Emma - likeable, honest and slightly down-trodden by the rest, but the central figure in the story nevertheless.

Her brothers Alfred, Cedric, and Harold are classic figures from the Christie family sagas. They represent the usual combination of the stuffed shirt, the shifty and the arty, and each makes a proposal to the hired help in a manner that reflects this.

Their brother-in-law Bryan Eastley is an ex-RAF officer still struggling to cope with peacetime (twelve years after the end of WWII). He also presses his attention on the hired help.

His young son Alexander has had to assume the adult role in the family, following his mother's death; he too tries to arrange a marriage for his father, i.e. with the hired help, the person responsible for so many delicious meals.

Alexander is staying at the Hall with his friend James Stoddart-West. They are indulged hugely by the investigating authorities, given that they appear to be aged about eleven. There are not many children visible in Agatha Christie's stories, but these two fit in well in this one.

Emma's suitor is Dr Quimper, to all intents and purposes a decent, hard-working pillar of the newly-formed NHS. He has no time for Emma's parasitic brethren, and is eventually given the opportunity to show it!

The hired help is, of course, Lucy Eylesbarrow. We see almost everything through her eyes but don't really get to know her. At the end of the book it is implied that she is going to take up one of her offers, but it is not obvious to the reader which one.

QUOTES AND ATTITUDES

Jane Marple reacts to her guest's claim to have seen a murder being committed:

True to the precept handed down to her by her mother and grandmother - to wit: that a true lady can neither be shocked or surprised - Miss Marple merely raised her eyebrows and shook her head ...

This book was written in 1957; in 1958-9 there was an Ashes series in Australia. Agatha Christie was very keen on cricket, and would have known that:

"What about it, Stodders?"
"Good-oh!" said Stoddart-West.
"He isn't really Australian," explained Alexander courteously. "But he's practising talking that way in case his people take him out to see the Test Match next year."

Two young boys are allowed to see the decomposed body of a murdered young woman lying in a sarcophagus:

"Take 'em in, Sanders," said Inspector Bacon to the constable who was standing by the barn door. "One's only young once."

'Only young once', indeed. The two young boys are then ushered in to hear the gory details at the inquest:

"We came on our bicycles," said Stoddart-West. "The policeman was very kind and let us in at the back of the hall. I hope you don't mind, Miss Crackenthorpe," he added politely.
"She doesn't mind," said Cedric, answering for his sister. "You're only young once. Your first inquest, I expect?"

Inspector Craddock considers ex-RAF pilot Bryan Eastley (a full twelve years after the end of hostilities):

"Now they find life tame. Tame and unsatisfactory. In a way, we've given them a raw deal. Though I don't really know what we could do about it. But there they are, all past and no future ..."

Each of the Crackenthorpe brothers would also have been expected to serve in World War II, but it is difficult to imagine Cedric finding life 'tame'. Far from it!

Here is a typical piece of Agatha Christie — not her opinion at all but put into the mouth of the local doctor (Morris) to expose the widespread, somewhat ridiculous insularity that pertained in the UK at the time:

"Ah well, I dare say he'd have lived to regret it if he had married a foreign wife."

There is room in this world for an analysis of Doctors in the Stories of Agatha Christie – on the whole she doesn't give them a good press. Finally, here is another typical piece of Christie - her fantastic economy in the outlining of character, studded with a dry wit:

> *"I don't really like air travel. I never have. Makes me nervous."*
> *"Saves a lot of time," said Harold.*
> *Lady Alice Crackenthorpe did not answer. It was possible that her problem in life was not to save time but to occupy it.*

SWIGATHA RATING 6/10

Once again, this story has an absolutely brilliant opening but tends to meander somewhat after then. There are plenty of different types of character, and their inter-action is always interesting. The question at the end about who Lucy will marry is an intriguing one, and is left satisfyingly unanswered.

But the solution does not ring true: the villain is a likeable, hard-working man who has a genuine affection for Emma; even so, he poisons her!

Of all the places to conceal a body, the grounds of a house with which the villain is closely associated would also seem a strange choice. The idea of a tontine, which provides the motive for the subsequent deaths of the family members, seems to have been inserted simply to pad things out.

How Miss Marple came up with the idea for this motive is a mystery in itself.

WHAT HAPPENED NEXT

Stoddart-West presumably went off to the Ashes series with his family (to witness England experience a 4-0 drubbing by Australia). Agatha Christie hinted later that the Crackenthorpe to win Lucy Eylesbarrow's affection would have been Cedric. A sequel that focussed on their life together would have been very interesting!

ADAPTATIONS

The first film adaptation featured Margaret Rutherford as Miss Marple (and, in effect, Elspeth McGillicuddy and Lucy Eylesbarrow as well). It is one of the better *Rutherford Marples* and very watchable, but the best adaptation I have seen is, yet again, the one with Joan Hickson.

It manages to make more sense of the plot: Miss Marple relying less on divine guidance to work out the motive, more on the Crackenthorpe family solicitor's hints. The character of Lucy Eylesbarrow is given free rein and Jill Meager steals the show. Unfortunately for her, in this adaptation she ends up with the incredibly dull Bryan Eastley rather than the louche Cedric ...

There was also a TV version, produced by ITV for its misleadingly-named *Agatha Christie's Miss Marple* series, that somehow manages to inject Noel Coward into the story.

NOTES

[1] Miss Marple uses a combination of Ordnance Survey maps and railway timetables to work out where and when the crime had taken place, and what opportunities had presented themselves to the murderer to successfully dispose of the corpse before the train stopped.

This aspect of the novel was the subject of a presentation during the Agatha Christie Conference at Lucy Cavendish College, Cambridge in 2017. It was entitled *Old Ladies on Trains: The Inherently Chronotopic Nature of Miss Marple's Detection in 4:50 from Paddington*. Great title!

Ordeal by Innocence (1958)

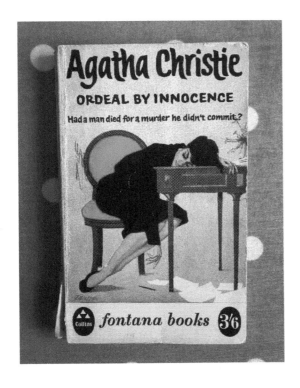 

THE BOOK   Fontana, 1963 pp 192

Fontana's pre-Tom Adams cover is typical of its type, with a somewhat rhetorical statement on the front - what a difference there was once Adams was engaged.

THE STORY

On his return from a two-year Arctic expedition, geophysicist Arthur Calgary discovers that Jacko Argyle has died in prison while serving a sentence for the murder of his adoptive mother, Rachel. Calgary realises that he could have confirmed Jacko's alibi for the time of the murder.

He travels to the family home, nervous as to his likely reception but confident that, at least, they would be pleased to have Jacko's name cleared.

The reaction of the family members proves not to be quite what he had expected ...

CHARACTERS

The story is pretty much confined to the house, Sunny Point, and its inhabitants. The murdered woman, Rachel Argyle, had adopted five children, four of them WWII refugees. Mary Durrant, Micky,

Tina and Hester are each strongly delineated, by contrast with the other, older members of the household (Rachel's husband Leo, his secretary Gwenda Vaughan and Kirsten, the 'home help').

The children are all grown-up, but (apart from Jacko) still live at or near to their childhood home. They remember their 'mother' with a mixture of devotion (Tina), loathing (Micky), exasperation (Hester) and indifference (Mary).

There are some similarities between this book and another dealing with murder in the past (*Five Little Pigs)*: the wrong person is convicted and dies in prison, the four remaining adoptees are each interviewed to find out what they remember, and so on. But in this case, rather too much time is spent with characters asking each other who they think did it or whether they know who did it

Still, at least the characters are not straight from central casting: Tina is a 'half-caste' daughter of a prostitute, Micky was sold by his mother for £100 and Hester is the unwanted illegitimate daughter of an Irish girl. And it is strongly implied at the end that there is new hope for all three of them: that is the gift that Calgary's unwelcome intervention ends up bestowing on them.

QUOTES AND ATTITUDES

Calgary meets Hester Argyll and is taken aback by his reception at Sunny Point:

> *"Going on about justice! What does it matter to Jacko now? He's dead. It's not Jacko who matters. It's us!"*
> *"What do you mean?"*
> *"It's not the guilty who matter. It's the innocent."*

This is very much a common Agatha Christie theme: it is more important that the innocent are free of suspicion or threat, than that the guilty should be apprehended[1].

Arthur Calgary meets Tina Argyll:

> *Her skin was dark, darker than an English skin could ever be. Her bones, too, were smaller. This was the half-caste child that Mrs Argyle had taken as a daughter into the family.*

Mary's husband discusses Tina, her half-sister:

> *"Tina's always the dark horse, to my mind," said Philip. "Perhaps it's the half of her that isn't white ... "*

Dr MacMaster raises an interesting point:

> "We all know what human nature is like. Do a chap a good turn and you feel kindly towards him. You like him. But the chap who's had the good turn done to him, does he feel kindly to you?"

Here he compares notes with another doctor:

> "She sounded - I can't explain to you how she sounded."
> "Irish blood," said MacMaster.
> "She sounded altogether stricken, terrified. Oh, I can't explain it."
> "Well, what do you expect?" the doctor asked.

Doctors rarely come out of Agatha Christie books well. Meanwhile, Micky Argyll is still haunted by his adoptive mother:

> She was dead, wasn't she? Why worry? What was the matter with him? Was it - that he couldn't hate her anymore because she was dead? So that was death ... He felt lost without his hatred - lost and afraid.

Micky still yearns for the comforts of his (slum) home and (drunken) birth mother, who had sold him to Rachel Argyll:

> "I didn't want to be taken away from my own home."
> "You might have been bombed," Tina pointed out. "You might have been killed."
> "What would it matter? I wouldn't mind being killed. I'd have been killed in my own place, with my own people around me."

But by the end, he is reconciled to his adoptive mother as he visits her grave:

> "There you are mum," he said. "I was a rotten son to you, and I don't think you were a very wise mother to me. But you meant well."

Some words of wisdom from Supt Huish about Kirsten:

> "She's of the age when women go slightly off their rocker in one way or another."

The book would have benefitted from better proof-reading. Here Calgary is accusing someone of killing Tina, and then justifying the accusation by announcing that she is still alive:

"You are saying I killed Tina and Philip?"

"Of course you killed them," said Calgary. "Tina has recovered consciousness."

EXTERNAL QUOTATIONS

There are three works quoted in the book, of varying degrees of significance but all of interest:

> *If I justify myself, mine own mouth shall condemn me.*
> *I am afraid of all my sorrows. I know that thou will not hold me innocent.*
> The Book of Job

> *O fair dove! O fond dove!*
> *And dove with the white breast!*
> *Let me alone, the dream is my own,*
> *And my heart is full of rest,*
> *My heart is full of rest.*
> Jean Ingelow [2]

> *Venus toute entière à sa proie attacheé*
> Jean Racine [3]

SWIGATHA RATING 6/10

This one is definitely a 'detective story that has a kind of passion behind it', but you could re-write the last 20 pages and insert almost any of the characters as the guilty party without making a nonsense of the previous 170. In fact, the BBC adaptation that was made in 2017 did just that.

For a writer of a species of fiction known as 'whodunits', it is strange that often Agatha Christie doesn't seem to care 'who'. Once again, like in *Five Little Pigs*, the killer just walks away after being found out. This is a very interesting 'Christie' but as a whodunit (and unlike *Five Little Pigs*) it is not in the top rank.

ADAPTATIONS

It was adapted for the annual BBC 'Christie for Christmas', to be shown in 2017, but was delayed and not shown until 2018, because of allegations of sexual impropriety against one of the cast. When it did come out, many were shocked by its distortion of the plot and the characters (particularly that of Arthur Calgary); many more loved it. I didn't.

NOTES

[1] Agatha Christie, *An Autobiography*:

> *One of the pleasures of writing detective stories is that there are so many types to choose from ... the light-hearted thriller ... the intricate detective story with an involved plot ... and then what I can only describe as the detective story that has a kind of passion behind it - that passion being to help save innocence. Because it is innocence that matters, not guilt.*

[2] A well-known (in her time) English Victorian poet

[3] Taken from *Phaedre*. It translates (very) roughly as *Venus, clinging on to her prey for dear life*. This somewhat unflattering comparison comes to Philip Durrant's mind as he considers his wife.

Cat Among the Pigeons (1959)

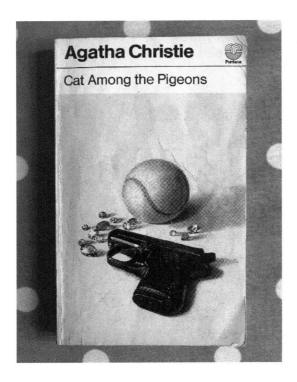

THE BOOK Fontana, 1976 pp 188

Tom Adams' cover is absolutely perfect, although it might be thought to give the game away somewhat. The blurb on the back is also excellent and enticing.

The original title of the book was *Death of a Games Mistress*: strictly speaking it should be *Death of a Games Mistress, a French Mistress, a German Mistress and a Deputy Head*.

Whoever came up with the new title came up with a better one.

THE STORY

Julia Upjohn is a new girl at Meadowbank, a girls' boarding school. It is the start of a new term, and as she is presenting her daughter to the headmistress, Mrs Bulstrode, Julia's mother is astonished to catch sight of someone she has met before in the Middle East. Fatally, Miss Bulstrode pays her no attention, having been distracted by the sight of one of the parents, Lady Veronica Carlton-Sandways, tottering around on the lawn outside in a drunken stupor. Mrs Upjohn departs for a tour of Turkey.

But soon the gym mistress is found battered to death after interrupting an attempted burglary in the new gymnasium; so, when her recently-acquired tennis racquet is found to contain jewels in its hollowed-out handle, Julia decides to break out of the school bounds, taking the jewels with her, and make her way to London to call on a friend of a friend of her mother ... to call on Hercule Poirot.

CHARACTERS

Most of the characters in the story are either teachers or pupils, unsurprisingly since Meadowbank is the setting. What is more surprising is that, by the end of the story, no fewer than four of them have been killed on the site.

Most of the characterisation is somewhat wan, and centres to a large extent around the suitability of staff members Miss Chadwick, Miss Vansittart and Miss Rich to take over from Miss Bulstrode when she retires.

The French teacher Miss Blanche is a worthless character and useless teacher - Agatha Christie seems to have had little respect for French mistresses and governesses[1].

The gym mistress who bites the dust has the splendidly appropriate name of Miss Springer.

Not one of the teaching staff is married, and the only male presence at the school is provided by the two gardeners; one of them, Adam, is a secret service plant (a *sinistra hopaless*, maybe?) but by the end of the book we know nothing more about him than that.

Mrs Upjohn is, however, definitely a woman of character, one prepared to take off for anywhere in the world at a moment's notice and without a by-your-leave. Poirot is unsurprised to hear from Julia that she is a close intimate of Maureen Summerhayes[2].

Poirot is hardly in this story, and to be honest it does not suffer as a result. After he has pulled his rabbit out of the hat at the end, and things have returned to normal (!), Miss Bulstrode finds that her problem has been solved: after all the mayhem, there is only one headmistress candidate left standing ...

QUOTES AND ATTITUDES

The characters' casual racism sounds painful to 21st Century ears, but that was the way that many people spoke at the time, especially ex-colonial types returning from a retreating Empire.

Here is laid bare the Meadowbank selection criteria:

But Miss Bulstrode had her rules, she did not accept morons, or juvenile delinquents, and she preferred to accept girls whose parents she liked.

Miss B also preferred to accept girls whose parents could afford the fees. Colonel Pikeaway instructs Adam on horticulture, using outrageously bad puns:

"Lovely Amabellis Gossiporia, and some of the wonderful new Chinese hybrids of Sinensis Maka Foolia. Try the rich blushing beauty of a clump of Sinistra Hopaless ..."

The British Empire was crumbling away in the wake of Indian independence and the Suez Crisis of 1956, but colonial attitudes would persist for a time yet:

"You think everyone you meet is dishonest."
"Most of them are," said Mrs Sutcliffe grimly.
"Not English people," said the loyal Jennifer.
"That's worse," said her mother. "One doesn't expect anything else from Arabs and foreigners, but in England one's off guard and that makes it easier for dishonest people."

This is not the author speaking, but the author mocking a particular English type that she had no time for. AC had a huge respect for the people of the Middle East, and her star character in this story, Mrs Upjohn, is observed at least trying to communicate with the locals on a trip to Turkey rather than barking at them.

As Empire metamorphosed into Commonwealth, the reigning monarch had a crucial role to play:

"Oh well," said Jennifer. "I expect the Queen often has to have people to lunch who don't know how to behave - African chiefs and jockeys and sheikhs."
"African chiefs have the most polished manners," said her father[3].

I don't think Elizabeth II would have had a problem with the jockeys. Adam keeps his boss informed of developments:

Her Highness arrived in style. Cadillac of squashed strawberry and pastel blue, with Wog Notable in native dress, fashion-plate-from-Paris wife, and junior edition of same (HRH).

Old Briggs warns Adam off chatting up schoolgirls, especially the Italian ones:

"Now you be careful, my boy. Don't you get mixed up with no Eye-ties. I know what I'm talking about. I knew Eye-ties, I did, in the first war ..."

Now it's the turn of the French, as the police consider one of their main suspects:

> *Angele Blanche was dismissed after a few more unimportant questions.*
> *"Touchy," said Bond. "All the French are touchy."*

In the wake of the introduction of the Welfare State and Education Act during the 1940s there were other options available for young girls than becoming a servant. Mrs Sutcliffe laments the 'servant problem':

> *"Old Mrs Ellis who is quite deaf and can hardly stand up and that half-witted daughter of the Bardwells who comes in to help on Saturday mornings."*

Now she considers removing her daughter from Meadowbank:

> *"Two murders! And a girl kidnapped. You can't send your daughter to a school where the mistresses are being murdered all the time."*

SWIGATHA RATING 6/10

Agatha Christie enjoyed herself writing this one, but the murderous side-plot introduced is, frankly, ludicrous. Otherwise, it is a good fun read, and indeed funny in places.

WHAT HAPPENED NEXT

Poirot hardly features in this story and was retired for another four years. The ash-bespattered Colonel Pikeaway was to become a regular in her later books, appearing with Tommy and Tuppence in *Postern of Fate* and also in *Passenger to Frankfurt*.

ADAPTATIONS

ITV's *Poirot* made a decent production with a screenplay by Mark Gatiss. Among the (inevitable) changes made was the inclusion of a javelin as a murder weapon ... Poirot was, of course, much more to the fore than in the book.

NOTES

[1] Mrs Summerhayes was Poirot's somewhat disorganised landlady in *Mrs McGinty's Dead*.

[2] See also the un-prepossessing Mademoiselle Brun (*The Secret of Chimneys*). There is an un-named governess in *The Hollow* who is described thus: *French governesses never seem to have any authority.*

[3] Re-reading this, sixty years after it was first published, it is incredible to think that the same Queen is still being dragooned into lunch with sheikhs ... and, no doubt, jockeys.

The Adventure of the Christmas Pudding (1960)

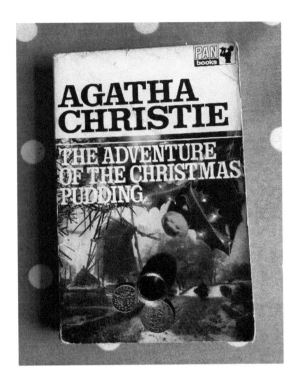

THE BOOK PAN, 1969 pp 219

The PAN edition which I read has a beautiful cover, with items traditionally that are stirred into a Christmas pudding (the ring, the sixpence) or placed on top of it (the holly) lying alongside a ruby, which most certainly isn't. In the background is a watercolour of a wintry English landscape. The book is still in great condition, nearly fifty years (and many re-reads) later. Even the blurb on the back is enticing.

THE STORIES

There are six of Agatha Christie's longer short stories in this collection. All of them had either been published before, or were based on stories that had.

The Adventure of the Christmas Pudding

Something of a self-indulgence, based on Agatha Christie's deliriously happy memories of Christmases spent at Abney Hall when she was a child. A shorter version of this story (*The Theft of the Royal Ruby*) had been published in *The Strand* 37 years previously.

Be careful when you swallow a spoonful of Christmas Pudding at King's Lacey ...

The Mystery of the Spanish Chest

This is a story in which Poirot 'considers he was at his best', but it is another one based on a shorter version (*The Mystery of the Baghdad Chest*), originally published in 1932. The 'Spanish' version features Miss Lemon, at her stolid and uncommunicative best, and Poirot laments the absence of the wild speculation and enthusiasm of his *vieux ami* Hastings:

> "It is indeed the irony," he said to himself, "that after my dear friend Hastings I should have Miss Lemon. What greater contrast can one imagine? Ce cher *Hastings, how he would have enjoyed himself.*" [1]

In the 'Baghdad' version, Poirot is indeed accompanied by Hastings, who narrates.

The Under Dog

One of her longest 'short' stories, sixty pages in this edition. It is unusual for a swigatha in that one of the characters proclaims from the start who the guilty person must be, based on her 'feminine intuition'; she never changes her mind, and is proved to be right. Compare and contrast with Mrs Oliver!

Four and Twenty Blackbirds

The third title taken by Agatha Christie from the nursery rhyme *Sing a Song of Sixpence*. It is not obvious what the connection is, although black*berries* in a pudding are a key feature of the plot.

The Dream

A typical Poirot yarn, first published in 1938. It shares the same plot device as the story before it and the one after it.

Greenshaw's Folly

This unremarkable Miss Marple story was written as a fund-raiser for a new stained-glass window at Agatha Christie's local church. She had originally offered a longer Poirot story with a remarkably similar title - *Greenshore's Folly* - but could not find a publisher for it at the time (!?).

SWIGATHA RATING 5/10

The title story is a great one to read in the late afternoon of Christmas Day, with a glass of port and in front of a blazing fire.

The other stories are ok, but this collection has been flung together somewhat messily, with the last three sharing the same plot device (the murderer impersonating someone else). All of these stories had already been published, so this would have been quite disappointing as an eagerly awaited 'Christie for Christmas', justified only by the title story.

WHERE IT LED

When Agatha Christie became interested in writing for the theatre in the 1950s, she reduced her novel output to one a year, and that became hailed by the publishers as 'A Christie for Christmas'. After the disappointment of this one, all the remaining Christies for Christmas (1961 - 1973) featured full-length, original novels.

The Mystery of the Baghdad *Chest* was eventually published in the posthumous collection *While the Light Lasts*.

ADAPTATIONS

The ITV *Poirot* series adapted each of the Poirot stories in this collection, but two of them are based on the original stories. So, even though one episode was entitled *The Mystery of the Spanish Chest*, it is actually based on the Baghdad version. In that episode, adapted by Anthony Horowitz[2], Hastings stands in for Miss Lemon, tying to make sense of her filing system.

ITV's *Agatha Christie's Miss Marple* series made a decent fist of *Greenshaw's Folly*. To pad it out, they introduced elements of one of the Thirteen Problems, *The Thumb Mark of St Peter*.

NOTES

[1] Miss Lemon and Captain Hastings never actually met in any of the original Poirot stories; in the much-lauded ITV adaptations, played by Pauline Moran and Hugh Fraser, they appear regularly together.

[2] Anthony Horowitz's *Magpie Murders* is an interestingly constructed book that has many, many references to Agatha Christie; the detective's side-kick is even named Fraser, after the actor who played Hastings in the *Poirot* tv series, and his flat is in Charterhouse Square, the real-life location of the building used for Poirot's flat.

The Pale Horse (1961)

THE BOOK Fontana, 1964 pp 191

Tom Adams cover is one of his early ones for this series, and hugely effective it is at conveying the 'black magic' elements of the story. Unusually, the back cover contains a close-up of one part of the painting depicted on the front - part of the right wing of the pinned bat.

THE STORY

Father O'Gorman, a Catholic priest, is murdered after hearing a dying woman's confession. In his pocket is found a list of names.

Meanwhile, Mark Easterbrook, a writer researching for a book about Mogul architecture, is in a London espresso bar when he witnesses a fight between two young women, in which one manages to pull out tufts of the other's hair. The girl on the receiving end, Thomasina Tuckerton, brushes off her experience, saying that it didn't hurt.

One week later, Mark finds her name in the Deaths column of *The Times*. He discovers that the name of Tuckerton was on Father Gorman's list. Mark finds himself investigating a coven that live in an expub known as The Pale Horse; the members claim to be capable of inflicting damage on their fellow beings from afar, via a combination of black magic ritual, spell and suggestion.

Mark presents himself to them as a potential client ...

CHARACTERS

There are a few characters in this story who seem almost to have stumbled into it from other ones: Ariadne Oliver, last seen enlisting Poirot's aid in *Dead Man's Folly* (1956); Colonel and Rhoda Despard, who met in *Cards on the Table* (1936); and Mrs Dane Calthorp, a refugee from Miss Marple's universe (*The Moving Finger*, 1943).

The story, although for the most part set in a typical English village, is very recognisably of its time: the Chelsea coffee-bar, Teddy boys, the smart-set girls getting their kicks. Mrs Oliver's reference to the difficulties of writing about 'beatniks and sputniks and squares and the beat generation' is clearly a heartfelt sigh from her alter-ego.

The characters are, as ever, described with wonderful economy, one sentence usually sufficing to make them clear; that sentence is rarely complimentary.

Agatha Christie often claimed that she didn't put her acquaintances into her stories, but there is one character in this book who is clearly based on someone she came across when working in a dispensary during WW1. To name this character here would give the story away somewhat, but it is pretty obvious to anyone who has read her autobiography that she was revolted by the man; that aversion comes through loud and clear in *The Pale Horse*.

ATTITUDES AND QUOTES

As always, quotations taken from a text cannot help but reflect at least some of the spirit and attitudes of the time when it was written. This is particularly the case here. For example, Mark Easterbrook is in conversation with the supposedly intelligent Dr Corrigan, who sounds here more like a refugee from *Doctor in the House*, a popular film of the time:

> *"You're not married then?"*
> *"No fear. And no more are you, I should say, from the comfortable mess in which you live. A woman would tidy all that up in no time."*
> *I told him I didn't think women were as bad as he made out.*

Now Mark assesses Thomasina Tuckerton's mother:

The eyes were pale blue and gave the impression that she was appraising the price of everything. She was the sort of woman who undertipped porters and cloakroom attendants.

And Thyrza Grey:

She was this evening the British country spinster to the life, pleasant, efficient, uninterested in anything beyond her immediate surroundings.

And Bella Stamfordis:

She spoke little, treating us to a far-away wrapped-up-in-higher-things mode. It ought to have been impressive.

Agatha Christie has many characters in her post-war books bemoaning the educational reforms that gave every child the chance to go to school, rather than enter service at the age of 12. Here is a different take on the subject.

Even Bella seemed tonight only a half-witted old peasant woman - like hundreds of other women of her kind - inbred, untouched by education or a broader outlook.

Mark Easterbrook in conversation with the prescient Mr Venables:

"Will computers take the place of men eventually?"
"Of men, yes. Men who are only units of manpower, that is. But Man, no."

Easterbrook and Venables are speaking in the wake of the nuclear arms race, a year before the Cuban Missile Crisis in 1962:

"Life is always dangerous - never forget that. In the end, perhaps, not only great natural forces, but the work of our own hands may destroy it. We are very near to that happening at this moment ..."
"No-one can deny that, certainly."

Poppy is a model-cum-spokeswoman for the so-called 'Smart' Set:

I poured some more champagne into Poppy's glass. Here, I felt, in front of me was someone who might be helpful if only you could tear out of her the disassociated facts that were flitting about in what she called her brain.

As usual, the book has a terrific beginning, the central idea is startling and the revelation of the perpetrator is satisfyingly surprising. There is plenty to cheer, therefore.

However, on re-reading it, I got the impression that the author was throwing the kitchen sink at her plot to drag it out to the usual 192 pages-worth. There is really no need for any of the 'guest stars', and the explanation at the end seems dashed off.

Good fun, though!

WHAT HAPPENED NEXT

The choice of thallium as the poison in use in this story had various unexpected consequences[1].

One was the press speculation that future murderers had chosen it for their own use having read *The Pale Horse* first. The year after it was published, Graham Young (who went on to become an insanely proficient poisoner) was arrested on suspicion of murdering his stepmother with thallium. This was the first known case of its kind in the UK, although Young denied having read the book.

Another was the occasion when a woman in South America, who had read *The Pale Horse*, was able to recognise the symptoms of thallium poisoning being perpetrated on a man by his young wife, thereby saving his life (because the hospital was able to treat the patient promptly with the correct medication).

ADAPTATIONS

There was an ITV version of this story that shoe-horned *Agatha Christie's Miss Marple* into it; I cannot stand that series, so I have yet to watch It. I should say, however, that the author herself had toyed with the idea of bringing Miss Marple into the plot, thereby re-uniting her with Mrs Dane Calthorp[2]. I think that that would have worked well, but it would have meant removing the characters from the Poirot Universe (Mrs Oliver and the Despards).

The BBC also adapted the story to show at Christmas in 2019. As seems to be becoming the norm with this series, all the humour of the original is excised, and the lead character of Mark Easterbrook is unrecognisable from the one in the book.

NOTES

[1] Kathryn Harkup *A is for Arsenic*

[2] John Curran *Agatha Christie's Secret Notebooks*

The Mirror Crack'd from Side to Side (1962)

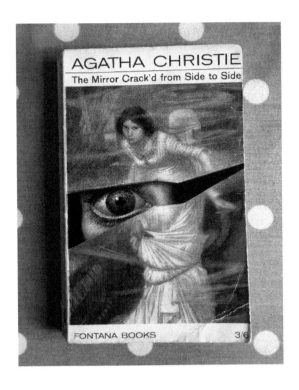
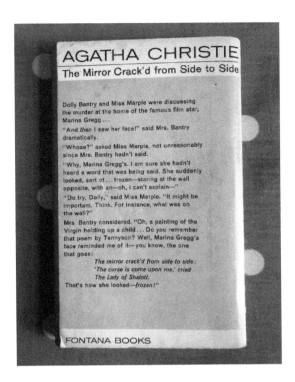

THE BOOK Fontana, 1967 pp 192

This is one of the most evocative covers (front and back) for me. I used to love the almost-quotes from the text on the back cover, and this is one of the very best. What a great job to have!

The book's title is inspired and the image is of the Lady of Shalott. The crack'd glass and wide eye are also items of wonder. Who wouldn't want to buy a second-hand book that looked like this? Strangely, Tom Adams was not pleased with this cover, because he didn't think his image of the Lady did the original Waterhouse picture justice. She does look a bit insipid, but I think that adds to its ghostly air.

The book is dedicated to 'Margaret Rutherford, in admiration.'[1]

THE STORY

Gossington Hall, once home to the Bantrys but now owned by the film actress Marina Gregg and her director husband Jason Rudd, is hosting a fête is aid of St John's Ambulance. At a reception for special guests inside the Hall, one of the St John's volunteers, Heather Badcock, dies after her drink has been poisoned.

The following day, Mrs Bantry hurries round to her friend Jane Marple's cottage to give her own personal eye-witness account of the events surrounding Mrs Badcock's death ...

CHARACTERS AND ATTITUDES

St Mary Mead in 1962 is hardly recognisable as the village portrayed 30 years before in the first Marple novel, *The Murder at the Vicarage*. The Development, a new housing estate being built there, is one of the main characters in the book. Miss Marple decides to acquaint herself with it, and is relieved to find that the people there are much the same characters as those that populated the old village.

There is a decided lack of hankering after the past in this story. The cheerful character of Cherry Baker epitomises the overall atmosphere, though she does have a disconcerting habit of referring to the Hall butler Guiseppe as 'the wop'.

The characters of the 'film set', on the other hand, are somewhat wan, with the exception of Jason, with his mournful clown's face, 'laughing at something terribly sad, that no-one else has seen', and Marina, who has received the shock of her life at the fête.

Otherwise, Hailey Preston, Ardwyck Fenn and Lola Brewster make no impression, and Rudd's PA Ella Zielinsky is not convincing at all with her absurd accusations.

QUOTES

One of the strengths of Agatha Christie was her ability to sum someone up in a sentence. Her characters are sometimes described (and sometimes rightly) as one-dimensional, but she can hit the bull's-eye. Here is a classic Christie one-liner, a description of a character to which no more need be added:

> *Miss Hartnell's house was still there, and also Miss Hartnell, fighting progress to the last gasp.*

Miss Marple braves The Development:

> *Mothers came out on doorsteps calling to their children, who, as usual, were busy doing all the things they had been told not to do. Children, Miss Marple reflected gratefully, never changed.*

Here is an example of Christie's brilliant economy and clue-handling:

"I shouldn't drink any more," said Marina. "I've had three already." But she accepted the glass.

Miss Marple remembers Alison Wilde, prototype of Heather Badcock:

"She was the sort of person who tells you what they have done and what they have seen and what they have heard. They never mention what any other people said or did. Life is a kind of one-way track - just their own progress through it. Other people just seem to them like - like wall-paper in a room."

What a great description that is.

Adoption in Agatha Christie's time was somewhat different to current practice. Rather than an option for orphans or children in care, it seems to have been the practice to adopt children from poor backgrounds to give them a leg up in life; the impact of that on a child was a theme that Agatha Christie returned to a few times. Miss Marple doesn't approve:

"In one case a mother, with a lot of children and very little money to bring them up in this country, wrote to her, and asked if she couldn't take a child. There was a lot of very silly sentiment written about that. About the mother's unselfishness and the wonderful home and education and future the child was going to have."

Adoptee Margot Bence confirms Miss Marple's analysis:

"She sold me because she was a damn' silly woman who thought I'd get 'advantages' and 'education' and have a wonderful life."

Very similar sentiments are expressed by Maureen Summerhayes in *Mrs McGinty's Dead.*

Finally, some things in St Mary's Mead have *not* changed:

One of the mysteries of St Mary Mead was what made the vicar remember certain things - only outstripped by the greater mystery of what the vicar could manage to forget.

SWIGATHA RATING 7/10

This is a lovely BOOK, and very enjoyable to read, for the most part. The pivotal moment - Marina Gregg freezing in shock at her own party, and the reason behind it - is a brilliant idea. All the clues are fairly placed, but the sideshows, including one which has a character ringing up each suspect and telling them 'I saw you do it', are unconvincing padding.

WHAT HAPPENED NEXT

This was Miss Marple's final appearance in St Mary Mead; for the rest of her career she was on her travels ...

ADAPTATIONS

There have been a few[2] - a Hollywood blockbuster (*The Mirror Crack'd*) featuring Elizabeth Taylor and Rock Hudson as Marina and Jason, a Japanese and an Indian film adaptation, and two versions for UK TV.

As is usually the case, the version produced by BBC TV with Joan Hickson as Miss Marple beats the rest hollow; it takes so much more care with the story.

NOTES

[1] Miss Rutherford had portrayed Miss Marple for the first time the year before in a version of *4.50 from Paddington* (in a film entitled *Murder She Said*), but it would be safe to say that the author's admiration had been generated more by her appearances in British comedy films of the 1950s and her stage performances than her Marple outings.

Twenty years later, the title *Murder She Said* was echoed by *Murder She Wrote*, the title of a long-running US TV series featuring Angela Lansbury as the Miss Marple / Mrs Oliver hybrid Jessica Fletcher. Angela Lansbury had herself already portrayed Miss Marple on screen in *The Mirror Crack'd*.

[2] *Agatha Christie on Screen*, Mark Aldridge

The Clocks (1963)

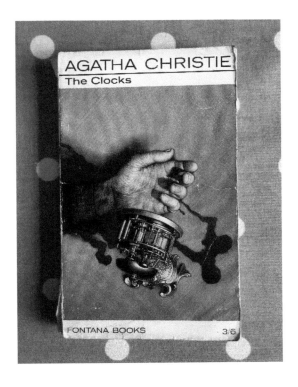
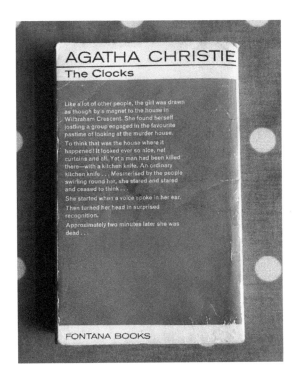

THE BOOK   Fontana, 1969 pp 220

Fontana's cover has many echoes of other 1960s covers that Tom Adams did for them, but I think it was by Ian Robinson, who often stood in for him in those days. This copy was the original I bought and read as a 14-year-old, and it still holds up well.

At the back of the book are three pages of *Also available in Fontana Books*, with three-line write-ups on a variety of books, including this one for *Appointment with Death*:

> *"Poirot has surpassed himself! Never has he been so brilliant, so accurate, so fair and so logical."* Evening News

Made this reader want to read it again …

THE STORY

Sheila Webb, a stenographer, is sent by the Cavendish Secretarial Bureau to 19, Wilbraham Crescent. On arrival, she finds the house unlocked and then discovers a man lying dead in a room full of clocks, with four of them stopped on the same time, 4:13[1]. Sheila screams, rushes out into the street and collapses into the arms of Colin Lamb, a secret service agent who just happened to be investigating Crescents in the area.

Lamb joins forces with Inspector Hardcastle to investigate the murder. When another employee of the secretarial bureau is later found dead in a telephone box in the same street, Lamb consults an old friend of his father's[2], Hercule Poirot ...

CHARACTERS

Most of the 'action' in the book takes place in the houses of Wilbraham Crescent which neighbour no 19. This small community contains Miss Pebmarsh, a blind woman with a remarkable ability to look after herself; Mrs Hemmings, a woman obsessed with cats; the McNaughtons, a whisky-toping retired couple; the Ramseys, a family whose father has defected to the Soviet bloc; and the Blands, a vulgar and tasteless builder and his wife.

Amongst that lot we also find a murderer, a Soviet spy and even Sheila's mother, long considered dead. Added to that strange mix is a standard Christie character - the walking murder victim, who wanders around muttering to herself and others about how 'it all seems funny', and makes her way to Wilbraham Crescent to be killed.

As for Poirot, when he finally enters the story after over 100 pages, we are told by his valet that he has been depressed; he is also becoming something of a bore on the subject matter of real-life crime and detective fiction writers (a warning to us all!).

QUOTES AND ATTITUDES

This book was written when the UK was still outside of the Common Market, its application to join having been rejected, in particular by France. Here, Mrs Curtin, the cleaner at No 19, explains to Inspector the anomaly of the clocks:

> "Each of these four clocks represented a time about an hour later than the cuckoo clock and the grandfather clock."
> "Must have been foreign," said Mrs Curtin. "Me and my old man went on a coach trip to Switzerland and Italy once and it was a whole hour further on there. Must be something to do with this Common Market. I don't hold with the Common Market and nor does Mr Curtin. England's good enough for me."

Brilliant! This should have been plastered all over the *Vote Leave* vans during the 2016 Brexit referendum.

Here one of the street residents describes Miss Pebmarsh, who teaches at an institute for blind children; the ramifications of the Education Act (which introduced grammar schools) are still being mocked some 20 years later:

> *"I merely think her views are bigoted and extravagant. After all, there are other things besides education. All those new peculiar grammar schools, practically built of glass. You might think they were meant to grow cucumbers in, or tomatoes."*

Here is another post-war theme that Christie often returns to: the fact that no-one lives at home anymore, 'home' being defined as where they and their family have always lived:

> *The lame and the halt and the old didn't live in their own houses any more, attended by a faithful domestic or by some half-witted poor relation glad of a good home. It was a serious setback to criminal investigation.*

... and criminal fiction authors! But she soldiered on. The Cuban Missile crisis was still fresh in the memory:

> *"They're having revolutions all over the world nowadays."*
> *"Let us not discuss the Bomb," said Hercule Poirot. "If it has to be, it has to be, but let us not discuss it."*

This is something of a non-sequitur from HP: no bomb spelt with a capital B has ever been part of a revolution.

SWIGATHA RATING 3/10

Apart from the startling start and the slightly ludicrous end, there is little to the story for the most part, and the characters do not exactly rise from the page. The emergence of Sheila's mother is ridiculous, and the coincidence of such a strange but inter-connected group of characters living in the same street is difficult to swallow.

As was becoming more common[1], Agatha Christie in her 70s was plundering her back catalogue for ideas, but fleshing them out was sometimes a bore, and that seems to be the case here.

WHAT HAPPENED NEXT

There was a film made in 1966, starring Peter Cook and Dudley Moore and called *Bedazzled*, in which they played the Devil and an unwilling disciple; one of their routine acts of evil was tearing out the last few pages of Agatha Christie books before they went on sale. In the film, the book that they desecrate is the first Fontana paperback edition of *The Clocks* (the one I read), which was first published in 1966.

Poirot disappeared for another three years, re-appearing in *Third Girl*. Thankfully, he had finished his magnum opus on crime fiction by then.

ADAPTATIONS

The Clocks was one of the later adaptations in the ITV *Poirot* series and, as a result, I approached it with some dread: some of the later series productions are dismally poor.

Happily, this one turned out to be one of the best of the later *Poirot* episodes: a fine cast, actually seeming to take their parts seriously, with a terrific Inspector Hardcastle played by Phil Daniels. The scene where Sheila finds the body in a room full of clocks and Pebmarsh walks in is electric.

This film makes more of the book than it deserves, and for once re-setting the story in 1936 makes sense.

NOTES

[1] This is the third time the author used this 'body-found-in-room-full-of-clocks' scenario. *The Seven Dials Mystery* was the first, and there was also a short story, *The Clock Stops*, written for a competition in which the entrants had to guess the ending.

[2] For his undercover work, Colin Lamb has had to change his name, because his father had made such a big name for himself in a similar field. From the hints given, especially by Poirot, who refers to him as 'the Superintendent', we can safely guess that Colin's father is Superintendent Battle.

A Caribbean Mystery (1964)

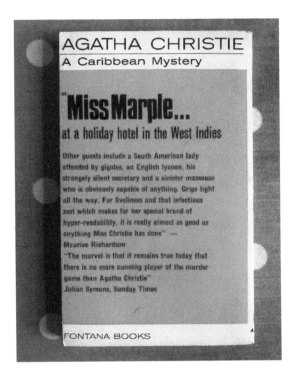

THE BOOK Fontana, 1970 pp 158

Tom Adams' cover captures the key moment in the whole story in more detail than one might normally expect. Shall say no more! It's a beautiful book, still in good condition some 50 years later; and, yes, it has been read a few times.

THE STORY

'Dear Raymond', Miss Marple's nephew, has packed her off to a hotel in the West Indies to help her recover from a bout of pneumonia. While there, she finds herself being entertained by the old Colonial bore Major Palgrave. Her attention drifts until she realises that he is relating a story about an unconvicted serial killer. The following morning, the major is found dead in his chalet, and Miss Marple finds herself regretting that she had not paid him more attention. For it soon becomes apparent that the serial killer is staying at the hotel ...

CHARACTERS AND ATTITUDES

In spite of the blurb on the back of the Fontana edition, most of the people staying at the hotel are much of a muchness, and are almost interchangeable. They are not an attractive bunch.

For example, there are four friends, Greg, Lucky, Edmund and Evelyn, who always holiday together; their love-lives seem interchangeable but it is difficult to remember or care who is doing what with whom and why.

Those people who are seen to be, or feel, out of their class, or financial depth, such as the masseur Jackson, are ignored, even despised by most. But not by Miss Marple ...

One of the more interesting characters is the maid, Victoria: competent, beautiful and charming, if somewhat immoral. She becomes one of the victims of the killer, but it is not clear whether this is because she told the killer what she had seen or was indulging in blackmail.

One of the themes that crops up again and again in Agatha Christie's Marple books is "How can one ever really know who anyone is?" Especially when in a hotel crammed with guests who all behave the same. Eventually Miss Marple finds a guest whom she respects - the amoral cripple Rafiel - which enables her to make progress and prevent the final murder. It is obvious who Rafiel is.

QUOTES

We are treated to an extract from the latest of (dear) Raymond West's (clever) novels:

> *"Do you mean that you've had no sexual experience at ALL?" demanded the young man incredulously. "At nineteen? But you must. It's vital."*
> *The girl hung her head unhappily, her straight greasy hair fell forward over her face.*
> *"I know," she muttered, "I know."*
> *He looked at her, stained old jersey, the bare feet, the dirty toe nails, the smell of rancid fat ... He wondered why he found her so maddeningly attractive.*
>
> *Miss Marple wondered too!*

Raymond West explains to Aunt Jane who'll be looking after her house while she is away:

> *"He'll look after the house all right. He's very house proud. He's a queer. I mean – "*
> *He had paused, slightly embarrassed - but surely even dear old Aunt Jane had heard of queers.*

Miss Marple meets Victoria Johnson.

> *The black West Indian girl smiled and said Good Morning as she placed the tray on Miss Marple's knees. Nice natures, all these girls, and a pity they were so averse to getting*

married. It worried Canon Prescott a good deal. Plenty of christenings, he said, trying to console himself, but no weddings.

The owner of the hotel explains the plight of Jackson:

"Well, how shall I put it - it's difficult for him socially. People are so damn snobbish - there's no-one here of his class. He's better than a servant - and below the average visitor - or they think he is. Rather like the Victorian governess."

Miss Marple consoles the supposedly dying Rafiel that his will to live is not odd.

"When you're young and strong and healthy, and life stretches ahead of you, living isn't really important at all. It's young people who commit suicide easily, out of despair from love, sometimes from sheer anxiety and worry. But old people know how valuable life is, and how interesting."

Rafiel is talking here about Esther Walters, and throws an interesting light on the social standing of school-teachers at the time:

"For one thing, there's class distinction. She's just a cut above him. Not very much. If she was really a cut above him it wouldn't matter, but the lower middle-class - they're very particular. Her mother was a school-teacher and her father a bank-clerk. No, she won't make a fool of herself over Jackson."

Rafiel considers black workers, over a century after emancipation.

"They've both worked like blacks, though that's an odd term to use out here, for blacks don't work themselves to death at all, as far as I can see. Was looking at a fellow shinning up a coconut tree to get his breakfast, then he goes to sleep for the rest of the day. Nice life."

SWIGATHA RATING 5/10

I enjoyed this book hugely as a boy, but on returning to it in adulthood I found it rather bland. As with too many of Agatha Christie's later books, it has a great beginning, but tends to drift after that. Although it is some 34 pages short of her usual 192, it dragged a bit in the middle.

One thing in its favour - it is the best version of the 'staring over my left shoulder' clue that she had been using ever since *The Man in the Brown Suit* in 1924. So, it's a shame that the cover of the version I read just about screams this book's answer to it.

WHAT HAPPENED NEXT

Miss Marple returned home. Five years or so later she finds out that Rafiel has died, and soon after that she is contacted by his solicitors with a letter from him. This forms the beginning of the novel *Nemesis*, which had been Rafiel's nickname for her in this Caribbean mystery.

ADAPTATIONS

There was a 1980s film starring Helen Hayes and a BBC adaptation that was one of the *Hickson Marples*. This latter is very well cast, with the great Frank Middlemas as Palgrave and the equally fine Donald Pleasance as Rafiel.

The plot is a bit slight to carry over two hours, so the producers inserted a bus-trip taken by Miss Marple to meet Victoria's aunt. They discuss Persian roses and the joys of Stockport. It's the best scene in the film, followed by another where Miss Marple attends Victoria's funeral.

At Bertram's Hotel (1965)

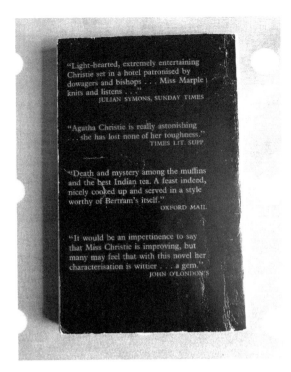

THE BOOK   Fontana, 1969 pp 192

Tom Adams' cover is one of my favourites. To explain the relevance of the image - commissionaire, bullet, chocolate - would give too much away about the plot.

The legend on the title page inside reads: *At Bertram's Hotel FEATURING MISS MARPLE THE ORIGINAL CHARACTER AS CREATED BY AGATHA CHRISTIE*. This is a dig at the Marple films, current at the time, that featured Margaret Rutherford in the title role and bore little resemblance either to her character or her original stories.

THE STORY

'Dear Raymond', Miss Marple's nephew, has (once again) paid for a holiday for her, this time to spend a fortnight at a favourite hotel in London that she had visited as a child. Miss Marple is initially delighted to be back, and marvels at how little has changed. Then she begins to feel uneasy - over the course of fifty years, some things *should* have changed.

Her unease proves to be justified when Canon Pennyfather, one of the guests, disappears. Murder follows ...

CHARACTERS AND ATTITUDES - spoiler!

The guests at Bertram's are a mix: a plethora of retired clergymen, impoverished old county ladies and ex-Army officers on the one side, and rich American tourists on the other. The former are there to provide the atmosphere that the latter seek - *My dear, it just* is *Olde Englande* - and so are given preferential rates.

The hotel staff are all perfectly cast, in more senses than one, from the Jeeves-ian master-of-ceremonies Henry to the Lemon-esque efficiency of Miss Gorringe on the front desk.

Into this mix are added members of the dysfunctional Sedgwick family - the daredevil Bess, one of her (many) ex-husbands, her troubled daughter Elvira Blake, whom Bess had disowned, and a racing driver who is having a fling with both of them.

This book was written at a time of huge change in the UK. At one point, Elvira's guardian Colonel Luscombe rails against these *long-haired Beatles or whatever they call themselves*, but Miss Marple / Agatha Christie's view is that change is healthy; stagnant ponds, on the other hand, are very unhealthy.

One irony is that the American visitors to Bertram's were looking for an England that no longer existed, oblivious to the fact that most of the post-war cultural changes in the UK had been inspired by imports from their own shores, in the form of rock and roll music, fast food, cinema and commercial TV.

QUOTES

Colonel Luscombe is Elvira's guardian. Not exactly the doting parent type:

> *His wife had died in childbirth and the baby, a boy, had been brought up by his wife's family whilst an elder sister had come to keep house for him.*

There is an interesting and unusually frank exchange with Elvira as he tries protect her from her mother. Maybe the author has put something of herself into it[1]:

> *"It's not always a happy thing to have a wonderful person for a mother."*
> *"You don't like speaking the truth very much, do you? But I think what you've just said is the truth."*

Here Miss Marple reflects on societal change since the Great War and a world that has disappeared ('can't get the servants'). She realises that Bertram's must be a fake:

All these elderly people - really very much like those she remembered when she stayed here fifty years ago. They had been natural then - but they weren't very natural now. Elderly people nowadays weren't like elderly people then - they had that worried harried look of domestic anxieties with which they are too tired to cope, or they rushed around to committees and tried to appear bustling and confident ...

What Miss Marple overlooks is that she herself fits in perfectly to the Bertram's *mise-en-scène*. Even so, she is not nostalgic for the past:

"I learned (what I supposed I really knew already) that one can never go back, that one should not ever try to go back - that the essence of life is going forward. Life really is a One Way Street, isn't it?"

Elvira tells Chief Inspector Davy that she was the intended victim:

"Someone tried to kill me ... Someone ... they shot at me ... If it hadn't been for him – "
She pointed down at the motionless figure at her feet.

Seasoned AC readers' antennae would leap into life at this point.

SWIGATHA RATING 7/10

This book came with me when I went to stay with my French cousins when I was 13. It was a memento of home, very English, and I still have a great affection for it. Reading it again, it was still very enjoyable, especially the superficially cosy scenes set in the hotel. But, of course, the author manages her usual trick of pulling the whole carpet from under her readers' feet with the un-cosiest denouement imaginable.

Although its setting was an Edwardian-style hotel, the book was very much of its time (1964-5), with references to the Beatles and motor-racing, and a plot that in part echoes the Great Train Robbery of 1963.

Unfortunately, I have to mark it down slightly. For no less than the fourth time, a woman at the heart of the story claims that someone's been trying to kill her, and for the fourth time they prove to be the murderer.

271

WHAT HAPPENED NEXT

Miss Marple returned home, for a well-earned six-year rest.

ADAPTATIONS

Directed by Mary McMurray, BBC's Miss Marple series served the book well, and, like Bertram's own staff, every part was perfectly cast, especially mother and daughter (Caroline Blakiston and Helena Michell).

NOTES

[1] I wonder whether this is a reflection on how difficult some aspects of author's huge fame must have been for her own daughter, Rosalind.

Third Girl (1966)

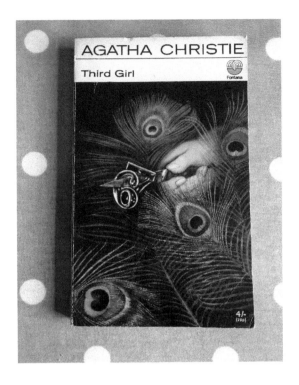
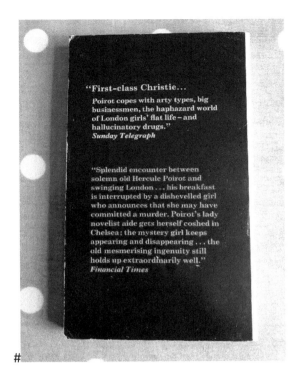

THE BOOK   Fontana, 1969 pp 190

The cover is a Tom Adams painting, I think a rather good one, but he wasn't fond of it. It refers to the numbers of the two flats connected with a murder (67 and 76, obviously!) and the character David Baker, who is referred to throughout by Mrs Oliver as 'the peacock.'

THE STORY

Hercule Poirot's breakfast is interrupted by a young woman, Norma Restarick, who announces that she thinks she might have committed a murder. Before Poirot can delve any further, she announces that he is too old to help her and leaves the flat. Fearing for the girl's safety and sanity, Poirot enlists the aid of his friend Ariadne Oliver to find her ...

CHARACTERS

Norma Restarick is the *Third Girl* of the title, sharing a flat with two other young women, Claudia Reece-Holland and Frances Cary. David Baker, a pretty boy dressed in the latest Carnaby St gear, is Norma's boyfriend.

One background scenario for this story is very much based on apartment life in the city of Swinging London in 1965, with young people very much to the fore, and drugs and pep pills freely available and freely used: a much freer world for those girls who could cope with it than their parents had enjoyed.

The other scenario is the classic Christie one of a family mansion in the country, with a Restarick family history that shares quite a few features with similar families from her other stories, lack of affection being one of them.

There is one character who is able to flit between the two settings quite seamlessly; that person is neither Norma nor David.

QUOTES AND ATTITUDES

Poirot judges his early-morning visitor. His views often echo those of his creator:

> She wore what were presumably the chosen clothes of her generation ... Anyone of Poirot's age and generation would have had only one desire. To drop the girl into a bath as soon as possible.

But he has some sympathy for a young girl unleashed into the world without parental guidance or support:

> "She is one of whom others will look around and say 'We want a victim. That one will do.'"

Poirot and Mrs Oliver are talking about Norma's boyfriend, David Baker, when Poirot makes a comment that you would not have heard in one of his earlier cases:

> "He looked very beautiful," said Hercule Poirot.
> "Beautiful?" said Mrs Oliver. "I don't know that I like beautiful men."
> "Girls do," said Poirot.

Norma's life is saved by Dr Stillingfleet:

> She saw a man of perhaps thirty-odd with red hair and a rather attractively ugly face

Dr Stillingfleet is not the first of his ilk[1].

Norma's grandfather, Sir Roderick Horsfall has a rant against the younger generation:

274

"They probably look like mods or rockers or beatniks or whatever they call these chaps nowadays with the long hair and dirty nails. One doesn't like to say 'Who the devil are you?' You never know which sex they are, which is embarrassing. I suppose they're Norma's friends. Wouldn't have been allowed in the old days. But you turn them out of the house and you find out it's Viscount Endersleigh or Lady Charlotte Marjoribanks ..."

Notwithstanding this, he ends up betrothed to Sonia, a girl at least 40 years younger than him.

Here is another of Poirot's wonderfully subtle put-downs, in this case aimed at Sonia:

"I am not like that. I am an intellectual."
"Aha," said Poirot. "That is always nice to know."

One of Dame Agatha's great characters is the information agent Mr Goby, a man incapable of talking face-to-face. He first appeared in *The Mystery of the Blue Train* in 1928, and was middle-aged then. Even so, as Poirot ages, he comes to rely more on him. Here Mr Goby takes his leave of his employer:

Mr Goby looked at the bookcase and said goodnight to it.

Another of her greatest hits is the redoubtable Miss Lemon:

She always knew what she was going to do and was she always right in what she did.

Even so, there are weaknesses ... here Miss Lemon betrays her insular attitude to her (foreign) employer:

"By the way, what did you think of that young woman who came yesterday?"
Miss Lemon, arrested as she was about to plunge her fingers on the typewriter, said briefly,
"Foreign."
"Yes, yes."
"Obviously foreign."
"You do not think anything more about her than that?"

Miss Lemon does not like to be drawn, but, wishing to get back to her typing, eventually offers this:

"Well, I always say that it's better to know where you are when you are employing someone, and buy British."

It does not occur to Miss Lemon that if everyone agreed with her, she would be out of a job.

Andrew Restarick opens up about Claudia Holland, a hugely impressive and capable employee:

> "I gave her pretty much carte blanche to put through this deal in Manchester on her own terms ... and she's done exceedingly well. She's as good as a man in some ways."

It's no wonder that the Women's Lib gathered pace in the UK in the 1960s.

SWIGATHA RATING 4/10

I think '4' might be being generous. The plot does not really work, and the solutions to both the murder and the theft are very unconvincing. I don't think Agatha Christie's heart was really in it.

Even with a stellar cast comprising Poirot, Mrs Oliver, Miss Lemon and Mr Goby, at times it is even boring. Still, it is interesting to get some sense of an author in her 70s trying to incorporate some of the huge changes in Britain during the 1960s into her books.

WHAT HAPPENED NEXT

The author cast herself / Mrs Oliver again in the final two Poirot novels that she wrote, *Hallowe'en Party* and *Elephants Can Remember*.

ADAPTATIONS

Although the Poirot stories were published between 1920 and 1972, there was an understandable desire by the producers of the ITV *Poirot* series (which covered almost all of them) to set most of them in 1936. It doesn't always work, and this one is a case in point. They might have got away with taking the *Swinging* out of London and providing a swing jazz accompaniment, but re-writing the story such that the identity of the first victim is changed, and the second is allowed to survive, is unnecessary and silly.

NOTES

[1] A character very reminiscent of Dr Lord in *Sad Cypress*, another ugly young medic who comes to the aid of a damsel in distress: *Dr Lord was a young man of thirty-two. He had red hair and a pleasantly ugly freckled face.*

Endless Night (1967)

 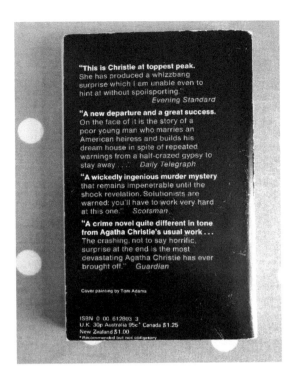

THE BOOK   Fontana, 1973 pp 191

In my opinion, this Tom Adams cover is one of his finest. In the forefront is a straightforward representation of an event in the story. The background is a brilliant evocation of Gipsy's Acre and the modern house that the architect Santonix built there.

The reviews quoted on the back reveal a general delight that the author was back on the top of her form.

THE STORY

Michael Rogers, a young ne'er-do-well from a poor background with an eye, and desire, for the finer things in life, dreams of building a magnificent house on a plot of land known locally as 'Gipsy's Acre'. He woos and marries Ellie Guteman, a rich American heiress, and his dream comes true ...

But warnings from all and sundry have been ignored by the happy couple, and the dream turns horribly sour.

CHARACTERS - spoiler!

Mike Rogers is the narrator throughout. Unlike other Christie narrators, such as Captain Hastings, Jerry Burton, Dr Sheppard, Nurse Leatheran, Anthony Cade and Charles Hayward[1], he has no Poirot, Marple or Battle looking on and providing cryptic hints for us as to what is actually happening.

Thus we see all the events through his eyes only, and have to judge the other characters in the book based on his descriptions. We have to base our understanding of his character on the same basis, and on first inspection he comes across as an easy-going, likeable and attractive young man. Yet there are plenty of hints, throughout his own narrative, to other sides of his character, and this makes him the finest, most complete character study in any of Agatha Christie's works.

His wife Ellie is often compared to the character Linnet Doyle from *Death on the Nile*, and she faces a similar betrayal, but, unlike Linnet, she is pure and generous at heart while remaining no-one's fool: she has a sense, almost an acceptance, of what is going on without comprehending the horror of it.

It is one of the most interesting and unusual aspects of the book that, whilst its readers have no idea what is happening, all the main characters in the story seem to know only too well.

QUOTES AND ATTITUDES

There is not a huge, twining plot in this book, but there is a great deal of revealing conversation that provides most of the clues.

Here, Mike discovers the level of resentment towards 'gipsies' around Gipsy's Acre; they are not to be trusted:

> *"Why doesn't anyone like gipsies?"*
> *"They're a thieving lot," he said, disapprovingly. Then he peered more closely at me. "Happen you've got gipsy blood yourself?" he suggested, looking hard at me.*
> *I said not that I knew of. It's true, I do look a bit like a gipsy.*

There are many comments about gipsies in the book, but this is the key one, connecting them to Mike. Here is another:

> *"The gipsies used to camp here a lot when I was a boy," he said. "I suppose I got fond of them, though they're a thieving lot, of course. But I've always been attracted to them. As long as you don't expect them to be law-abiding, they're all right."*

The speaker, Major Philpott, is attracted to Mike as well. Mike's architect friend Santonix can see straight through him.

> "Born poor doesn't mean you've got to stay poor. Money's queer. It goes where it's wanted."
> "I'm not sharp enough," I said.
> "You're not ambitious enough. Ambition hasn't woken up in you, but it's there, you know."

Mike's ambition proves to be boundless. Santonix, too, is attracted to Mike, but feels something else as well talking to him, without being able to define what it is:

> "Don't you recognise, haven't you often felt, that I am partly evil myself? Always have been. That's why I know when it's near me, although I don't always know exactly where it is ..."

Santonix can sense the presence of evil in Mike just as Shakespeare's Witch can feel a 'pricking in her thumbs' when Macbeth comes towards her; neither Mike nor Macbeth is aware of the evil in themselves.

Michael's mother is under no illusions about him:

> "You don't want me to see her in case I should say to you 'Don't'. Is that it?"
> "I wouldn't pay any attention if you did."
> "Maybe not, but it would shake you. It would shake you somewhere inside because you take notice of what I say and think. There are things I've guessed about you - and maybe I've guessed right and you know it."

And Mike has no illusions about himself either:

> I wanted - there were the words again, my own particular words - I want, I want ... I could feel all the feeling surging up in me. I wanted a wonderful woman and a wonderful house like nobody else's house and I wanted my house to be full of wonderful things. Things that belonged to me. Everything would belong to me.

Mrs Rogers had warned her son about his ambitions:

> "I don't know what good ambition's ever done to anybody. It's the kind of thing that turns to dead sea fruit [2] in your mouth."

As his original plan comes to fruition, Mike's ambition grows:

'And then'. They were the two words of the future. I used them in the same way I had once used those other two words 'I want' ...

He finally thinks he has everything:

I was me - me - me as I wanted to be. Me as I'd always wanted to be. I'd got everything I'd wanted and I was going home to it.

As it turns out, he has just lost everything. Looking back, he remembers the last time he felt truly happy: Ellie had just sung *Endless Night*, and Mike asks her to sing another song by William Blake:

Little Fly
Thy summer's play
My thoughtless hand
Has brushed away ...

SWIGATHA RATING 10/10

This is a genuine psychological thriller, not so much a *who-dun-it* as a *who-am-I*, the answer to which everyone seems to know bar the narrator. Most readers will be surprised by the denouement, but on re-reading it I found that the answer leapt from every page.

This is one of the best things that Agatha Christie ever wrote, and in Michael Rogers she has created her finest and most credible villain. This astonishing late flowering is in a different league to the other stories written around the same time.

Of all the 80 or so books that made up my re-read of the Christie canon, this is this one that has surprised me the most.

WHAT HAPPENED NEXT

Whether intentional or not, the sensation of the presence of evil is explored further in Agatha Christie's next book, featuring Tommy and Tuppence, entitled *By the Pricking of My Thumbs ...*

ADAPTATIONS

There is an interesting film, made in 1971, starring Hywel Bennett, Hayley Mills and Britt Ekland - very much stars of that time, and perfect for their parts; the supporting cast is a bit weak. The film sticks pretty closely to the original plot, but removes all the 'gipsy' elements, apart from the name of Michael's dream house.

There was also a version made as part of the ITV *Agatha Christie's Miss Marple* series. That sentence alone should be enough to put you off.

NOTES

[1] Jerry Burton narrates *The Moving Finger* (featuring Miss Marple); Dr Sheppard : *The Murder of Roger Ackroyd* (Poirot); Nurse Leatheran : *Murder in Mesopotamia* (Poirot); Anthony Cade : *The Secret of Chimneys* (Battle). Charles Hayward, narrator of *Crooked House*, confides in his father, the Assistant Commissioner of Scotland Yard.

[2] 'Dead sea fruit' is an expression for something that appears to be beautiful or full of promise, but is in reality nothing but illusion and disappointment (which Mike will soon discover for himself).

By the Pricking of my Thumbs (1968)

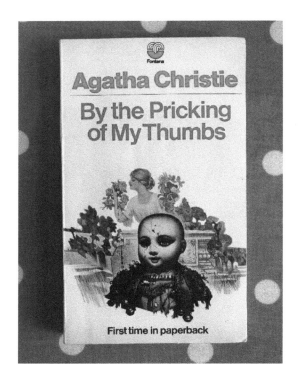

THE BOOK Fontana, 1971 pp 191

The Tom Adams cover is focussed on a doll found stuffed in a chimney, which proves to be a crucial part of the story. It is a very appropriate cover for a book which features a deranged serial killer of children. There has always been something eerie to me about broken dolls.

THE STORY

Tommy and Tuppence visit his Aunt Ada in her nursing home. Tuppence is thrown out of the irascible old lady's room. While waiting for Tommy to come out, she meets Mrs Lancaster, another resident. The latter inexplicably asks Tuppence whether it was her 'poor child' walled in behind the fireplace.

Aunt Ada dies soon afterwards and amongst her effects is a painting of a house by a canal that haunts Tuppence with memories of having seen it before. The painting had been given to Aunt Ada by Mrs Lancaster, who is no longer staying at the home when Tommy and Tuppence collect it.

Intrigued, and with Tommy away, Tuppence sets out to find the house.

THE TITLE

The title is a quote by one of the witches in *Macbeth*:

> *By the pricking of my thumbs, something wicked this way comes*

There is an old superstition that tingling in the fingers (or other bodily reactions) presaged something bad about to happen. In the play, the 'pricking' is the witch's reaction to the arrival on the scene of Macbeth; in the book, Tuppence feels a shudder of fear in the company of Julia Lancaster, but misunderstands the reason for it.

CHARACTERS AND ATTITUDES

Tommy and Tuppence are as Tommy-and-Tuppence-y as ever, with their habit of reliving their old cases again to the fore. Once she has set out on her own, Tuppence becomes a much less annoying character as she probes the spooky atmosphere of an out-of-the-way village, and reaches out to any inhabitants who remember a time long gone.

It is an enjoyable read; there is a great deal of gossiping about the past along the way, much of it repeated, but there again that is surely what one might expect.

Then Tommy returns, and all of a sudden we are on the trail of a gang of master-criminals that appears to have been in operation for at least fifty years. The story goes a bit haywire from then on.

When children and old ladies feature prominently in the later Agatha Christie stories they rarely conform to type: children are never innocent (and are often murdered, as in this story) and old ladies are never 'fluffy', but menacing and murderous (again, as in this story).

QUOTES

Something similar to this exchange occurs in two other Christie novels, both written before this one[1]:

> *"I see you're looking at the fireplace."*
>
> *"Oh. Was I?" said Tuppence, slightly startled.*
>
> *"Yes. I wondered - " she leant forward and lowered her voice, "- excuse me, was it your poor child?"*
>
> *Tuppence, slightly taken aback, hesitated.*
>
> *"I - no, I don't think so," she said.*

"I wondered. I thought perhaps you'd come for that reason. Someone ought to come some

time. Perhaps they will. And looking at the fireplace, the way you did. That's where it is, you

know. Behind the fireplace."

"Oh", said Tuppence. "Is it?"

"Always the same time," said Mrs Lancaster, in a low voice. "Always the same time of day."

This time at least it proves germane to the plot. I sometimes wonder whether the author was haunted by some broken dolls of her own past.

There is a great deal of rambling conversation in this story. Here, Sir Philip Starkie bewilders Tuppence (and this reader) with an adaptation of a famous quotation from *Peer Gynt* to describe his wife:

" 'Who was she? Herself? The real one, the true one

Who was she - with God's sign upon her brow?'

Did you ever read Peer Gynt*, Mrs Beresford?"*

He went to the window. He stood there a moment, looking out – Then he turned abruptly.

"She was my wife, God help me."

This is an indication to me of an author with ideas still buzzing around her head that beg to be included in the story, even if doing so corrupts the logic and flow of it[2]. Whoever was supposed to be editing these late stories must have been frightened of upsetting her.

SWIGATHA RATING 5/10

This is the eeriest swigatha, with a horrific protagonist. It has the perfect title and some good opening chapters, but tends to drift from then on.

It is still worth reading, but just that one reference to *Peer Gynt* symbolises a loss of control in comparison with her heyday that is evident throughout.

WHERE IT LED

Having re-introduced Tommy and Tuppence after a break of more than a quarter of a century, Christie brought them back five years later for one last outing in her final book, *Postern of Fate*. By then, sadly, she had almost literally lost the plot …

ADAPTATIONS

The ITV series *Agatha Christie's Miss Marple* adapted this book, with Geraldine McEwen as Miss Jane Marple joining Tommy (Anthony Andrews) and Tuppence (Greta Scacchi) for the ride. There is an amazing cast of bit-part players - Steven Berkoff, Claire Bloom, Bonnie Langford all playing tiny roles - but June Whitfield steals the show. The screenplay takes bizarre liberties with the original - Tuppence is portrayed as an alcoholic - but at least they had the good sense to drop the sub-plot about criminal masterminds and jewel thieves.

NOTES

[1] *Sleeping Murder* and *The Pale Horse*

[2] *Peer Gynt* is a play in verse by Henrik Ibsen. Over 20 years previously, in *The Hollow*, Agatha Christie had quoted the original, as Henrietta Savernake dumps a clay model of a face that she had been working on in the bin and considers death and personality: *'Where am I, myself, the whole man, the true man? Where am I with God's mark upon my brow?'* As quoted in *The Hollow*, the quote from *Peer Gynt* is relevant; it illuminates character and explains attitude. Its mutated presence here is unexplained and obscure.

Hallowe'en Party (1969)

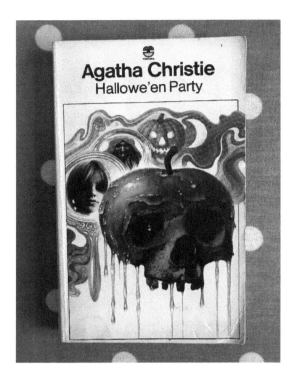
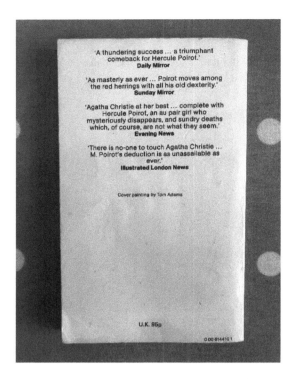

THE BOOK Fontana, 1969 pp 189

Tom Adams' cover is a straightforward representation of elements associated with Halloween, with the apple morphing into the top half of a skull that he had used in his painting for *The Hound of Death*.

THE STORY

During a Halloween Party given for teenagers, 13 year-old Joyce Reynolds boasts to Ariadne Oliver, writer of crime fiction, that she once witnessed a murder. At the end of the party Joyce is found drowned, with her head in a pail of water that had been used for bobbing for apples.

Mrs Oliver contacts Hercule Poirot and asks him to investigate ...

CHARACTERS

The cast of this story are unusual for an Agatha Christie book, because so many of the key roles are given to youngsters: Joyce, her older sister Ann and her younger brother Leopold; the elfin adolescent Miranda; and the intrepid teenagers Nicholas and Desmond, who are given an extraordinary level of responsibility by Poirot towards the end.

By contrast, the adult characters are almost peripheral until the emergence of Michael Garfield, a landscaping Narcissus with an obsession about creating his own Garden of Eden, and an apparently unhealthy obsession with Miranda. The chapters set in this garden seem to have come from a different writer, one more interested in her subject.

One other interesting character, who only appears in a lengthy flashback, is Olga Seminoff, yet another refugee from Central Europe[1] who inculcates herself into the affections of a wealthy employer, but one who is very sympathetically portrayed.

QUOTES AND ATTITUDES

There is a great deal of repetitive dialogue in the 'plot' section of this book, which in some cases point to an underlying theme but in others indicate sloppy editing.

Here are three takes on mental health provision at the time from Inspector Spence, Rowena Drake and Dr Ferguson respectively, all within the first 60 pages, and all saying the same thing:

> *"We had our mentally disturbed, or whatever they call them, but not so many as we have now. I expect there are more of them let out of the place they ought to be kept safe in."*

> *" ... someone of highly disturbed mentality, I suppose, the kind of people who are let out of mental homes simply because there is no room for them there, as far as I can see."*

> *"A lot of people who ought to be under mental restraint aren't under mental restraint. No room in the asylums."*

Although the actual deaths that occur in the story are the murder by an adult of a girl aged 13 and a boy aged 10, there are repeated examples given of the murderous nature of young children:

> *"Boy of 13. Wanted to kill someone so he killed a child of 9 ..."*

> *It was not unknown in the present age for children to commit crimes, quite young children. Children of 7, of 9 and so on.*

> *It was even possible that the killing which had occurred two or three years ago might have been committed by a boy, youth or adolescent of 14 to 12 years of age. Such cases had occurred in recent newspaper reports.*

And, finally, there is the matter of Poirot's footwear. It is difficult to believe that the author was making a particular point here (all these examples occur within twenty pages of each other):

> *"You know, if you'll excuse me saying so, you oughtn't to wear patent leather shoes in the country."*

> *"But why don't you wear proper country shoes?"*
> *"Madame, I like to look soigné in my appearance."*

> *"You'd be more comfortable in canvas shoes or sandals."*
> *"Ah, ça, non."*
> *"I see you are sartorially ambitious."*

> *"My feet. I am not very suitably attired as to footwear for the country. A change of shoes would be desirable."*

This is not one of those books that could have been set in any period. Here's a quote that pins the story into the late 1960s (I love the idea of 'Flower Pot'!):

> *"You know the sort of thing. Peculiar drugs and - what do they call it? - Flower Pot or Purple Hemp or L.S.D., which I have always thought just meant money, but apparently it doesn't."*
> *"I suppose it costs it," suggested Ariadne Oliver.*

Like David Baker in the previous 1960s Poirot novel, *Third Girl*, the 'Eden' section of the story has another representative of the Beautiful People, Michael Garfield. He has a limitless store of self-regard, and at the end Poirot softly intones an extremely appropriate old French song to sum him up[2]:

> *Regarde, Narcisse*
> *Regarde dans l'eau*
> *Regarde, Narcisse, que tu es beau.*

> *Il n'y a au monde*
> *que la beauté*
> *et la jeunesse,*
> *Hé-las, et la jeunesse.*

> *Regarde Narcisse*
> *Regarde dans l'eau.*

SWIGATHA RATING 5/10

I have to admit that I enjoyed this book more than I had expected or remembered, but it definitely reads as if an editor never touched it. Besides all the unnecessary repetitions mentioned above, there are also instances wherein seemingly pertinent developments are never explained. For example, there is one intriguing scene between Poirot and the headmistress Miss Emlyn, who has guessed the identity of the murderer, but we have to work out for ourselves why; she is never mentioned again.

It is difficult to swallow a ten-year old boy as a blackmailer, and Poirot's selection of a pair of teenagers to keep on the trail of a killer and save the life of Miranda seems very unlikely.

Still, I enjoyed it!

WHAT HAPPENED NEXT

Poirot and Mrs Oliver were re-united for the final time in *Elephants Can Remember*, three years later.

ADAPTATIONS

ITV's *Poirot* adaptation ignores all the talk of the mentally deficient and tones down the child elements: Nicholas, Ann and Desmond disappear, Leopold is almost twice the age of the book character and no-one discusses seven-year old delinquents. Poirot's shoes DO get a mention, but just the once.

It is one of the better later Poirot adaptations, but for some strange reason Ariadne Oliver (played by the terrific Zoe Wanamaker) is kept confined to bed for almost all of it. This does not happen in the book, and I fail to see the need for it.

NOTES

[1] Before Olga there had been Katrina (*How Does Your Garden Grow?*) and Sonia (*Third Girl*).

[1] Michael as 'Narcissus' – one of the Flower People?! The things that Poirot quotes / hums / sings softly are usually worth digging out, but I have not been able to find the origins of this song anywhere. Here is a rough translation:

Narcissus look,

Look on the water,

See how beautiful you are.

There is nothing to this world

But beauty and youth, alas,

Beauty and youth.

Look, Narcissus

Look on the water.

Maybe Agatha Christie wrote it ...

Passenger to Frankfurt (1970)

THE BOOK   Collins, 1970 pp 256

This book was a 1970 Christmas Present (my first 'Christie for Christmas'). The book had been published that year and was already into its second edition. The author describes it as 'an extravaganza'.

The paperback did not come out until 1972, by which time the wonderful 60s Fontana cover template had been abandoned. The one shown here for the first paperback edition is a mess, with its pitiful pseudo-Gothic script and Tom Adams' artless cover. For once, his bug-on-the-cover doesn't work, possibly because of the swastika graffiti-ed on to it.

THE STORY

Sir Stafford Nye, a bored, unsatisfied diplomat, is approached at Geneva Airport by a young woman who appeals for his help. Intrigued, he agrees to hand over to her his passport, and allows his drink to be drugged by her. She escapes; when he awakes, he determines to find her.

Before long, he finds himself entwined in a spider's web of world anarchy and a global conspiracy to re-assert the master race. Washington has been raised to the ground, and the powers that be are plotting to spray the legions of student demonstrators with 'Benvo', a miracle drug that spreads contentment.

I kid you not.

And Stafford marries the young woman, with a toy panda as his best man.

CHARACTERS AND ATTITUDES

There are quite a variety of characters in this book, from *Almanac de Gotha* leftovers to an asylum full of Adolf Hitlers. The story is so 'extravagant' that the interaction between these characters is totally unconvincing, and the climactic, senseless discussions about the use of 'Benvo' expose their lack of credibility.

Amongst the cast:

> - Sir Stafford Nye, a world-weary diplomat: *ce n'est pas un garçon serieux*
> - Countess Renata Zerkowski, a fearless heroine with great persuasive powers, reminiscent of Anna Scheele in *They Came to Baghdad*
> - Grafin Charlotte von Waldhausen, a huge Shelob of a woman, wallowing in her fat and bent on world domination
> - Lady Matilda Cleckheaton, Marplesque aunt of Stafford Nye and an old school chum of Charlotte
> - Mr Robinson, a 'regular' in late Christie books, large, yellow and world expert on money
> - Colonel Pikeaway, another late Christie regular, covered in ash and shrouded in cigar smoke
> - 25 people in a lunatic asylum convinced that they are Adolf Hitler, thereby shielding the real one, who had been hurriedly placed there in 1945 to escape the Russians entering Berlin
> - The Young Siegfried, a charismatic youth leader who may or may not be Hitler's son.

This is the daftest story I have ever read to the end.

QUOTES

Here are some comments on the times as seen through the author's eyes, beginning with an extract from her own introduction:

> *Hold up a mirror to 1970 in England ... Everyday there is a killing. A girl strangled. Elderly*
> *woman attacked and robbed of her meagre savings. Young men or boys - attacking or*

attacked. Buildings and telephone kiosks smashed and gutted. Drug smuggling. Robbery and

assault. Children missing and children's murdered bodies found not far from their homes.

That's not quite my over-riding impression of life in the UK in 1970. Here are some more signs of the times from the mouths of her characters:

She said, "Safe is a four-letter word but not the kind of four-letter word that people are interested in nowadays." (Renate)

A girl had been strangled in the park. Girls were always being strangled. One a day, he thought callously. No child had been kidnapped or raped this morning. That was a nice surprise. (Stafford Nye)

"Impossible to get anything down here now. Our own grocer ... turned suddenly into a supermarket, six times the size, all rebuilt, baskets and wire trays to carry round and try to fill up with things you don't want and mothers always losing their babies, and crying, and having hysterics. Most exhausting." (Lady Matilda)

Many of Agatha Christie's later novels suffer from a lack of editing; maybe the editors were baffled by what they were reading. This is an extract from a speech that starts off being made by Mr Robinson, the fat financier, and ends up in the mouth of James Kleek, secretary to Lord Altamount:

"It's quite simple," said Mr Robinson. "There are big movements afoot. There has to be money behind them. We've got to find out where that money is coming from ... I know a lot about money ... That's what you mean, sir, isn't it?" He half turned towards Lord Altamount. "That's the way you more or less put it to me."
"Yes, you're expressing things very well, James."

An editor might have pointed out that Peru is still part of South America:

"South America, as I say, is one of the strongholds. And Peru and South Africa also."

And again:

" ... there are four, five different divisions of power in South America, Cuba, Peru, Guatemala and so on."

The real Agatha Christie does still come through in patches. Here is Mr Robinson again:

"If you know a thing," he said, "it is always a great temptation to show that you know it; to talk about it, in other words. It is not that you want to give information, it is not that you have been offered payment to give information. It is just that you want to show how important you are. Yes, it's just as simple as that."

So, so true.

SWIGATHA RATING 1/10

It is almost impossible to succinctly summarise this book. It is described as an extravaganza, which should indicate a spectacular production, but it is nothing of the kind: it is a rambling, repetitive saga that splutters to its end. The best writing is contained in the first two pages of the author's introduction, which itself has deteriorated into nonsense by page four. From an unbelievable opening, the story goes steadily downhill until it arrives at an ending that defies analysis.

It gets one point because the physical book is great to hold, and Mr Robinson's strategy for uncovering the leaders of the conspiracy ('Follow the Money') at least makes sense, and anticipates the strategy that untangled a real-world political cover-up (Watergate) two or three years later.

WHERE IT LED

Straight to the top of the best-seller lists. When you are such a huge 'name' your publisher can get away with anything.

ADAPTATIONS

Unsurprisingly, there have been none, although there is a 'talking book' version read by Hugh Fraser, brave man.

Nemesis (1971)

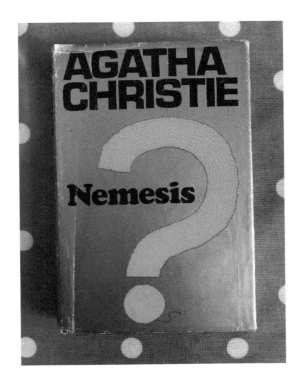
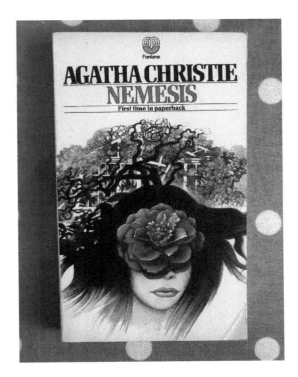

THE BOOK   Collins, 1971 pp 256

The hardback first edition cover refers to the pink woollen scarf that Miss Marple was wearing when she announced herself to Jason Rafiel as 'Nemesis' in *A Caribbean Mystery*. This book was another 'Christie for Christmas' present in 1971, and has worn well.

Tom Adams' cover for the paperback reflects the body of a young girl buried under a collapsed greenhouse, but what looks like a red camellia is a strange choice to represent the rampant white-flowering Russian vine (*polygonum baldschuanicum*) that was planted over her.

THE STORY

Miss Marple receives a post-mortem commission from Jason Rafiel, a man who had helped her prevent a murder in the Caribbean a couple of years previously. She has been hired to investigate a crime which Rafiel believed had resulted in a miscarriage of justice: the murder of Verity Hunt.

She is given no other indication, apart from a ticket for a coach tour, but she has confidence in Rafiel's planning, so she accepts her commission and joins the tour ...

CHARACTERS

The coach tour proves to be a journey into the past. All of the characters on the coach that are unconnected with that past fade almost immediately into the background, and we are left with the small cast invited by Rafiel to progress the plot:

- Professor Wanstead, a home office pathologist
- Miss Temple, the retired head of a girls' school
- Miss Cooke and Miss Barrow, an enigmatic pairing who seem to be spying on Miss Marple
- Lavinia, Clotilde and Anthea, the three erstwhile Bradbury-Scott sisters, trapped in their family home like characters out of Chekhov.

In the background are the ghosts: Rafiel himself, the murdered Verity Hunt and Nora Broad, plus Michael Rafiel, who is serving a life sentence for Verity's murder (the fate of Verity and Nora echoes a similar plot-line in an earlier Marple story, *The Body in the Library*).

Then there is Miss Marple herself. Unusually, she is the central character in a Marple story. Everything is seen through her eyes, and her thought processes are made clear - again and again, in some cases. But she is a very old lady, and the repetition does not jar as it does in some of the other Agatha Christie books of the period.

She has only one clue to work with, provided by Miss Temple: that Verity died of 'Love'. But there are many variations within that particular emotion ...

QUOTES AND ATTITUDES

A quotation from Longfellow comes to her mind when Miss Marple reads of Jason Rafiel's death:

Ships that pass in the night, and speak to each other in passing, only a signal shown, and a distant voice in the darkness ...

Miss Marple presumes that will be the last she hears of him, but the 'signals' and 'a distant voice in the darkness' are to continue from beyond the grave.

Miss Marple has a dream:

"I was talking to someone, not anyone I knew very well. Just talking. Then when I looked, I saw it wasn't that person at all I was talking to. It was somebody else. Very odd."[1]

Consciously or not, Agatha Christie has put a lot of herself, far more than usual, into the Miss Marple that appears in this book:

> Miss Marple had never quite succeeded in abandoning her Victorian view of foreigners. One never knew with foreigners. Quite absurd of course, to feel like that - she had many foreign friends from various countries. All the same ...

Miss Marple may have had many foreign friends from various countries but over the previous forty years of stories they had never been mentioned, nor the countries where they lived. Agatha Christie, on the other hand ...

Miss Marple considers the Three Sisters:

> They were what Miss Marple would have called in her youth by the now obsolete term 'ladies' - and what she once recalled calling 'decayed ladies'. Her father had said to her: "No, dear Jane, not decayed. Distressed gentlewomen."

Her own description turns out to be more appropriate than her father's correction.

1971 was clearly still a perilous time for young girls. An old man in a churchyard delivers a verdict on the young girls buried in it:

> "Silly girls, I call most of 'em. And their mums haven't got time to look after them properly nowadays - what with going out to work so much."

'Most of 'em'! How many young girls were buried in that churchyard?

The 1970s saw a long-overdue dawn of feminism in the UK. This comment by Professor Wanstead would have raised eyebrows even in 1971, but both it and similar lines elsewhere are leading the reader up the garden path:

> "Girls, you must remember, are far more ready to be raped nowadays than they used to be."

Everything is turned on its head when the truth is revealed. Gentle humour is such an important element of Agatha Christie's writing. Here is one of my favourite examples:

> "He had six camels, the boy's father, she said, and a whole troop of horses, and she was going to live in a wonderful house, she was, with carpets hanging up all over the walls, which seems a funny place to put carpets."

Archdeacon Brabazon comments on the relationship between Verity and Michael:

> *"Young women like bad lots. They always have. They fall in love with bad lots. They are quite sure they can change them."*

It reminds me of the hopeful bridal Wedding Vow: *Aisle Altar Hymn* ... but Brabazon believed that Verity would have done so. This was to be the last Jane Marple story that the author wrote. And what an appropriate exit she is given:

> *"Mr Rafiel would have liked me to have fun," said Miss Marple. She went out of the door.*

SWIGATHA RATING 6/10

Robert Barnard's summing up of this story ends: *All the usual strictures about late Christie apply.*[2] For once, I do not agree with him. Unlike the other 'murders in the past' stories written around this time, this plot is coherent and there are very few loose ends.

The opening idea was (once again) original and inspired: a commission from beyond the grave to investigate a crime that is otherwise devoid of useful leads. One might say that Miss Marple has been hired to conduct a 'Verity Hunt' – a search for the truth. The editing is still somewhat shoddy, but I enjoyed re-reading it, and it stands head and shoulders over both the book that preceded it and that which followed.

WHAT HAPPENED NEXT

One may presume that Rafiel's money meant that Jane Marple was no longer dependent on her nephew, 'dear Raymond', who had paid for the Caribbean trip and for many of her other holidays. She was now going to have some fun.

One of her earlier cases, *Sleeping Murder*, was published later, after the author had died, and later still some short stories, *Miss Marple's Final Cases*, appeared. But those had been written many years before. This was Marple's final appearance, and it is appropriate that her last act was to leave the room.

ADAPTATIONS

The BBC adaptation in 1987 is excellent, and I have to say that it improves the original. The main way that it achieves this is by its introduction to the heart of the story of two people 'down on their luck': Michael Rafiel and Lionel Peel, Miss Marple's godson.

Michael has not been jailed for life in this production, but is living, penniless, among down-and-outs in London. Lionel is a new character, one who has been thrown out of his home by his wife, and taken sanctuary with his godmother. She takes him on the coach tour with her, and it proves to be the making of him. The scene where Lionel and Michael meet at the end is a memorable one.

By contrast, I draw a veil over the ITV 2007 production, which has Verity in a nun's sanctuary and - oh, forget it.

NOTES

[1] This is another manifestation of Agatha Christie's childhood nightmares about 'The Gunman', who could assume the character and face of others at will, but only she could see it. (Agatha Christie *An Autobiography*, p 36).

[2] Robert Barnard *A Talent to Deceive*

Elephants Can Remember (1972)

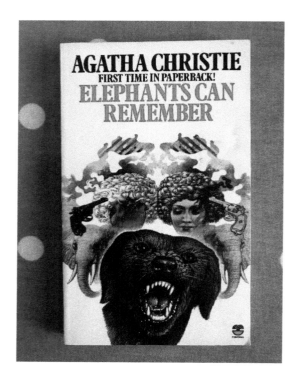
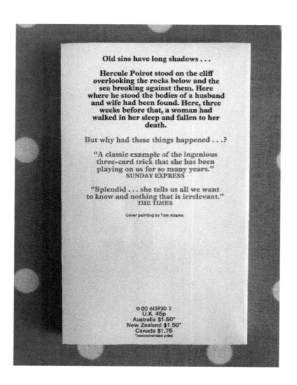

THE BOOK Fontana, 1975 pp 160

Tom Adams' cover references recognisable elements of the story and cleverly twins (a clue!) some of them, almost suggesting a Rorschach test.[1]

THE STORY

Mrs Ariadne Oliver (Agatha Christie in disguise) is button-holed at a literary luncheon by the overbearing Mrs Burton-Cox, who announces that her son Desmond is planning to marry Celia Ravenscroft (Mrs Oliver's god-daughter). Both of Celia's parents had died of gunshot wounds in a tragedy some dozen years previously, and Burton-Cox asks whether Celia's mother had killed her father and then shot herself, or whether it was *vice versa*.

Somewhat unbelievably, Mrs Oliver has no idea what happened, her excuse being that she had been on a literary tour of America at the time, but resolves to find out what she can, enlisting the aid of Hercule Poirot *en route*. He advises her to talk to as many people connected with the event as she can.

So she does, and finds out (again) that *Old Sins Have Long Shadows ...*

CHARACTERS

General Ravenscroft is married to Molly, a woman some 25 years younger than him, having previously been engaged to Molly's twin, Dolly. Molly is devoted to Dolly, but not vice versa ... *vice versa* is almost the main theme of the book.

The General and Molly had two children, both of whom were away at school at the time of the shootings. They had also employed two governesses to look after the children as they were growing up, first Maddy, then Zélie (not their real names, but the children's nicknames for them, presumably taken from their governess title *Made-moi-Selle*).

Mrs Oliver interviews a variety of characters (her 'elephants') who each remember a bit of, but never the whole of, the story. As in many late Christies, she uncovers cases of child-murder, with the culprit never being brought to justice, but it is Poirot who, by tracking down Zélie to Paris, is able to confirm what happened.

Also, as-in-many-late-Christies, Poirot's enquiries are supported by ex-Superintendent Spence and the wonderful Mr Goby.

QUOTES AND ATTITUDES

Once again, as was becoming increasingly the case, a late Christie is crying out for stricter editing, if only to reduce the amount of repetition. I am not sure, however, whether an editor would have allowed this strange comment to stay in or not:

> *"That's where you're going to, isn't it? Famous Writers of 1973 - or whichever year it is we've got to now."*

That is a strange statement for Mrs Oliver's maid-cum-dresser, Maria, to make. The year was 1972; whereas some people might imagine that they are still living in the previous year, it is rare indeed to find someone who think they are in a future one.

One of the persistent themes of late Christie[2] is child-murderers - in both senses: children who murder children, or their parents, or adults who murder children. Here, Mrs Oliver is asking about the Ravenscrofts' son Edward:

> *"There was no - no mental trouble, I suppose, in the family?"*
> *"Oh, you mean the boy - yes, that might be, of course. You do hear very strange things. There was that boy who shot his father - that was somewhere near Newcastle."*

Edward would have been about eleven years old at the time of his parents' murder. Here's a potential child-killer who would probably be even younger:

> *"Well, these things, as you know, happen quite often among children. Children are pushed in a perambulator into a pond sometimes because an older child, being jealous thinks that 'Mummy will have so much less trouble if Edward, or Donald, or whatever his name is, wasn't here ...'"*

These things 'happen quite often'? I have been alive for over 60 years, and I can think of only two cases in the UK where a child of 10 or 11 has killed another child. Maybe it would have happened more often if *this* had truly been the average day in the life of the UK:

> *"But look at what you read in the paper every day now. Young men, practically only boys still, shooting a lot of people for nothing at all, asking a girl in a pub to have a drink with them and then they see her home and the next day her body's found in a ditch. Stealing children out of prams from their mothers, taking a girl to a dance and murdering her or strangling her on the way back."*

'Every day'? Not quite how I remember 1972! This is almost a reprise of some of the author's introduction to *Passenger to Frankfurt*.

SWIGATHA RATING 3/10

Nothing actually happens in the present, apart from Mrs Oliver's interviews, and there were only three characters involved in the actions in the past, so as a 'swigatha' (i.e. a whodunit) it is not a difficult one to twig.

The solution is fairly clued, but if I ever have to read 'did the father kill the mother or did the mother kill the father?' one more time, I shall scream.

WHAT HAPPENED NEXT

This was the last Poirot story to be written, but it was followed a couple of years later by the publication of *Curtain*, which Agatha Christie had kept locked in a safe for some 30 years. One gets the impression from this book that she wishes she could have locked Poirot up with it: he hardly appears.

ADAPTATIONS

ITV's *Poirot* (2013): to paraphrase Robert Barnard, 'all the usual strictures about late ITV *Poirot* adaptations apply'. This production introduces a new character who murders another new character, then tries to strangle a man twice her size, and ends up trying, again unsuccessfully, to throw Celia off a balcony.

The producers clearly felt that not enough happens in the book, which is true, and try to compensate, but it might have worked better if they had stuck with the original plot and cut the running time to one hour.

On the positive side, there is another fine performance by Zoe Wanamaker as Ariadne Oliver.

NOTES

[1] Rorschach Test: 'The Rorschach test is a psychological test in which subjects' perceptions of reflective inkblots are recorded and then analysed using psychological interpretation ... ' In the book, Mrs Oliver asks a string of people about their memories and impressions of an event in the past, and receives a variety of interpretations of it.

[2] See also *By the Pricking of my Thumbs*, *Halloween Party* and *Nemesis*.

Postern of Fate (1973)

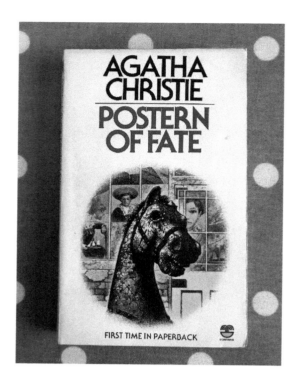
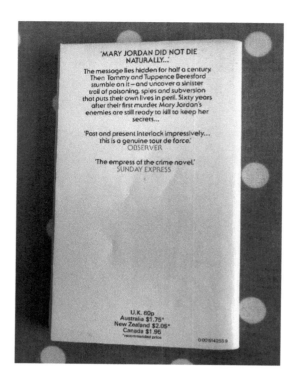

THE BOOK Fontana, 1976 pp 221

Tom Adams' cover references a tumble-down conservatory, a rocking-horse (Mathilde) found within it and the Edwardian era children who used it. French editions of this book are named after the rocking horse (*Le Cheval à Bascule*), which seems more appropriate than an irrelevant quote from James Flecker.

Like many of the paperback editions from the mid-1970s, this book has not survived well, with whole sections coming apart.

THE STORY

Just before the First World War, a boy, Alexander Parkinson, leaves a coded message in his copy of RL Stevenson's *The Black Arrow*:

> *Mary Jordan did not die naturally. It was one of us. I think I know which.*

About 60 years later, Tommy and Tuppence Beresford move to their new home and discover the book and the message. They also discover that Mary Jordan did indeed die young, as did Alexander (at the age of fourteen). They decide to investigate further, and come across plenty of people who were around at the time and pleased to reminisce about it.

CHARACTERS

Tommy and Tuppence Beresford have moved house. They are now 50 years into their career (having begun it as Bright Young Things) and at least it shows. Their usual jolly banter is toned down somewhat, mainly because Tuppence assumes the character of the author herself.

As she investigates her new home, like a child exploring, Tuppence comes across many items from Agatha Christie's own childhood at Ashfield, such as an old greenhouse named "KK" containing Mathilde, a clapped-out rocking horse; Truelove, a horse and cart that had belonged to Agatha's brother Monty, and a croquet set. On the bookshelves in the bedrooms are favourites of young Agatha such as Mrs Molesworth's *The Cuckoo Farm*, plus *Four Winds Farm*, *The Prisoner of Zenda* and *The Black Arrow*. Mrs Molesworth has nothing to do with the plot but gets mentioned at least as often as some of the characters who have.

Here is an example of an autobiographical reference:

> *"Yes," said Tuppence. "I read when I was five years old. Everybody could, when I was young. I didn't know one even had to sort of learn. I mean, somebody would read stories aloud, and you liked them very much and you remembered where the book went back on the shelf and you were always allowed to take it out and have a look at it yourself, and so you found you were reading it too, without bothering to learn to spell or anything like that."*

(Agatha Christie taught herself to read at the age of five; she did not go to school as a child, and her mother wouldn't teach her.)

An exasperated Tommy retreats into the smoke-filled rooms of power that house the by-then ubiquitous Colonel Pikeaway and 'Mr Robinson'[2]. The latter is simply described as 'yellow', and no explanation is proffered as to who he is or what he does, but he seems to know everything. Robinson is Christie's equivalent of Ian Fleming's 'M': in this case, M stands for Money. All we get to know about Pikeaway is that he smokes a lot.

Tuppence's investigations lead to interminable conversations with groups of very elderly people, who appear to have very contradictory memories about events of 60 years before - a touch of *verismo*, at least! There are over twenty of these people, and it is very difficult to differentiate between any of them.

There is also a group of 10-year-old children who seem to know as much about the events of 60 years before as their great-grand-parents.

Neither the old nor the young ever come up with anything concrete; instead, there are 150 pages of hints, repetitions and contradictions. Tuppence's investigation is one massive shaggy dog story, and indeed it is a dog, based on one of the author's Manchester terriers, who points the way to the culprit.

ATTITUDES AND QUOTES

Here is a sample of the text that reflects its inconsistencies. At the end of Chapter XI, Pikeaway tells Thomas he 'knows all about it' (an attempt on Tuppence's life) and advises him to stay where he is:

> *"Colonel Pikeaway?"*
>
> *"Ah, it's you, Thomas Beresford, isn't it?"*
>
> *"Ah, you recognised my voice. I wanted to tell you that – "*
>
> *"Something about Tuppence. I've heard it all," said Colonel Pikeaway. "No need to talk. Stay where you are for the next day or two or a week. Don't come up to London."*

On the very next page, at the start of Chapter XII, Tommy is in London to tell Pikeaway about what happened to Tuppence:

> *"Good man," said Colonel Pikeaway, puffing out smoke. "Sorry to send for you so urgently but I thought I'd better see you."*
>
> *"As I expect you know," said Tommy, "we've been having something a little unexpected lately."*
>
> *"Ah, why should you think I know?"*

You could not really blame an author in her 80s for these contradictions, but someone should have spotted this (and many other examples).

Elsewhere, there are plenty of (usually approving) references to the 'Common Market' - the UK had joined what was then the EEC at the beginning of 1973, the year the book was written. The sub-plot involves the re-awakening of some kind of fascist youth conspiracy (again - see *Passenger to Frankfurt*) and a properly-run pan-European state is seen by Colonel Pikeaway as the strongest bulwark against it:[3]

"It's a good thing, the Common Market. It's what we always needed, always wanted. But it's got to be a real Common Market. That's got to be understood very clearly. It's got to be a united Europe."

The title quote comes from *The Gates of Damascus*, by James Ellroy Flecker.

Four great gates hath the city of Damascus ... Postern of Fate, the Desert Gate, Disaster's Cavern, Fort of Fear ...

The same four lines are quoted again and again in the book, but I am at a loss as to their relevance.

SWIGATHA RATING 2/10

Postern of Fate was the last book that Agatha Christie wrote and it shows: there is far too much rambling on, non-sequitur and repetition in the scenes featuring Tommy and Tuppence. This bespeaks a lack of reading and editing prior to publication, but in fact It was previewed. Perhaps they didn't want to bother the old lady.

For fans of Agatha Christie, the story has a certain charm and interest, because she has put so many of her memories into it: some pages could have come directly from the early pages of her Autobiography. As a *swigatha*, however, it is a dead loss: we never find out who killed Alexander Parkinson, the murderer of Mary Jordan is not given a name, and the latter-day villain only turns up with about twenty pages to go, having not been previously mentioned.

The original idea is a great variation on the 'old-sins-have-long-shadows' groove that she had become stuck in, but by the end it would take a Bletchley Park super-brain to provide a fluent solution to this puzzle.

WHERE IT SHOULD LEAD / ADAPTATION

The book was a best-seller for Christmas 1973, but by then people would buy anything by her (I know, I did!). I think that it would be worth trying to create a version of this story that has been properly edited and proof-read; it would lose many pages but could lead to something interesting, such as a different type of adaptation to those to which we have become accustomed.

I am not aware of any versions of this story on screen, TV or radio so far, and maybe the Christie estate is happy to leave it at that. All the same, there is an opportunity for a talented writer to strip away all the fluff and nonsense from the original and create a genuinely nostalgic mystery out of what remains. It would not make a gripping film or serial, but it could provide a very interesting play for voices-only on the radio, exploiting some of the ramblings of characters both young and old, with reference also to the author's *Autobiography* and maybe including extracts from the recordings that she herself made for BBC Radio.

NOTES

[1] Agatha Christie, *An Autobiography*. Although completed in 1965, the book was not published until 1977, after she had died (and after *Postern of Fate*, so no original reader would have got the autobiographical references).

[2] Both of these shady characters also appear in *Passenger to Frankfurt*. Prior to that, they had the pleasure of encountering Hercule Poirot (*Cat Among the Pigeons*), and the thrice-blessed Mr Robinson appears in a case for Miss Marple (*At Bertram's Hotel*).

[3] One wonders what Pikeaway would have made of Brexit; I suspect he'd have hired Mr Robinson to 'follow the money' to some very interesting places.

Poirot's Early Cases (1974)

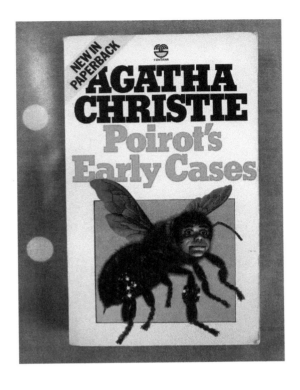

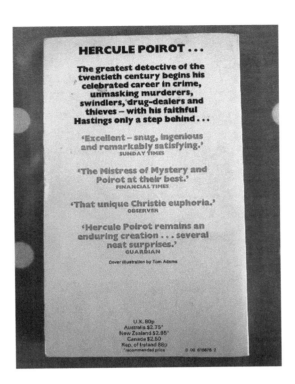

THE BOOK Fontana, 1979 pp 222

The Tom Adams cover, featuring a bee, jewels and a ventriloquist's dummy, references three of the stories in the collection. He sure liked his insects! The original painting would have looked great on the old Fontana style cover, but doesn't here. Also, once again with these editions, the book has not survived the test of time: whole chunks of pages have detached themselves from the binding.

THE STORIES

There are eighteen stories in this collection. They were written in the 1920s/30s. Many had appeared in magazines, but never in a collection in the UK until this book came out shortly before the author's death. Hastings narrates all but three of them, and the final story features the first appearance of Miss Lemon as Poirot's confidential secretary.

The Affair at the Victory Ball

Six people attend a fancy-dress ball in the guise of characters inspired by the *Commedia dell'Arte*. One is murdered. Agatha Christie had a set of these figures in her childhood and used **them a few** times in her stories.

The Adventure of the Clapham Cook

Poirot is hired to investigate the disappearance of a cook. He receives a cheque for one guinea for his pains

The Cornish Mystery

Mrs Pengelly contacts Poirot and says that she thinks she is being poisoned. Poirot goes to Cornwall the following day and finds that she has died.

The Adventure of Johnny Waverley

Kidnappers announce that they intend to take away a young boy at a particular date and time. In spite of the precautions taken to prevent this, the time arrives and the boy disappears. This is an early example of Poirot allowing the culprit to escape justice.

The Double Clue

Poirot's first encounter with Countess Vera Rossakoff. A jewel theft enables him to display his command of the Cyrillic alphabet. Once again, the culprit is allowed to evade exposure.

The King of Clubs

An odious man is found dead at his home. The person who caused his death is allowed to escape any workings of the law.

The Lemesurier Inheritance

The inheritance in this story refers to both the genetic make-up of an eldest son and also the title and country house which he is apparently doomed not to inherit.

The Lost Mine

Poirot tells Hastings a story involving Chinamen in Limehouse. His rendering of their reported English speech consists of the addition of -ee as a suffix to each noun and verb. Very unlike Poirot – a dreadful story.

The Plymouth Express

This mystery, set on the train to Plymouth, was later to provide the core plot for *The Mystery of the Blue Train*, a full-length story written a couple of years later (when the author was recovering from a breakdown).

The Chocolate Box

Poirot tells Hastings another story, this time set in Belgium when he was a policeman there. For the first (and last) time, he makes a mistake in his deductions; also for the first (but not the last) time he allows the culprit to go unpunished.

The Submarine Plans

Poirot investigates the disappearance of some plans at the home of a future prime minister. Once again, he allows the secrets he uncovers there to be hushed up afterwards. Re-worked as a longer story, *The Incredible Theft*, in the *Murder in the Mews* collection.

The Third Floor Flat

Four young people find themselves locked out of their flat. Two of them try to break in using the service lift, only to find themselves in the wrong flat with the body of the dead woman. Poirot investigates and solves the case, allowing the culprit to get away in the process.

Double Sin

Poirot and Hastings take a coach tour and find themselves involved in a hunt for some stolen antique miniatures. Agatha Christie's titles are usually pretty apposite but I'm blowed if I know what this one refers to.

The Market Basing Mystery

Market Basing appears a few times in swigathas[1]. This particular story has a plot that was re-used almost exactly for the slightly longer *Murder in the Mews*. I'm surprised that Japp and Poirot, who appear in both, didn't notice.

Wasps' Nest

Poirot prevents a 'murder'. This is an excellent story, one of her best; there is no Hastings, so I would think that this was written later than most of the others.

The Veiled Lady

Poirot is hired to steal some jewels. The plot, involving a blackmail letter, just does not bear close scrutiny.

Problem at Sea

A classic story, with a perfect setting for the 1990s TV series that featured all but one of these stories. Featuring ventriloquism, hence the dummy in Tom Adams' painting. No Hastings or Japp in this one, so no quips from the latter about Hastings being 'Poirot's dummy'.

How Does Your Garden Grow?

Poirot is contacted by Mrs Barrowby, who is frantically worried about something that she does not specify. He goes to visit her and finds that she has died. An ok short story that assumes a greater significance as far as Dame Agatha's readers are concerned: it is the first time he is seen working with Miss Lemon. No Hastings in this story – not surprisingly as he and Miss Lemon never actually met.

SWIGATHA RATING 6/10

This is a stronger (and longer) collection of stories than the previous group narrated by Captain Hastings (*Poirot Investigates*, 1924). This volume was first published in the UK 50 years later, which allowed some of Dame Agatha's later stories to be included.

On no fewer than six occasions, Poirot allows the culprit to go unapprehended by the forces of the law.

WHERE IT LED

Three of these stories were re-used in longer formats and published under different titles between 1928 and 1937, which may explain why this collection took so long to see the light of day.

Hastings would only narrate one more published short story – *The Mystery of the Baghdad Chest*, which appeared posthumously in the 1997 collection *While the Light Lasts*. Exactly the same story, except this time with Miss Lemon rather than Hastings, had appeared already, with the only noticeable difference being that the chest was Spanish.

In the 1930s, Agatha Christie started working on what some people consider her finest set of short stories – *The Labours of Hercules*. The stories appeared in *The Strand* magazine and come out as a book in 1947. Those were the last short-format stories featuring Poirot that she *wrote*, although some earlier ones were not published until later.

ADAPTATIONS

All of the stories in this collection, with the exception, for some reason, of *The Lemesurier Inheritance,* appeared in their shorter or longer format in the ITV *Poirot* series. Many are beautifully done, with *Wasp's Nest* in particular standing out.

NOTES

[1] For example, *The Secret of Chimneys*, *Dumb Witness* and *By the Pricking of my Thumbs*.

Curtain (1975)

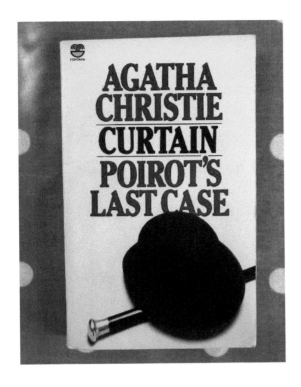
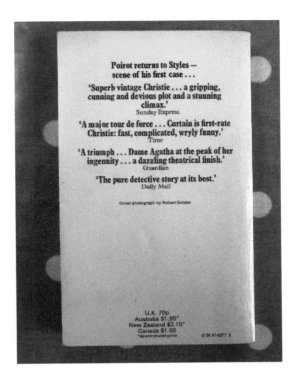

THE BOOK   Fontana, 1977 pp 188

The photographic cover of the Fontana paperback first edition is quite different to those that it had previously published by the same author. There must have been a decision made not to commission a cover from Tom Adams, although he did return for Sleeping Murder. It works, though ...

THE STORY

Captain Hastings, recently widowed, has returned to England. He receives a letter from Hercule Poirot inviting him to come and stay with him at Styles, the scene of their first adventure in England together. An ailing Poirot tells him that they are going to hunt down a murderer once more - one staying at Styles.

As the title implies, it is to be the last time that they would hunt together ...

CHARACTERS - spoiler!

Strangely, for the 1940s saw Agatha Christie at the peak of her powers when it came to characterisation, the cast at Styles (apart, of course, from Poirot and Hastings) are a pretty unattractive bunch, with some taken out of central casting and some hardly described at all. The killer, and victim, becomes interesting only in retrospect.

So we have Boyd Carrington, retired from Empire and very old school, the type of colonial buffer that Agatha Christie often satirises: a pompous old bore who repeats other people's stories back to them; Colonel Luttrell, an incompetent failure and his shrewish wife; Major Allerton, a philanderer (ex-Army officers are rarely upstanding in Agatha Christie); Dr Franklin, a genocidally-inclined scientist obsessed with his experiments to the exclusion of all else, and his wife, permanently tired and taking the vapours. Nurse Craven hardly emerges from the page.

At least Hastings' daughter Judith rings true: fearless, she is her mother's daughter all right, and her exasperated affection for her muddled father matches that of her 'uncle' Hercule.

But that does not bring light relief: this is a dark book, with its reference to 'an epidemic' of pain and torture 'in the world of late years' and plenty of talk of the desirability of ridding the world of degenerates.

Even Judith's father, the genial, genuine and likeable Arthur Hastings, is revealed as the thwarted would-be murderer of an innocent man, and as for his long-time associate Poirot ...! This *bon catholique*, who 'does not approve of murder', commits a mortal sin by carrying out the cold-blooded murder of another person.

QUOTES AND ATTITUDES

Seasoned readers would sit up and take notice immediately when Hastings warms to someone from 'the old school': so many prove to be blackmailers, drug dealers or killers:

> *He was very good-looking, though a man well over fifty, with a deeply tanned face. He looked as though he had led an outdoors life, and he looked, too, the type of man that is becoming more and more rare, an Englishman of the old school, fond of out-of-doors life, and the kind of man who can command ... Governor of a province in India ... first-class shot and big-game hunter ... the sort of man, I reflected sadly, that we no longer seem to breed in these degenerate days.*

Interesting that Christie gives Hastings the line about 'these degenerate days': she was writing just after the Battle of Britain, Britain and its Empire's 'finest hour'. They were at the time fighting the overwhelmingly superior Axis Powers on their own; the Nazis, of course, had their own views about 'degenerates' (and what to do about them).

Hastings' daughter Judith weighs in with her solution to the degeneracy problem:

> *"Unfit, useless lives - they should be got out of the way. There's so much mess about. Only*
> *people who can make a decent contribution to the community ought to be allowed to live.*
> *The others ought to be painlessly put away."*

She is obviously under the malign influence of Dr Franklin, whose opinions are strong:

> *"If an imbecile - a cretin - dies, it's a good thing."*

> *"It's an idea of mine, you know, that about eighty percent of the human race ought to be*
> *eliminated. We'd get on much better without them."*

What a nice idea to have, especially at a time when death camps were being built as the final solution to rid the world of Jews, Roma, homosexuals and, yes, 'cretins'. What shocks this reader is the realisation that whereas Captain Hastings is prepared to murder the womaniser Allerton, whom he mistakenly thinks is going to seduce his daughter, he is quite happy at the end to endorse her going off to marry a genocidally-inclined lunatic.

There are few innocent young children in Agatha Christie's stories; rather too many are reported as being murderous or sadistic:

> *"I have known a child, annoyed by its kitten, say 'Keep still or I will kill you' and actually do*
> *so - to be stunned and horrified a moment later when it realises the kitten's life will not*
> *return ... "*

Almost as light relief, here is a classic, and typical, example of Poirot and Hastings in conversation (although they had worked together off and on for over twenty years, Hastings never has an inkling of what Poirot is thinking or how he is feeling):

> *"I find it painful to be here, in a way, and yet it brings back to me a hundred old thoughts and*
> *emotions that I'd quite forgotten I ever felt. I dare say you feel the same."*
> *"Not in the least. I do not feel like that at all."*
> *"They were good days," I said sadly.*
> *"You may speak for yourself, Hastings. For me, my arrival at Styles St Mary was a sad and*
> *painful time. I was a refugee, wounded, exiled from home, existing by charity in a foreign*
> *land ..."*
> *"I had forgotten that," I admitted.*

> *"Precisely. You attribute always to others the sentiments that you yourself experience. Hastings was happy - everyone was happy!"*

No-one is happy in this book.

It was a brilliant idea to start and end the partnership between Poirot and Hastings at the same place: *à la fin comme au commencement* … Nothing has changed in their 20-year relationship, as Poirot writes in his confessional letter:

> *You should, mon ami, have been able to arrive at the truth. I saw to it that you had every indication. If you have not, it is because, as always, you have far too beautiful and trusting a nature.* A la fin comme au commencement.

SWIGATHA RATING 7/10

Agatha Christie had two brilliant ideas as to how to crown Poirot's career (and polish him off!): the return to Styles, and the creation of an Iago-esque villain, with Poirot as his judge, jury and executioner. But I don't think it is one of the best. There is too much padding: pages and pages of dialogue with Hastings demanding that Poirot take him into his confidence and Poirot refusing, for example.

Indeed, the character of Hastings is so dominant that hardly anyone else gets a look in. Yes, he is the narrator, but too much of his narration revolves around his own reactions and what he is thinking.

WHAT HAPPENED NEXT

The story was written during the Blitz on London in 1940, which Agatha Christie was not sure she would survive: maybe that contributed to the underlying tone of the book. It was to be locked away in a vault and published after her death; in the event, the book was published in 1975, the year before it. Poirot's death attracted an obituary on the front cover of *The New York Times*.

Poirot and Hastings never did hunt together again, but Poirot, having already made one appearance that year (*Sad Cypress*), soon came back to life to make another one (*One, Two Buckle My Shoe*), followed in 1941 by *Evil Under The Sun*. Maybe writing took Agatha Christie's mind off things; certainly, those books were less dark.

ADAPTATIONS

There has been one: for ITV's *Poirot* series. It features a quite remarkable performance by David Suchet, who shed two stone to age himself and look weak, and a very good one by Aidan McArdle as his adversary, Stephen Norton. Thankfully, for once, no-one in the production team saw fit to try and improve the original story.

Sleeping Murder (1976)

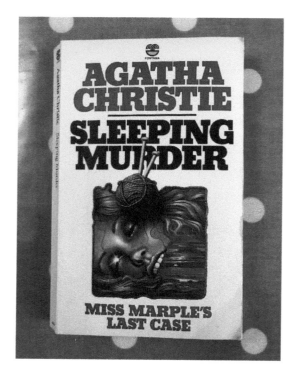
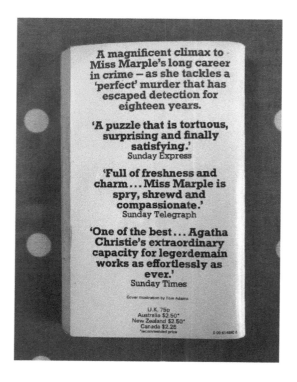

THE BOOK Fontana, 1978 pp 192

Tom Adams' scope for this cover was limited by the demands of the publisher, who wanted a Marple memorial that included large text and her knitting[1].

Unlike most of the Fontana paperbacks I have from the 1960s, but like most of their paperbacks from the mid-70s, my edition is coming apart a bit.

THE STORY

Newly-wed orphans Gwenda and Giles Reed are house-hunting in Devon. Gwenda believes that she has found the perfect place, and they buy Hillside, but when they move in she is haunted by the feeling that she knows the house very well. Too well. A visit to a performance of *The Duchess of Malfi* shocks her into a memory of a murder that she had witnessed there as a young child.

Fortunately, Miss Marple is beside her in the theatre ...

This story was written at some time in the 1940s-1950s (it is not very clear when, exactly[2]) and locked away in a vault, to be published as a Marple swansong after the author's death.

CHARACTERS

The characterisation in this book is not memorable. The newly-weds are charming, intrepid *et cetera* but it takes some believing that two young orphans (Gwenda is 21) would be able to buy a huge house with a large garden in Devon.

The most interesting characters in this story - Gwenda's father, Kelvin Halliday, and his wife Helen - are both already dead when it starts, but they come alive in the story from descriptions by others.

Helen's supposed suitors (Messrs Fane, Erskine and Affleck) are very succinctly described - e.g. Walter Fane, 'the ghost of a spider' - but none of them really seems to have much of a motive for murder and they each disappear from the memory once they have left the page.

It is a slightly strange book, because it does not seem to be set in any particular time. Most of the swigathas written during the late 1940s and early 1950s, which this one presumably was[2], either reference World War II in some way, or the privations that followed it, or the introduction of the Welfare State into the UK, or the establishment of a National Health Service, or all four: not this one. Maybe this was deliberate, given that the story was going to be locked away until sometime after the author's death.

QUOTES AND ATTITUDES

One thing, however, that does come across as very much of the time that the book was written are the little Englander prejudices expressed.

Mr Galbraith describes the Jellaby-esque Elworthys, previous owners of Hillside:

> *"Elworthys - that's it - pack of women - sisters. Changed the name - said St Catherine's was Popish. Very down on anything Popish - used to send out tracts. Plain women, all of 'em - took an interest in n*****s - sent 'em out trousers and bibles."*

Here is another character very down on anything Popish:

> *"Robert is in the Army." Mrs Fane sniffed. "Married a Roman Catholic," she said with significance. "You know what that means!"*

The maid Lily comments about her fellow-servant, the Swiss nursemaid Léonie:

"That Layonee, she was a bit stupid like all foreigners, couldn't understand proper what you said to her - and her English was something awful."

There are many Lily Kimbles still around the UK today, wondering why silly foreigners can't speak English properly. Léonie's English may not have been perfect, but Lily's French would have been non-existent; Agatha Christie's French was pretty good, and this is another example of her gentle ribbing of Anglo-Saxon attitudes. Another one is Mr Kimble's reply:

"'Don't you pay no attention to foreigners, my girl,' I said. 'One and all they're liars. Not like us.'"

Dr Kennedy confides to Giles that people should know their place:

"I'm old-fashioned, young man. In the modern gospel, one man is as good as another. That holds morally, no doubt. But I'm a believer in the fact that there is a state of life into which you are born - and I believe you're happiest staying in it."

Maybe Giles might have pointed out to him that one man was held to be as 'good as another' in the original gospels too.

SWIGATHA RATING 6/10

The identity of the villain is not a huge surprise, given their presence in the story and the shallowness of the other characterisations within it. What was a surprise to me on re-reading was that there were (at least) four victims on that villain's conscience - I could only remember two.

This is an ok-to-middling Agatha Christie, just begging for a good adaptation that fleshes out the minor characters a bit (which it got).

WHAT HAPPENED NEXT

Although this book is subtitled *Miss Marple's Last Case*, chronologically her final case was actually *Nemesis* in 1971. She re-appeared in 1979, when some old short stories featuring her were published with an equally misleading title (*Miss Marple's Final Cases*).

ADAPTATIONS

There was an excellent BBC adaptation for its *Miss Marple* series in 1987. It was very faithful to the original text, but gave the suitors and Halliday's servants more of a share of the limelight. The casting director did a superb job: the minor parts are beautifully played, with John Bennett hugely sympathetic as the put-upon Erskine and Frederick Treves the opposite as Helen Kennedy's brother.

There was also another, inferior version made in 2006 for ITV's *Agatha Christie's Miss Marple* series which is 'not really pretending to be true to the original'[3].

NOTES

[1] *Tom Adams' Agatha Christie Cover Story*

[2] John Curran *Agatha Christie's Secret Notebooks.*
The legend had been that this book was written during the Blitz (as Hercule Poirot's own swansong *Curtain* had been) but Dr Curran proves, from the references to it in the notebooks, that it must have been a few years later than that.

[3] Mark Aldridge, *Agatha Christie on Screen*

Miss Marple's Final Cases (1979)

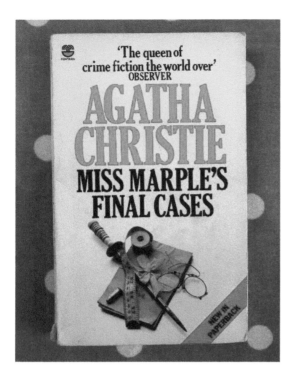
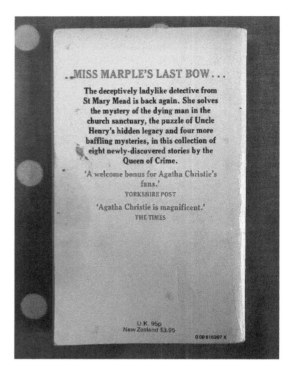

THE BOOK   Fontana, 1979 pp 154

The cover above features some items from the stories - the dressmaker's tape-measure, some envelopes ... The noticeable thing about this cover Is the font-size used for the author's name. It had been getting steadily larger since the covers of the 1960s.

THE STORIES

There are eight stories in this collection, with six featuring Jane Marple.

These stories were published for the first time as a collection after the author had died. Four had been published in *The Strand* magazine and three in *Woman's Journal*, the last one in 1954.

The final one, *Miss Marple Tells a Story*, was a commission for BBC radio in 1934 (and the story was told on air, appropriately enough, by Agatha Christie herself).

Sanctuary

Agatha Christie returns to Chipping Cleghorn, which had been the setting for *A Murder is Announced*.

Vicar's wife Bunch Harmon comes across a dying man whilst decorating the church with chrysanthemums; he gasps a few words before dying. Two people claiming to be relatives come to the vicarage and identify the man, but arouse Bunch's suspicions whilst doing so. She decides to consult her godmother ...

Strange Jest

Two young people are set a test of their ingenuity by their uncle as they try to secure their inheritance after he has died. Jane Helier[1] advises them to consult Miss Marple.

Tape Measure Murder

An excellent and original murder story, set in St Mary Mead and featuring some familiar village names - Constable Palk, Inspector Slack, Miss Hartnell, Colonel Melchett - plus some names that Agatha Christie ended up using elsewhere - Ted Gerard, Murgatroyd, Harmon.

The Case of the Caretaker

A young scapegrace returns home to St Mary Mead having married a rich heiress. Soon afterwards, his wife is thrown from her horse, which had apparently been startled by the sudden appearance of an old woman cursing and waving her arms about. Dr Haydock is not convinced that all is as it seems, and sets Miss Marple the challenge of working out what actually happened.

The Case of the Perfect Maid

Miss Marple's maid, Edna, asks her to help restore the reputation of her cousin Gladys, who has been dismissed from service on suspicion of attempted theft. A classic St Mary Mead story, beautifully done, with Miss Marple in fine form:

> *"They won't get away with it this time! I'm not going to have one of our village girls' character for honesty taken away like that! Gladys Holmes is as honest as the day, and everyone's going to know it! Good afternoon!" Miss Marple had stalked out before Inspector Slack had recovered ...*

Miss Marple Tells a Story

An old solicitor friend of hers, Mr Petherick[1], asks Miss Marple to investigate the murder of a woman, for which one of his clients is almost sure to be convicted. She uncovers a story steeped in genuine tragedy.

The Dressmaker's Doll

Two dressmakers are terrified and haunted by a puppet doll that seems to be able to please itself. This story has one of Agatha Christie's rare punning jests contained in it: the name of the Pekinese dog accompanying a customer to a fitting is Fou-Ling ...

In a Glass Darkly

During a leave of absence from the battlefields of the First World War, a man has a vision in a mirror of a girl being strangled in a bedroom. Four years later, he finds himself in a bedroom with his hands around the same girl's throat ...

SWIGATHA RATING 6/10

There are some excellent stories in this collection, but one gets the impression one has heard many of them before.

For example, compare the start of *Sanctuary* with that of *Why Didn't They Ask Evans?*, in which a vicar's son comes across a dying man, who gasps a last few words before dying; two people claiming to be relatives come to the vicarage and identify the man but arouse suspicions ... etc.

Similarly, *The Case of the Caretaker* is an early version of *Endless Night*, and *Strange Jest* is almost an identical plot to one of the stories in *Poirot Investigates*.

Having said that, this book is a treat for fans of Miss Marple's home ground: not many of the Marple novels are set in her home village, but most of these stories are set in St Mary Mead or nearby.

ADAPTATIONS

In a Glass Darkly was adapted for the small screen as one of the stories in ITV's *The Agatha Christie Hour*, but none of the other stories have been.

NOTES

[1] Characters that originally appeared in *The Thirteen Problems*.

THE BOOK   Fontana, 1992 pp 227

A rather dashed-off Fontana cover presumably features elements of some of these stories - for example, a champagne glass from *Yellow Iris* - but I am blowed if I know what the rest are. The back cover mentions three of the stories that feature stalwart Christie characters, but gives no indication of the two that don't.

These stories were written between 1925 and 1971. A typical AC paperback from 1971 would have had 40 lines on a page. This similarly-sized 1992 paperback has 30, so if these stories had been published in a collection at the time when the last of them was written (and Agatha Christie was alive), the book would have been 55 pages shorter.

THE STORIES

There are eight stories in this collection: two feature Parker Pyne, two Hercule Poirot and two Harley Quin. Reading them now, one cannot but help think (again) that one has read many of them before.

Problem at Pollensa Bay (first published in 1936)
In which Parker Pyne resolves a mother's fears for her son's future with the help of Madeleine de

Sara, aka Dolores Ramona, aka Maggie Sayers, whom the mother condemns thus: *"The creature's a Dago."* Madeleine had performed a similar role in *The Case of the Discontented Soldier*, from *Parker Pyne Investigates*.

The Second Gong (1932)

Hercule Poirot is hired by a man who thinks he is being swindled. He travels to the man's home only to find that he has been killed by the time he arrives. Basically the same plot as *Dead Man's Mirror*, one of the stories from *The Murder in the Mews*.

Yellow Iris (1937)

Hercule Poirot receives a mysterious phone call begging him to come to a restaurant late at night to prevent a murder. He manages to do so. The basic plot of this story is fleshed out in the later novel *Sparkling Cyanide*, apart from the presence of Poirot, which might explain why the murder attempt in that story is successful.

The Harlequin Tea Set (1971)

Mr Satterthwaite's car breaks down (again - see *At The Bells And Motley*, from *The Mysterious Mr Quin*) and he repairs to a café where he meets Harley Quin. Lots of references to red hair, dark skin and genetic inheritance (not for the first time) and a fatuous plot line about a mother switching her one-year-old son and her one-year-old stepson around, and the father of the stepson not noticing.

The Regatta Mystery (1936)

Clever-ish nothing of a romp concerning an expensive jewel being stolen in plain sight. When first published, it featured Hercule Poirot; here it has Parker Pyne.

The Love Detectives (1950)

Satterthwaite has car problems (again!). The one in which he is travelling to a crime scene, as guest of the Chief Constable of the district, is pranged by one being driven by Harley Quin. Somewhat incredibly, Quin is then asked to hop in and also attend the scene by Colonel Melrose, the said Chief Constable. Sadly, the plot provides another example where two people who connived at a murder individually admit to it, both implausibly[1].

Next to a Dog (1929)

A young girl at her wits' end looking for work finds her only comfort in the person of her ageing terrier, Terry. When Terry has an accident and is put down, her outlook improves. Slightly nauseating, but an interesting insight to the plight of young women in general, and especially young widows, after WW1, a subject to which Agatha Christie returned often in her early short stories.

Magnolia Blossom (1925)

A woman is persuaded by her desperate, ne'er-do-well husband to 'present herself nicely' to another man, one with whom she had in any case been planning to run away. Not one of the author's finest twists.

SWIGATHA RATING 3/10

Most of these stories are ok individually as a light read, but putting them out as a collection is not. Nowadays, of course, if anyone ever does come across a hitherto unpublished known story by her, it could just go out in electronic format.

Strictly speaking, *Problem at Pollensa Bay* does not come within the original 'swigatha' remit[2], because the book did not come out until I was in my thirties. It is included for the sake of completeness; if one were to be kind, one would say that it was published for the same reason.

WHAT HAPPENED NEXT

What happened next was an ongoing rummage through the Christie archives for further stories with which to entice her growing global readership. So, in 1997, we had the desperately weak collection *While the Light Lasts*, which the author would have been horrified to see published.

So, what also happened next was the closure of the swigatha files – enough!

ADAPTATIONS

Yellow Iris was adapted for TV by ITV as part of their *Poirot* series. It is not one of their better ones.

NOTES

[1] Compare and contrast *The Murder at the Vicarage*.

[2] The original idea was to re-visit all the Agatha Christie books I read as a child and teenager, in the editions that I read, and compare the impact of the books now with what I remembered from then.

Appendix A: Titles Quotes

INTRODUCTION

When she first started writing detective fiction, Agatha Christie (or her publisher) tended to give the stories titles that were self-explanatory: The *Mysterious Affair at Styles, The Murder on the Links, The Murder of Roger Ackroyd, The Murder at the Vicarage* and so on.

As her confidence (and popularity) grew, and she gained more control over the publication of her work, she started to use fancier titles. The first such was 'Sing a Song of Sixpence', a short story included in the *Listerdale Mystery* collection in 1934. Time and again over the next twenty years she would mine nursery rhymes (and *Sing a Song of Sixpence*) for her titles, sometimes to witless effect as she tried to manipulate her plots to match the lyrics.

Agatha Christie had always included liberal amounts of quotation from English literature in her text. Beginning with *Sad Cypress* in 1940, she started to turn to it for her titles; eventually it would be

Shakespeare, Tennyson and the King James Bible that would be quoted on her front pages, replacing the nursery completely.

NURSERY RHYMES

Sing a Song of Sixpence
A Pocketful of Rye
Four and Twenty Blackbirds (from *The Adventure of the Christmas Pudding*)
The first three lines of 'Sing a Song of Sixpence' provided three titles for Christie – two for short stories and one, *A Pocket Full of Rye*, that gave the author the opportunity to have a riot with the book's plot as she makes it follow the verses of the eccentric rhyme that inspired it.

And Then There Were None
My 1977 edition of this story *has Ten Little N*****s* as its title. When attitudes as to what kind of language was and was not acceptable took a turn for the better in the UK, a new title was required, and it was found in the rhyme's final line. That had been the title adopted in the US when it was first published there in 1940. It is a great title for the book, even if gives away the ending somewhat.

One Two Buckle My Shoe
Each of the chapters contains a line from this children's counting song as the author tries to squeeze her plot into it.

Five Little Pigs
This is a great story, and there *are* five protagonists, but the attempt to fit each of them in to the role of 'This Little Piggy' doesn't quite succeed: for example, a girl who survives being disfigured by her sister as a child to become a renowned scholar is characterised as the little pig who cried 'wee! wee!' all the way home.

Crooked House
From 'There was a Crooked Man....' and a very appropriate title it is too!

Mrs McGinty's Dead
A character called Mrs McGinty dies.

Hickory Dickory Dock
A title based on the name of the street where the killings take place and nothing else. The formula was getting tired by now, and thankfully she realised it – this was the last use of a nursery rhyme as plot device.

How Does Your Garden Grow

> *Mary, Mary quite contrary*
>
> *How does your garden grow?*
>
> *With silver bells and cockle shells*
>
> *And pretty maids all in a row*

Poirot duly finds a clue in the shells in a garden bed. Published as one of *Poirot's Early Cases* in 1974 but written decades before.

QUOTATIONS FROM LITERATURE

Come, Tell Me How You Live

The title of Agatha Christie's memoirs of her trips to Syria and Iraq, with her archaeologist husband Max Mallowan, this line is taken from *Alice Through the Looking Glass*, by Lewis Carroll. Here is the full verse:

> *I shook him well from side to side*
>
> *Until his face was blue:*
>
> *'Come tell me how you live,' I cried,*
>
> *'And what it is you do!'*

She uses the line in a poem at the start 'with apologies to Lewis Carroll'.

Sad Cypress

Taken from *Twelfth Night* by William Shakespeare. The clown Feste's song *Come away. come away, death, and in sad cypress let me be laid ...* is quoted in full at the start. A good choice for a story that has been described as 'elegiac'.

The Hollow

From *Maud*, a 'monodrama' by Alfred Tennyson. The opening lines are:

> *I hate the dreadful hollow behind the little wood,*
>
> *Its lips in the field above are dabbled with blood-red heath,*
>
> *The red-ribb'd ledges drip with a silent horror of blood,*
>
> *And Echo there, whatever is ask'd her, answers 'Death.'*

This verse is quoted by Poirot in the text. The obvious connection is the name of the house where death occurs, although one of the characters considers that the man killed is more alive than anyone else – they are all but 'Echoes'.

Taken at the Flood

From *Julius Caesar*, by Shakespeare. Brutus to Cassius:

> *There is a tide in the affairs of man which, taken at the flood, leads on to fortune …*

This a very appropriate title for a story about someone who sees an outlandish opportunity and seizes it, with no regard for the consequences.

Evil Under the Sun

From the Bible (the *Book of Ecclesiastes*):

> *I have seen another evil under the sun, and it weighs heavily on mankind.*

The same thought occurs to Poirot and the Rev Stephen Lane as they watch people sunbathing – that there is evil everywhere under the sun; it is especially manifest when Poirot is around.

N or M?

This title comes from the Catechism in the Book of Common Prayer which asks:

> *"What is your Christian name? Answer n. or m."*

The original Latin version had *"nomen vel nomina"*, meaning "name or names"; this was shortened to *'n or nn'* for the English language version. By a mistake in the transcription that was not picked up, 'nn' came to be represented by "m": hence 'n or m'.

The Moving Finger

From *The Rubaiyat of Omar Khayyam*:

> *The moving finger writes, and having writ, moves on.*

A great title for a book – what is done cannot be undone – but in this case the writing concerned is in the form of poison pen letters which refer to things that had NOT happened.

The Pale Horse

From the Bible (the *Book of Revelation*): *And I looked, and behold a pale horse: and his name that sat on him was death, and Hell Followed with him.*

In the book, it is the name of a (sinister) pub.

The Mirror Crack'd from Side to Side

From *The Lady of Shalott* by Tennyson:

Out flew the web and floated wide

The mirror crack'd from side to side:

"The curse is come upon me," cried

The Lady of Shalott.

An absolutely inspired choice of title, perfectly fitting the crucial moment in the story, as described by Mrs Bantry to Jane Marple.

Endless Night

From *Songs of Experience* by William Blake.

Every Night and every Morn

Some to Misery are born

Every Morn and every Night

Some are born to Sweet Delight,

Some are born to Sweet Delight

Some are born to Endless Night.

This story is about a person whom even the mother who bore him knew would come to no good.

By the Pricking of My Thumbs

From *Macbeth* by Shakespeare:

Second Witch: *By the pricking of my thumbs, something wicked this way comes.*

A 'pricking of the thumbs' is the witch's reaction, similar to a shudder, to the approach of Macbeth. It's also how Tuppence feels when she first meets the person who proves to be the murderer, though she misreads the cause.

It is also how *I* feel when I watch the start of another Walliams *Tommy and Tuppence* adaptation on BBC.

Postern of Fate

From the *Gates of Damascus* by James Ellroy Flecker:

Four great gates has the city of Damascus … Postern of Fate, the Desert Gate, Disaster's Cavern, Fort of Fear...

Difficult to know why this title was chosen, but then again everything about this book is difficult, including reading it.

In a Glass Darkly

From the Bible (St Paul's *First Letter to the Corinthians*). The King James version is the most common one: *For now we see through a glass darkly …*

… but there are many translations, and this is one of them. This story was published in *Miss Marple's Final Cases* (even though she is not in it) after Agatha Christie's death.

While the Light Lasts

Not sure where this comes from – it was used *in memoriam* of quite a few British and Commonwealth soldiers who died in WW1. Many online websites say it comes from a poem by Tennyson, but I have not been able to trace it:

> *While the light lasts*
> *I shall remember*
> *And in the darkness*
> *I shall not forget*

Some websites even claim that these are Christie's own words, and they were used for the memorials and graveyards that were still being built in the 1920s. Whichever it is, this was the title story of another collection published posthumously. In this story, a widow had used this quote in the obituary to her husband, presumed killed in WW1. He returns under the alias of 'Enoch Arden', to find her married again. *Enoch Arden* is the name of an actual Tennyson poem, and the name also features in *Taken at the Flood*.

Appendix B: Old Sins Have Long Shadows: Childhood and *A Pocket Full of Rye*

'One of the luckiest things that can happen to you in life is to have a happy childhood. I had a very happy childhood.'

These are the opening lines of Agatha Christie's *Autobiography.* General consensus has it that Agatha Christie did not reveal much of herself in her crime novels, but I think that this particular conviction comes through loud and clear in her 1953 novel *A Pocket Full of Rye*.

In the middle period of her writing (1940-1955), there were many books with titles taken straight from the nursery – *One, Two Buckle My Shoe, Hickory Dickory Dock, Five Little Pigs* and so on. None of them had dealt directly with childhood as a subject, but the concept of a happy childhood, or the lack of one, informs much of the characterisation in this book.

YEWTREE LODGE

Most of the action takes place at Yewtree Lodge, a dark mansion that is home to the dysfunctional Fortescue family. It is owned by the rich swindler Rex Fortescue, and it houses various members of his unhappy family: his much younger second wife Adele, his sister-in-law, his elder son and daughter-in-law, and his daughter. The household is presided over by a housekeeper who has no time for any of them.

When Rex is poisoned, his Prodigal second Son stages a surprise visit, resulting in the immediate death of the maid, Gladys.

OLD SINS HAVE LONG SHADOWS

Many of Agatha Christie's later stories quote this proverb, which I believe is originally Danish. In those books, the crimes of the past very much influence events in the present.

In *A Pocket Full of Rye*, it is a comment made by Rex's sister-in-law Miss Ramsbottom to Inspector Neele, hinting that Rex's past unscrupulousness was the motive for his death.

The housekeeper at Yewtree Lodge, Mary Dove, describes the members of the household thus: *'They are all quite odious.'* One of the reasons why this may be is that, in the case of members of the household of Yewtree Lodge, many of the 'old sins' were perpetrated *on* them, rather than *by* them.

For example, **Percival, Lance and Elaine Fortescue** had been 'brought up' by an unscrupulous, humiliating bully of a father and a self-proclaimed invalid mother, who had little time for them when alive and died when they were young. Lance explains to his wife Pat what it was like:

> *"She wore lots of clinking things and lay on a sofa and used to read me stories about knights and ladies which bored me stiff. Tennyson's* Idylls of the King. *I suppose I was fond of her …*
> *She was very – colourless, you know. I realise that, looking back."*
> *"You don't seem to have been particularly fond of anybody," said Pat, disapprovingly.*

Each of the children was named after characters in the same Tennyson poem. After his wife's death, Rex washed his hands of his children and handed over their care to his sister-in-law – the fire-and-brimstone breathing Miss Ramsbottom.

Neither their father nor their mother was remotely interested in the children. No wonder Lance doesn't seem 'particularly fond of anybody'.

Ruby MacKenzie had also lost a parent when she was young. She was seven when her father died, possibly as a result of skullduggery by Rex Fortescue.

To make things worse for her, her mother was driven out of her already-feeble mind by this. Every night, she would make her children swear that they would murder Rex when they grew up.

Ruby changed her name to *Jennifer*[1]. Having nursed Percival back to health, she married him; her mother never spoke to her again. Jennifer was profoundly unhappy ever after.

The maid at Yewtree Lodge, **Gladys Martin,** did not even have the dubious privilege of parents such as these, having been abandoned at an orphanage.

> *"It sounds rather cruel," said Pat.*
>
> *"Yes, my dear," said Miss Marple, "life is cruel, I'm afraid. One doesn't really know what to do with the Gladyses …"*

No matter what the best intentions of the orphanage or Miss Marple might have been, Gladys emerged from their care without family or friends. She was thus easy meat for the murderer, who knew *exactly* what he could 'do with the Gladyses …'

Mary Dove, the housekeeper who looks on the rest of the household (and the world) with amused contempt, was also herself an orphan.

ON THE BRIGHT SIDE

Contrast those characters from within the household with those of two from outside it. First, let us consider **Inspector Neele**. Unusually, we are given some detail about the Inspector's upbringing (imagine a similar paragraph about, say, Inspector Slack):

> *Call it a lodge indeed! Yewtree Lodge! The affectation of these rich people! The house was what he, Inspector Neele, would call a mansion. He knew what a lodge was. He'd been brought up in one! … The lodge had been small and attractive from the outside, and had been damp, uncomfortable and devoid of anything but the most primitive form of sanitation within. Fortunately these facts had been accepted as quite proper and fitting by Inspector Neele's parents … Mrs Neele had never discovered the pleasures of electric irons, slow combustion stoves, airing cupboards, hot and cold water from taps, and the switching on of light by a mere flick of a finger. In winter the Neeles had an oil lamp and in summer they went to bed when it got dark. They were a healthy family and a happy one, all thoroughly behind the times.*

From out of this happy childhood has emerged a confident, able man who has no need to prove himself to anybody else. As Miss Marple says: "You're a very, *very* clever man, Inspector Neele. I've seen that from the first." You would not expect to hear her pay such a compliment to the likes of Slack.

Then there is the thrice-married **Pat Fortescue**, ill-favoured by fortune but the most sympathetic character in the book. Pat shares Agatha Christie's sentiments about the importance of a happy childhood in building resilience against fortune's slings and arrows:

> *Miss Marple said gently:*
> *"You've had a good deal of unhappiness, haven't you, my dear?"*
> *"Oh, I've had some very good times, too. I had a lovely childhood in Ireland, riding, hunting, and a great big, bare draughty house with lots and lots of sun in it. If you've had a happy childhood, nobody can take that away from you, can they?"*

After an idyllic childhood, Pat has to cope with troubles a-plenty as an adult: her fighter pilot husband shot down soon after they were married, her second husband blowing his brains out to avoid a betting scandal - and now she is married to Lance Fortescue …

Pat thinks she's unlucky; Miss Marple knows that, at least in one crucial way — the happiness of her upbringing — she is not. She cannot bring herself to tell Pat what further misfortune she is about to face, but is quietly convinced that Pat will have the character to bounce back from it in a way that, say, Jennifer and Miss Dove would not. For, as her creator saw it, a child growing up in a happy and caring home would be far better able to cope with the problems and setbacks of adulthood once they left it.

And she should know. Twenty or so years earlier, in 1926, Agatha Christie had certainly had more than her own fair share of setbacks: her beloved mother dying, her husband leaving her, a single parent with a six-year-old daughter, followed by her own breakdown and disappearance.

She bounced right back, to become the most successful writer ever, and, soon afterwards, one with a happy family home to boot.

NOTES

[1] Another *Idylls of the King* reference: *Jennifer* is a form of the name Guinevere, King Arthur's Queen (and Lancelot's lover …!).

Appendix C: Who's Who in Chipping Cleghorn

Like many of Agatha Christie's stories of the 1940s, *A Murder is Announced* is set firmly in the time that it was written (1947-9), with every character in it affected in one way or another by common features of the post-WW2 period in the UK: the rationing of everything, and the difficulties of finding one's way and place in a hugely-changed world, whether as a refugee, demobbed soldier, ex-Land Girl or whoever.

Underlying the story, however, there are also elements driven by the angels and demons of the author's own childhood that add hugely to its quality.

A combination of the two creates a picture of a village way of life (in Chipping Cleghorn) that is unrecognisable from that described in her earlier stories.

Village Life in King's Abbot

Dr James Sheppard, the narrator of *The Murder of Roger Ackroyd* (published in 1926), includes a brief chapter "Who's Who in King's Abbot". He describes it as *very much like any other village* where the *hobbies and recreations can be summed up in one word, 'gossip'*.

Everyone knows everyone else; Ackroyd has lived there all his life and is *the heart and soul of our peaceful village*, and everyone is very fond of his son Ralph. Houses have maids and under-gardeners, fishmongers and butchers have delivery boys, and the village grapevine is in full operation, enabling the doctor's sister Caroline to know everyone's business without leaving her home.

The First World War had come and gone but village life remained much the same.

Village Life in Chipping Cleghorn

Twenty-four years later, that picture of a typical English village would be unrecognisable.

The knock-on effects of the Second World War – troops returning after years away, deserters roaming the countryside, refugees, rationing, shortages and the shrinkage of empire – are pivotal to the plot and the background of almost every character in it.

During and following the War, most households had had to learn to manage without servants and butchers without boys. Straitened means meant that previously well-to-do people had had to sell up and leave, or downsize households that their families had lived in for generations, as Miss Marple explains:

> "Take this place, Chipping Cleghorn, for instance. It's very much like St Mary Mead where I live. Fifteen years ago, one knew who everybody was. The Bantrys in the big house – and the Hartnells and the Price Ridleys and the Wetherbys ... They were people whose fathers and mothers and grandfathers and grandmothers, or whose aunts or uncles had lived there before them. If someone new came to live there they brought letters of introduction ...

> "But it's not like that any more. Every village and small country place is full of people who've just come and settled there without any ties to bring them. The big houses have been sold, and the cottages have been converted and changed. The people just come – and all you know about them is what they say of themselves ..."

If a Chipping Cleghorn version of Caroline Sheppard had wanted to know what was happening in the village she would have had to get a copy of the *North Benham News and the Chipping Cleghorn Gazette* – the old grapevine had gone.

Such a village, where no-one really knows who other people are, provides a setting that allows Agatha Christie to explore in more detail one of her common themes: How do you really know *who* someone else is?

Refugees

The household at Little Paddocks, the scene of the crime, consists almost entirely of refugees of one sort or another who have settled there since the end of the War. Mitzi, the cook, is an actual refugee from the post-war horrors of Central Europe, whereas the others – Mrs Haymes, Dora Bunner,

Patrick and Julia Simmons - could be classed as economic refugees scrounging off the householder, Miss Blacklock. Two of them are twins ('Pip and Emma') who do not even recognise each other.

Miss Blacklock herself is also in hiding: Dora Bunner is the only person who knows who she really is, but is happy to collude with her in concealing her identity.

Of the neighbours who drop in on the fatal day that the murder is announced, four, the Swettenhams and the Easterbrooks, are themselves refugees of a kind – from a shrinking British Empire.

Open Doors and Shortages

Although no-one can be quite sure who anyone else is in Chipping Cleghorn, everyone is happy to leave their doors wide open when they go out. This might seem strange at first, and the police cannot understand it.

The houses, however, were left open not as a sign of mutual trust – no-one had anything worth taking anyway. Open doors enabled the village's own version of the post-war black market to function, and it is the one thing that everyone in the village *does* know about.

Everyone was forced to collude with each other as they coped with the shortage of every essential, from food to fuel to clothing. Strictly speaking, such a black market means that just about every person in the village is breaking the law, something it is difficult to imagine the redoubtable Mrs Price-Ridley, Miss Wetherby and Miss Hartnell doing in days gone by.

As Inspector Craddock realises, it is the Chipping Cleghorn 'open door policy' that allows the murderer to get hold of the weapon, and to smuggle Rudi Scherz into Little Paddocks to perform his comedy before he is shot with it.

One thing Craddock fails to grasp is the implication of the central heating being left on at Little Paddocks when it wasn't really necessary. It is mentioned by every visitor because, at a time of coupons for every necessity, they clearly each found it worthy of comment that vital fuel was being squandered in such a way. That proves to be the key to unlocking the mystery.

Agatha Christie and Identity

This book was Agatha Christie's 50th, and it is but one of many that has a character concealing their identity or stealing someone else's.

In this book, though, identity is a theme that runs right through the story. The question is asked of every character: 'How do we *really* know who this is?' Agatha Christie's interest in such a question, and its answer, goes back to her early childhood.

The Gunman

From the age of about 6, Agatha Christie had a recurring nightmare featuring someone she called *The Gunman*:

> *The gun was part of his appearance ... that of a Frenchman in grey-blue uniform, powdered hair in a queue and a kind of three-cornered hat, and the gun was some old-fashioned kind of musket*[1].

In her dreams, this Gunman would appear at a normal tea-party at home, happily joining in the conversation; only Agatha knew who he really was. Sometimes she would look into the face of her sister or mother at the party and realise that it was actually the Gunman looking back at her.

The childhood Gunman nightmare left its traces in the adult. In 1926, Agatha Christie was alone and vulnerable after her mother's death. She was also on the verge of a breakdown as she cleared her mother's effects from Ashfield, her childhood home. One day, her then-husband Archie visited from London. She describes recalling

> *... that old nightmare of mine – the horror of sitting at a tea table looking across at my best-loved friend, and suddenly realising that the person sitting there was a stranger.*[1]

In fact, Archie had come to tell her that he loved someone else, and this tips her over the edge. Agatha went into hiding, running away to a place where no-one would know her. There, for eleven days, she herself adopted a false identity, using the surname of Archie's lover.

Her second husband, Max Mallowan, served in North Africa during WWII, and she had similar fears that she would not know him when he returned after a long period on duty. Thankfully, she did, and the Gunman was perhaps finally put away for good, but the possibility that people were not who they seemed to be continued to inform her plotting.

Old School – Hinchcliffe and Murgatroyd

Apart from the vicar and his wife, there are two other people in Chipping Cleghorn about whom there are no doubts as to their identity: Miss Hinchcliffe and Miss Murgatroyd, two late middle-aged ladies who have been living together for some time.

Hinchcliffe is the strong character, with 'a short man-like crop and weather-beaten countenance'. She is fiercely protective of the 'fat and amiable' Murgatroyd.

These two characters had been gestating in Agatha Christie's mind for half a century. She had not been to school as a young girl and had few friends of her own age, so she invented her own pretend-school for girls, known simply as *The School*.

She populated it initially with young girls around her own age (6-11), and kept developing them in her imagination well into their (and her) adulthood. Each had a specific character, and the first she invented were Ethel and Annie.

> *Ethel was … clever, good at games, had a deep voice and must have been rather masculine in appearance. Annie … was shy and nervous and easily reduced to tears … She clung to Ethel, who protected her on every occasion …*

> *Ethel never married but lived in a small cottage with the gentle Annie – very appropriate, I think now: it's exactly what they would have done in real life.* [1]

Hinchcliffe and Murgatroyd are, unlike most of the other characters at Little Paddocks on the night of the murder, amusingly and sympathetically portrayed. Also, unlike everyone else, no-one seriously questions who they are.

That is because Agatha Christie knew exactly who they were – she had been carrying them around in her head since childhood, and she treats them with great care. Many of the characters populating her books were based on people she spotted on buses or in cafes, about whom later she could not care less. It is therefore rare in her books that genuine grief at the passing of another is depicted, but it is in this one:

> *Nobody offered Miss Hinchcliffe sympathy or mentioned Miss Murgatroyd's death. The ravaged face of the tall vigorous woman told its own tale, and would have made any expression of sympathy an impertinence.*

The presence of these two genuine Agatha Christie characters, whom she loved and knew so well, helps lift this story up to a different level from most of the others.

Aftermath

After the murderer has been apprehended, two of the ex-suspects get engaged to be married, but even so there is little likelihood that everything in Chipping Cleghorn will be settling back to normal, as would usually be the case in a swigatha.

For one thing, in the wake of the Second World War there was no 'normal' to settle back into, and, for another, Hinchcliffe would forever be haunted by the ghost of her friend.

NOTES

[1] All these quotes are taken directly from Agatha Christie, *An Autobiography.*

References

During the re-read of Agatha Christie, I became aware for the first time of the huge amount of reference material devoted to her works, and these are the ones that I referred to most often.

Starting with the most obvious:

Agatha Christie – an Autobigraphy *(1950-65)*

A hugely revealing narrative, even though it skips describing the eleven days that were the most famous of her long life. Agatha Christie always said that she never drew her characters from real life, but there are quite a few candidates that leap to the eye when reading this book.

Agatha Christie's Secret Notebooks / Murder in the Making *by Dr John Curran (2009-11)*

An analysis of the creative process based on archive material found at Greenway. The genius of Agatha Christie lay in her ideas and these books comprehensively show how they were developed.

Come Tell Me How You Live *by Agatha Christie (1940-46)*

A very enjoyable diary of the Mallowans' trips to Syria and Iraq that gives insight into her resilience and what really mattered to her. Her true appreciation of other cultures comes across very strongly, and should give pause for thought to those people who consider her work to betray personal racist tendencies.

A Talent to Deceive: An Appreciation of Agatha Christie *by Robert Barnard (1979)*

The best, most balanced analysis of Agatha Christie's work that I have so far come across: not a hagiography, which makes a refreshing change. The sort of writer whose opinions you will disagree with, but respect.

Agatha Christie Cover Story *by Tom Adams and Julian Symons (1981)*

Essential reading for anyone interested in the story and ideas behind the amazingly distinctive series of covers painted for Fontana by Tom Adams from 1963-73: my memory of those covers was the original inspiration for both the re-read and *Swigatha* online. A follow-up volume, *Tom Adams Uncovered,* covers much the same ground, but also includes a variety of covers inspired by other writers.

Agatha Christie on Screen by Dr Mark Aldridge (2016)

An excellent and comprehensive history of all the adaptations of Christie works worldwide. The way things are going, it will need to be brought up to date on a regular basis. Aldridge's analysis of *Agatha Christie's Poirot: The Greatest Detective in the World* was published in 2020.

The Agatha Christie Who's Who by Randall Toye (1980)

A listing of over 2,000 of the characters created by Agatha Christie. Randall Toye estimates that there are over 7,000 referenced in some way in the stories published in her lifetime, but that needed pruning, so the hundreds of butcher's boys, postmistresses and village parallels have been discarded. For obvious reasons, there is also no room for the characters in the tired short story re-hashes of the 1990s and since.

The Agatha Christie Miscellany by Cathy Cook (2013)

Exactly what it says, but fun to dip into and well-researched.

A is for Arsenic by Kathryn Harkup (2015)

A qualified chemist and 'science communicator' considers the different poisons used in swigathas, with examples from 14 books, and then reveals their chemistry, action and history.

Who Killed Roger Ackroyd (Qui a tué Roger Ackroyd)? by Pierre Bayard (1998)

The Professor of Literature at the Sorbonne University of Paris is convinced that Poirot's solution to the murder of Ackroyd is delusional, and provides an alternative that best fits with the facts as described by the narrator.

This books hints at the question: "If the narrator is allowed to hide information from readers in an effort to deceive them, how can we know which bits we can trust?"

Agatha (2014) by A Martinetti, G Lebeau and A Franc

A graphic biography, beautifully done, somewhat in the style of a Tintin book, with Poirot, looking just like one of the identikit detectives Thomson and Thompson, constantly turning up to plague the author! A very moving tribute.

The Act of Roger Murgatroyd (2006) by Gilbert Adair

A spoof 'homage' to the Queen of Crime – a fun read, with a brilliant ending that would have had Professor Bayard falling off his chair. Since followed up by *A Mysterious Affair of Style* and *And Then There Was No One*, but one spoof is enough for me.

Other very useful sources of reference included:

Greenway House (Churston Ferrars, Devon)

One of Agatha Christie's homes, now a National Trust property, almost a family museum, but well worth a visit for the grounds alone, and also the wider landscape. The Torquay Riviera, the River Dart, Burgh Island and elsewhere appear in a few of her stories, and there is an annual Agatha Christie festival based in Torquay around the time of her birth day in September.

A great time and place to meet fellow enthusiasts.

Online (Facebook)

There are some excellent (and some not-so-great) pages around, often attracting real experts on the subject. Surprisingly, Facebook fan pages have proved to be an invaluable source of interesting content and comment; the official Agatha Christie websites and facebook pages are somewhat worthy and almost patronising.

Apart from the @swigatha page, here are some that I have been following:

Agatha Christie Brazil
The Agatha Christie Fan Group
Greenway – the loveliest place on earth
Agatha Christie Locations

You do sometimes find that many of the thousands of followers of similar pages are more interested in the TV and screen adaptations (and actors) than the books, but I have made some very knowledgeable and likeable contacts on these pages.

Legacy (Nick Smart and Raye Green)

As a result of people meeting at a dinner at Greenway during the Festival, and the judicious use of Facebook, contributions were solicited to create *Agatha Christie: The Legacy*, a magazine celebrating the centenary of *The Mysterious Affair at Styles.* It came out in March 2020, and it is hoped that it will be the first of a few! The first issue contained articles by Drs Curran and Aldridge, indeed by yours truly too.

Second-hand Bookshops

The 1960-70 edition Fontana and Pan paperbacks that I was seeking tend to fly off the shelves of UK bookshops as soon as they arrive, but there are two that always had a good stock:

- *The Torquay Museum*, which houses a floor dedicated to Christie, always has an excellent collection, principally because staff there scour local second-hand bookshops to keep the stock levels high

- *Henry Pordes Books*, In London's Charing Cross Road, has a stack dedicated to Agatha Christie paperbacks just inside its entrance.

Second-hand bookshops are where it all started for 'swigatha' and so it feels appropriate that this is where it all should end.

Lightning Source UK Ltd.
Milton Keynes UK
UKHW050401140222
398611UK00003B/17

9 781914 288159